Born in Vienna in 1909, Peter F. Drucker was educated in Austria and England. From 1929 he was a newspaper correspondent and an economist for an international bank in London. Since 1937 he has been in the United States, first as an economist for a group of British banks and insurance companies, and later as a management consultant to several of the country's largest companies, as well as to leading companies abroad. From 1942 to 1949 Mr Drucker was professor of philosophy and politics at Bennington College; since 1950 he has been professor of management at New York University's Graduate School of Business. His books include *The Effective Executive*, *The Practice of Management*, *Managing For Results*, *The Age of Discontinuity* and *Technology, Management and Society*, all published by Pan Books.

Management Series

The New Markets...
and other essays

PETER F. DRUCKER

UNABRIDGED

PAN BOOKS LTD : LONDON

First published 1971 by William Heinemann Ltd
This edition published 1974 by Pan Books Ltd,
33 Tothill Street, London SW1

ISBN 0 330 23821 3

Major portions of this work were previously published in
*Harper's Magazine, Harvard Business Review, The Public
Interest, Review of Politics, Sewanee Review* and *Virginia
Quarterly Review*. The author's book, *Men, Ideas and
Politics* (New York: Harper & Row, 1971) also republishes
some of the same essays.

Some new footnotes for the British reader have been added
here and minor textual amendments made, but nothing of
substance has been omitted or altered. Each essay has
a new introduction.

*Printed and Bound in Great Britain by
Cox & Wyman Ltd, London, Reading and Fakenham*

Contents

Preface

'But this is not a management book', many readers may say. It does not deal with what goes on *inside* business enterprise or specifically with the tasks of the executive. Indeed it is addressed to the general reader as much as to the executive in business or government. But the subject of this book is the environment in which executives and institutions work and perform. Few subjects that are commonly considered 'management' are anywhere near as important to the executive as an understanding of the economic, social and political – and even spiritual – environment to which all the essays in this book address themselves.

These essays, written over a quarter-century, cover a wide diversity of topics – and at first they may not seem to have much in common. An essay on 'The New Markets', which treats the financial fads and follies of the nineteen-sixties as symptoms of structural change in economy and society, finds itself cheek by jowl with an essay on Kierkegaard, surely the least 'market-oriented' thinker of the modern West. An evocation of Henry Ford as the 'Last Populist', and fulfilment and denial alike of the nineteenth century's agrarian and Jeffersonian dreams, might seem unrelated to the internal stresses of the Japanese 'economic miracle' or the pathos and bathos of this 'Romantic Generation' of today's educated young people.

Yet all these pieces, despite the diversity of their topics, have a common subject matter and a common theme. They are all essays in what I would call 'political (or social) ecology'.

This term is not to be found in any university catalogue. But the only thing that is 'new' about political ecology is the name. As a subject matter and human concern, it can boast ancient lineage, going back all the way to Herodotus and

Thucydides. It counts among its practitioners such eminent names as de Tocqueville and Walter Bagehot. Its character is Aristotle's famous definition of Man as *zoon politikon*, that is, social and political animal. As Aristotle knew (though many who quote him do not) this implies that society, polity, and economy, though Man's creations, are 'nature' to Man, who cannot be understood apart from and outside of them. It also implies that society, polity, and economy are a genuine environment, a genuine whole, a true 'system' to use the fashionable term, in which men, ideas, institutions, and actions must always be seen together in order to be seen at all, let alone to be understood.

Political ecologists are uncomfortable people to have around. Their very trade makes them defy conventional classifications, whether of politics, of the market place, or of academia. Was de Tocqueville, for instance, a 'liberal' or a 'conservative'? What about Bagehot? 'Political ecologists' emphasize that every achievement exacts a price and, to the scandal of good 'liberals', talk of 'risks' or 'trade-offs', rather than of 'progress'. But they also know that the man-made environment of society, polity, and economics, like the environment of nature itself, knows no balance except dynamic disequilibrium. Political ecologists therefore emphasize that the way to conserve is purposeful innovation – and that hardly appeals to the 'conservative'.

Political ecologists believe that the traditional disciplines define fairly narrow and limited tools rather than meaningful and self-contained areas of knowledge, action, and events – in the same way in which the ecologists of the natural environment know that the swamp or the desert are the reality and ornithology, botany, and geology only special-purpose tools. Political ecologists therefore rarely stay put. It would be difficult to say, I submit, which of the essays in this volume are 'management', which 'government' or 'political theory', which 'history' or 'economics'. The task

determines the tools to be used – but this has never been the
the approach of academia.

Students of Man's various social dimensions – government, society, economy, institutions – traditionally assume
their subject matter to be accessible to full rational understanding. Indeed they aim at finding 'laws' capable of
scientific proof. Human action, however, they tend to treat
as non-rational, that is, as determined by outside forces such
as their 'laws'. The political ecologist, by contrast, assumes
that this subject matter is far too complex ever to be fully
understood – just as his counterpart, the natural ecologist,
assumes this in respect to the natural environment. But
precisely for this reason the political ecologist will demand –
like his counterpart in the natural sciences – responsible
actions from Man and accountability of the individual
for the consequences, intended or otherwise, of his actions.

An earlier volume of essays of mine – *Technology, Management, and Society* (Heinemann 1970, Pan, 1972) – centred on
what used to be called 'the material civilization': business
enterprise, its structure, its management, and its tools; technology and its history, and so on. The present volume is more
concerned with economic, political and social processes: the
early diagnosis of fundamental social and economic change;
the relationship between thought – economic, political or
social – and actions; the things that work and don't work in
certain traditions, whether those of America or those of
Japan; or the conditions of effective leadership in the
complex structures of industrial society and giant government. But in the last analysis, the present essays, and those
in the earlier volume, have the same objective. They aim at
an understanding of the specific environment 'natural' to
Man, his 'political ecology', as a prerequisite to effective and
responsible action, as an executive, as a policymaker, as a
teacher, and as a citizen.

*   *   *

Not one reader, I am reasonably sure, will agree with every essay – indeed I expect some readers to disagree with all of them. But then I long ago learned that the most serious mistakes are not being made as a result of wrong answers. The truly dangerous thing is asking the wrong questions. I do hope that readers, whether executives in a business or administrators in a government agency, parents or their children, policy-makers or citizens, teachers or students, will agree that this volume addresses itself to right questions. And even the reader who disagrees heatedly with the author's prejudices, opinions, and conclusions will, I hope, find these essays enjoyable reading. Above all, however, he will, I hope, find that they help him understand the world in which he manages his institution and performs his tasks.

Montclair, New Jersey   PETER F. DRUCKER

1. The New Markets and the New Entrepreneurs

[From *The Public Interest*, Autumn 1970]

This is one of the more recent essays in this book – it dates from 1970. Its subjects, at first glance, are the trends in finance, stock market, and international economy that have provided headlines for the financial pages for a decade. Its occasion is the collapse of the heady boom in 'conglomerates' and 'growth ventures' that had dominated the world stock exchanges these last ten years. But its subject-matter is the profound changes in economy and society of which the boom and its collapse were only symptoms.

I

The third merger wave to wash over the American economy in this century is receding fast. It leaves behind a landscape changed even more fundamentally in economic structure than its predecessors did, sixty-five and forty years ago.

The first merger wave, the one that reached its climax between 1900 and 1910, was the merger wave of the 'tycoons', with J. P. Morgan's US Steel and John D. Rockefeller's Standard Oil Company as their prototypes. In these mergers a dominant industrialist or financier tried to gain and occupy a commanding height in the economy by obtaining control of a major material or a major industry. They were 'offensive' mergers.

The second merger wave, in the twenties, was, by contrast, one of 'defensive' mergers. Its prototype, indeed its earliest example, was General Motors, put together between 1910 and 1920 as a merger of medium-sized car companies for common defence against Henry Ford's near-monopoly. The aim of these 'defensive' mergers was to create a 'number two' who would be able to hold its own against the giants which the first merger wave had spawned. And while a good many of the creations of this period – such as General Motors itself – in turn became the leading company in their industry, the 'defensive' mergers made for less concentration of power in the country's major industries and for more vigour and equality in competition. It often resulted in 'oligopoly'; but it more often thwarted 'monopoly'.

The third merger wave, the one which has now peaked, began with 'defensive' mergers, very similar to those of the twenties. Typical are the railroad mergers, such as the one which created the Penn-Central and the new railroad system in the Northwest between Chicago and Seattle. It is no coincidence that the plan for these railroad mergers is forty years old, that is, goes back to the period of 'defensive' mergers in the twenties. But the mergers among the major New York banks in the late forties and early fifties – such as the merger that put the Chase Bank and the Bank of Manhattan together into the Chase Manhattan Bank, the National City Bank and the First National into the First National City, or the Chemical Bank and the New York Trust Company into Chemical New York – these mergers were also 'defensive'. As a result, commercial banking in New York – and commercial banking internationally – has become far more competitive. There are fewer players, to be sure, but they are far stronger and far more aggressive. These 'defensive' mergers of the last twenty years aimed, as did the mergers of the twenties, at creating enterprises large enough for a national or international market and strong enough to withstand competition on a national (or, as in the case of the banks, an international) scale. Mergers of this kind have been taking place also in manufacturing industry. The merger between two medium-sized forest products companies, Champion Paper and US Plywood created, for instance, a thousand-million dollar business producing all kinds of forest products from sawn timber and plywood veneer to fine paper. Still, the combined company is considerably smaller than the country's largest paper company, International Paper, itself created by mergers before World War II.

THE 'DIVERSIFICATION MERGER'

But the typical mergers of the post-war period, and especially of the last ten years, resemble neither the 'offensive' merger of 1900, nor the 'defensive' merger of 1925.

To begin with, there were two very different and yet 'typical' kinds. In the 'diversification merger' which dominated the early years of the period, say, up to 1964 or so, a large company, though distinctly not one of the leaders in its industry, merges with companies of the same kind but in totally different lines of business. One leader in this kind of merger activity has been IT & T – the initials standing for International Telegraph and Telephone. Originally this was a company operating telephone businesses abroad, especially in the Latin-speaking countries. It also manufactured telephone equipment for these companies. It was, in fact, originally the foreign counterpart to the American Telephone and Telegraph Company, the Bell System. During the last forty years, the company gradually gave up or lost one operating telephone company after the other. It became instead a world-wide manufacturer of electronics, very large in its total, but no better than third or fourth in every one of its markets or technologies. And then, in the last ten or fifteen years, it expanded through the acquisition increasingly of businesses that have nothing to do, at least at first glance, with its main business. It acquired Avis-Rent-A-Car, the Sheraton hotel chain, Levitt, the country's largest mass-builder. It is planning to merge with Hartford Fire Insurance, one of the large casualty insurance companies, a merger blocked so far, however, by the anti-trust division and the Connecticut Insurance Commissioner.

In a similar 'diversification through merger', American Radiator & Standard Sanitary Corporation, an old and large, but stagnant, producer of plumbing and heating equipment, merged first with Westinghouse Air Brake, a large, and also rather stagnant, producer of railroad brakes and signals, then with Mosler Safe, a medium-sized and rapidly growing company, making mostly equipment for banks, and then with Lyons, a California-based mass-builder. In the process the company became 'American-Standard'.

Two of the many hundreds of 'diversification mergers' exemplify the phenomenon. One of these is the merger in which Montgomery Ward, a large retail and mail-order chain, came together with Container Corporation of America to form a new company, Marcor. The other example is the acquisition of the country's second-largest medium-term finance company, Commercial Credit, by Control Data, the one computer manufacturer other than IBM (and very much smaller) who has so far shown any profits making computers. At first sight Montgomery Ward and Container Corporation have nothing in common and the merger makes no economic sense. But both companies, while absolutely very large, are no more than 'also-rans' in their respective industries with less than one-third of the sales of the industry leader (Sears Roebuck and American Can respectively). In their problems, their opportunities, and their strategic decisions, they may therefore be akin to each other.

Similarly producing big computers and providing instalment loans to automobile buyers have, it seems, nothing in common. But the central problem of the successful computer manufacturer is to finance his machines which, as a rule, are leased rather than purchased. The central problem of a finance company, especially the smaller and weaker one, is a dependable and steady supply of high-quality borrowers. Again, there is a high degree of 'fit' even though the respective businesses are as diverse as can be.

THE 'TAKE-OVER MERGER'

'Diversification mergers', though continuing right through the sixties, passed their peak around 1964 or 1965. From then on, for five years until the end of 1969, the mergers that made the headlines were something quite different, 'merger by take-over'. This merger is forced upon a reluctant, and often loudly resisting, management by organizing a stockholders' revolt against it. And the one who 'takes over' is almost invariably a very much smaller company, a total outsider, indeed, typically a brash newcomer who did not even exist a few years earlier. In the 'diversification mergers', both parties plighted their troth with the promise of 'synergism' which would somehow make the combined business be more productive than the two alone. But in the 'take-over', the slogan is 'asset management', that is, the maximization of the value of the shareholders' equity through financial management. In effect, the 'take-over' is far less a merger of businesses than a *coup d'état*. A guerilla leader, himself owning practically no part of the company he acquires, gets the outside shareholders of large publicly owned companies to oust their own, entrenched 'professional business management' and put him into the saddle instead. And the more successful ones of these new corporate guerilla captains went from one 'take-over' to another. Starting with nothing, they built within a few years 'conglomerates' showing total revenues in the thousands of millions.

Among the 'take-over' victims have been some of the oldest and best-known companies in the country, companies run by entrenched 'professional management'. They include two of the world's largest steel companies, Jones & Laughlin and Youngstown Sheet & Tube, both with sales around the thousand-million dollar mark. They were taken over respectively by Ling-Temco-Vought controlled by James Ling and built by him in a few years from a small electronics shop into a medium-sized aerospace company with sales around $160 million, and by Lykes Bros Steamship Company, a New Orleans-based shipping line which never in all its forty years of history had had sales of more than $70 million.

In another bitterly fought take-over, AMK, a company of whom a few years earlier nobody had even heard, took over the old United Fruit Company in Boston – a company with over $400 million in assets and almost $400 million in sales. This was AMK's second leap – in the first one a year earlier, it had taken over one of the oldest meat-packers, Morrell – but its base had been a small company making industrial machinery. The United Fruit shareholders sided with the raider not because management had failed, but because it had been so successful in its attempt to turn around and save an old and ailing enterprise that it had accumulated a large amount of cash. The most spectacular of these take-overs would have been the take-over of the country's sixth-largest bank, Chemical New York – with assets of $9,000 million – by a company, called Leasco. Leasco was not even mentioned in the financial handbooks of 1966, two years before it made this attempt, albeit an unsuccessful one, to engulf a huge commercial bank into what had started out, a few years earlier, as a small computer leasing operation without any capital to speak of.

There thus came into being a whole new group of entrepreneurs. They were not 'owners', but they know how to mobilize the vast multitude of shareholders of big publicly owned companies against management. They have been able again and again to unseat 'professional management' in the name of 'asset management', that is, by promising to maximize financial returns. And their aim is not the 'synergism' (whatever that may mean) of 'diversification'. It is the 'conglomerate' built by financial manipulation and based on financial control.

THE NEW 'GROWTH' COMPANIES

Perhaps even more significant, however, is another development, and one that never before coincided with a wave of mergers. It is the emergence of yet another group of new entrepreneurs far more numerous than the 'asset managers', but perhaps a good deal sounder, though neither as colourful nor as spectacular. These are the men who have been building new 'growth' businesses in very large numbers. Now businesses are, of course, being started all the time. But these new businesses were started as 'growth' businesses, and from the beginning with large investments from the capital market. In every year from 1965 to 1969, eight to ten thousand brand-new businesses got going. Many new entrepreneurs went to the capital market for anything up to a million dollars before their business had even been started, produced its first product or made its first sale. A year or two later most came back for another substantial sum of money, ranging from $1 million to $10 million apiece. These companies were still sufficiently small and their investors sufficiently few in number – and also what the securities laws call 'sophisticated investors' (that is, primarily investment institutions) – not to have to register their securities with the Securities Exchange Commission. Yet they were sufficiently large already to have to apprise the Commission of their existence. All told, these new businesses raised about $5,000 million to $10,000 million each year from the 'sophisticated investors' during the last five years.

'Science-based' companies, most non-financial readers

will probably say. Indeed the 'science-based' companies that sprang up in the fifties around Boston or on the Peninsula south of San Francisco, were the forerunners. But while 'science-based' industries such as 'learning' or computer application are to be found among the new 'growth' ventures of the sixties, they constitute a small fraction of the total. Among the 'glamour' stocks for which the 'sophisticated investors' bid, were franchise restaurants, magazine and book publishers, nursing homes and hospitals, manufacturers of prefabricated housing and of mobile homes, and many others.

Some of these new 'growth' companies are even to be found in finance, both on Wall Street and as managers of investment trusts. The first of these financial growth ventures – and the most successful one to date – Donaldson, Lufkin & Jenrette – was started ten years ago by a group of young business school graduates and had become by 1969 the seventh largest Stock Exchange firm. Then it single-handedly achieved what Franklin D. Roosevelt, with all the power of the US Government behind him, had failed to bring about thirty years earlier: to force the Stock Exchange out of being a private club. When Donaldson, Lufkin & Jenrette outgrew its capital base in 1969 and threatened to quit the Exchange unless permitted to sell shares to the public – something always strictly forbidden by the rules which, in effect, limited investment in Stock Exchange firms to wealthy individuals – it had become so important that the Stock Exchange had to give way. Donaldson, Lufkin & Jenrette raised $12 million by selling shares to the public in April 1970.

Very few of these new companies can be compared with Xerox, the growth company *par excellence* of the American economy in post-World War II – a company having barely $1 million in sales as recently as 1950, still having less than $15 million in sales in 1960, and, in 1969, reporting sales of $1,500 million. But a good many of these new companies grew, within a very short period, to very respectable middle size – $50 million, $60 million, $70 million, sometimes even $100 million in sales. An even larger number grew to the point where their founders could sell them at a considerable capital gain to older, staider, and less 'dynamic' companies bent on 'diversification', or could, in a few cases, become 'take-over entrepreneurs' in their own right. Not since the railroad and banking ventures of the 1830s has there been any comparable explosion of new ventures getting, from the start, broad financial support in very large amounts.

THE DEVELOPMENTS THAT 'COULD NOT HAVE HAPPENED'

And neither the 'take-over merger' nor the new 'growth' ventures could really have happened, according to 'what everybody knows' about the structure of the American economy. This is brought out clearly by the cleavage between the actual developments and the magisterial announcements regarding what could happen – just when the actual developments were approaching their peak.

Nineteen sixty-seven was the year in which take-overs exploded – and not only in the US – and in which also the largest number of new 'growth' businesses appeared on the capital market. It was also the year, however, which produced the all-time best-seller by an American academic economist, John Kenneth Galbraith's *The New Industrial State. The New Industrial State* has two fundamental theses. One, professional management in the big corporation is so firmly entrenched that it cannot be challenged, let alone be overthrown from inside or outside. The dispersed 'public' stockholder is completely disenfranchised, to the point where management need not, and indeed does not, aim at maximizing profitability but can run the business comfortably to perpetuate itself in power. Secondly, *The New Industrial State* asserted that new businesses simply cannot come into existence in this economy of large corporations which manipulate the market, both that of goods and that of capital. Small new businesses certainly cannot possibly grow.

What makes the contrast between the theses of this best-selling book and the reality of the very moment when it appeared particularly significant is, however, that Galbraith in this book is not the innovator and iconoclast, and the exploder of the conventional wisdom which he had been in his earlier books. The two theses of *The New Industrial State*, however provocatively phrased by Galbraith, were the most conventional and most widely accepted theses regarding American economic structure. They go back indeed to the years before World War I, when John R. Commons, the father of American institutional economics, first propounded them. They underlay, of course, Veblen's work in the years of World War I. They were given full documentation in the classic on American corporate structure, Berle and Means' *The Modern Corporation and Private Property*, which came out in 1932. They were restated in the three books which initiated, one way or another, the tremendous interest in and study of the American business corporation over the last twenty-five years: James Burnam's *The Managerial Revolution* (1941) and my own books *Concept of the Corporation** (1946), and *The New Society* (1950†). For once, in other words, Galbraith in *The New Industrial State* was the very voice of the 'conventional wisdom'. But this makes it all the more apparent that something significant must have happened in the very structure of the American economy in these last few years.

Indeed, not even the 'diversification merger' is truly compatible with the prevailing and generally accepted doctrine of 'managerialism'. The doctrine preaches that entrenched management in the large publicly owned company does not need the outside financial market altogether. Large, well-

* Published in the UK as *Big Business*.
† Published 1951 in the UK.

established companies, so said the received wisdom of the last forty years, are capable of financing themselves through 'retained earnings'. But if this were indeed correct, the 'diversification mergers' would not, indeed could not, have happened. The accepted doctrine also teaches that such a company does not have to compete for management. Management can perpetuate itself and can offer competent mediocrities safe careers. In these mergers one top management voluntarily abdicated – for of course the new, merged company needs only one top management. No top management, one would conclude, would commit suicide if immune to stockholder control in the first place, and capable of providing itself the resources for its own success. And indeed none has ever done so, under these conditions.

Unlike the 'defensive' mergers of yesterday, the 'diversification mergers' do not strengthen a company in the markets for its products or in manufacturing efficiency. The only explanation why managements in companies that are apparently doing quite well – as did Commercial Credit and Control Data, Montgomery Ward and Container Corporation, Sheraton Hotels, American Radiator and Westinghouse Air Brake – might be willing and often eager to merge, is that they find themselves under pressures they cannot neglect, that is being unable to attract resources they must have to survive yet cannot generate just by being big and established. The 'diversification merger', like 'takeover' and the new 'growth' entrepreneurs, was a seismic disturbance that argues some major structural shift somewhere deep below the economy's surface.

THE MULTINATIONAL COMPANY

One more, equally significant, development occurred in economic structure during these last few years – and it too 'could not have happened'. Fifteen years ago all but a handful of the major American businesses were entirely 'American' (or at least 'North American', i.e. with a subsidiary in Canada) in their geographic distribution. Today the great majority of major manufacturing companies are 'multi-national', with 20 to 50 per cent of their output produced outside the US. Indeed, as Jean-Jacques Servan-Schreiber pointed out in his book, *Le Défi Americain* [The American Challenge] (which followed Galbraith's *The New Industrial State* as the international economics best-seller for 1968), the American companies producing in Europe are the world's third largest industrial power, out-produced only by the US and Russia, and in turn out-producing even Japan and Germany. Nor is 'multinationalism' confined to manu-facturing companies. The large US banks, the Bank of Am-erica, the First National City Bank, and the Chase Manhattan, have today an even larger proportion of their business outside the US than have most multinational manufacturing companies. Several stock exchange houses also, White Wold, for instance, are truly 'multinational' and have become leading underwriters in the European capital markets. And then there are the off-shore investment trusts, American-managed but domiciled outside the US and confined, by law, to doing business exclusively with non-Americans. One of them, Investors Overseas Service, started only in 1956 by a former social worker from Philadelphia, Bernard Cornfeld, had, by the end of 1969, amassed almost \$2,500 million in assets and had become the leading asset-manager in many European and Latin American countries, only to become, six months later, the first major casualty of the 1970 slump.

This development began in the US; and for the first few years 'multinational' was synonymous with 'US-based'. Around 1965, however, the move to 'multinationalism' became truly 'multinational'. The fastest growers these last few years have been the Swedes. Today three out of every ten men working for Swedish-owned manufacturing plants work outside of Sweden – a few short years ago the figure was one out of ten. Then the Japanese, around 1968, began to move. Every issue of the *Oriental Economist*, Japan's counterpart of the *Wall Street Journal*, reports a new manufacturing plant, built by a Japanese company abroad, a new joint-venture with a non-Japanese company to produce abroad, a new Japanese manufacturing subsidiary abroad. The development has been so sweeping that one student, Judd Polk, an economist at the International Chamber of Commerce, argues that we should replace the old theory of international trade which deals with the 'international distribution of the fruits of production', with a new theory of the international allocation of the factors of production. Another observer, Professor Howard Perlmutter of the University of Pennsylvania, predicts that, by 1985 or so, the bulk of the world's supply of manufactured goods will come from 300 world-wide companies, producing in all the major countries, managed multinationally, and owned by shareholders from all the major countries.

More than half of the production of the US-based multinationals outside of the US has been added in the last five years. Yet five years ago, every economist 'knew' that American multinational expansion had been stopped, that indeed the American multinational company was in for a sharp contraction. For in 1965 the US Government banned further investment of US funds in American multinational businesses abroad, especially in the developed countries (other than Canada and Japan). The ostensible reason was concern for the US balance of payments – though a major reason was surely also the desire to placate our European allies, especially de Gaulle, who were complaining loudly that the US was using its payments deficit to buy up the European economies. The ban has been strictly policed and is faithfully observed. Yet every year since 1965, the US multinationals have invested more in Europe. The answer is simply that America never financed the European acquisitions and new businesses of American 'multinationals'; the Europeans did it all along. They exchanged their holdings in their own national companies, trading in a restricted national market, for holdings in a multinational company world-wide in scope and management. Europe actually during these last ten years invested quite a bit more – several thousand million dollars – in shares of US-based companies than US-based companies invested in production in Europe, whether through starting a business or through acquisition of an existing European one. The result of this is that Europeans, in the aggregate, now probably own as much of the leading American businesses – perhaps as much as 20 per cent in some cases – as US businesses own of major industries in Europe. So far no one has paid much attention to this. But predictably we will one day soon discover this; and then 'foreign domination of American industry' is likely to become as much of a political slogan in this country as 'American domination of French (German, British, Italian, Dutch, etc) industry' has become a political slogan in Europe.

The Swedish and Japanese examples are even more amazing. In both countries the government has all along exercised the tightest control over investment abroad. In both countries investment in manufacturing plants abroad was officially banned and currency for it was simply not available. The 'multinationalism' of industry in these two countries is, in other words, also being financed by the 'multinational' investors – especially the investor in the countries in which the investment is being made – who exchanges his ownership of a local business against a share in the ownership of a multinational one.

But this is as incompatible with the 'verities' of international economic theory as the 'take-over' wave or the emergence of the new entrepreneurs are incompatible with the received wisdom of the doctrine of 'managerialism'. It is not only Keynesian theory that assumes the fiscal and financial sovereignty of the national state – all economic theory these last fifty years has done that. But no sooner did the most powerful state, the US, exercise this sovereignty, when, totally unplanned, the 'Euro-dollar market' sprang up through which the Europeans channelled their capital into American-based multinational companies, thus defeating both the US Government and their own governments as well.

It can be argued that the new mergers, whether 'diversification' or 'take-over', are 'temporary phenomena', and also that many of these were neither sound nor desirable. It can be argued that the new entrepreneurs are simply the froth on a stock market boom. It can be argued – as General de Gaulle did – that the 'multinational' company is an abomination and a flagrant violation of the immutable laws of politics and history. There is indeed little doubt that a good many of the conglomerates were jerry-built, the result of financial sleight of hand and 'asset exploitation' rather than 'asset management'. A good many of the new businesses, the shares of which were eagerly bought up by the 'sophisticated investors' were certainly fad and folly, and little else. One need not be an ultra-nationalist to see some real problems in multinational companies who have revenues larger than the national income of some of the countries they operate in, and who make their decisions in headquarters that are far away from the countries that depend on them and far beyond the reach of these countries' governments.

But that these developments of the last ten years may not be to everybody's liking; that they may not all have been desirable or sound; and that not all their results may be enduring, does not alter two facts. They happened; and they have fundamentally affected economic structure, domestically (in every developed country) and internationally. Whether one likes them or not – and I personally have great reservations – one must ask the question: What explains them? And one must assume that such far-reaching changes which, moreover, fly in the face of so much we considered

'knowledge' in the field, must have their causes in major
shifts in the structure of the economy and in the structure of
the society.

II

The developments of the last ten years are, I submit, the first
responses to the emergence of two new major 'mass-
markets', a mass-market for capital and investment, and a
mass-market for careers for educated people doing knowledge work. Like all first responses, they were in all probability, the wrong responses or, at best, inadequate
responses. But they were responses to real new challenges –
and the challenges will not go away.

Every economy, whatever its structure or its level of development, has three dimensions. One dimension is that of
goods and services, their production, distribution, and consumption. It is the 'here and now' of the economy. The
second dimension is that of allocating resources to the
future, the dimension that deals with the formation and investment of capital. Finally, in every economy, there is
work, there are jobs, and there are careers.

Each of these dimensions, at whatever level the economy
operates, needs some way of allocating resources.

But it is only when an economy has reached the stage
where it produces, in each dimension, more than the merest
subsistence, that choices begin to become important. Only
then can there be a 'market' or 'planning'. And a 'mass-
market' can only come into being when there is enough
supply in each area for large numbers of people to make
meaningful choices.

The 'mass-market' level in respect to the first dimension,
the production and consumption of goods and services, was
not reached any place in the world until about 200 years
ago. This was the essence of what the textbooks in economic
history call the 'commercial revolution' of the early eight-

eenth century – concentrated, of course, until the Napoleonic Wars almost exclusively in England and the Low Countries. But even in England the well-being of the populace was still measured far into the nineteenth century, indeed until the repeal of the Corn Laws in 1846, by the fluctuations in the price of the standard loaf of bread. Even in England, in other words, the great mass of the people, until well into the nineteenth century, had very little choice in respect to goods and services and were not yet capable of forming a mass-market. They could not choose, let alone refuse to buy. If they did without it was because they lacked the means to buy rather than the appetite. In Japan, by the way, the price of the basic rice unit remained the standard measurement of economic welfare until the time of World War I.

The emergence of the mass-market in goods and services in the eighteenth century explains why there suddenly arose a discipline of economics. For until there is meaningful choice, there can be no economics.

But early economics, whether classic, neo-classic or Marxist, did not produce a theory of money capital and investment, let alone a theory for the dimension of work and jobs. There was no need for this because supply in these two areas had not yet reached the level where there was significant choice except marginally. There had been markets for credit for many centuries. They go back all the way to the great Fairs of the late middle ages. Still, as late as the early 1930s, when I was a young investment banker in London, then still the financial capital of the world, it was axiomatic that no more than one out of every three or four hundred people, even in a highly developed economy, had enough savings to invest in anything but those financial necessities, life insurance and the mortgage of his home. In other words, even in highly developed economies, as late as 1930 the great mass of the people, in respect of capital and investment, were totally incapable of allocating it, to any significant degree, among

choices. And all earlier economic theory, from Adam Smith
through Marx to Marshall at the turn of the century, assumed essentially that jobs were, by necessity, scarcer than
available labour supply, whether this was being expressed in
Marx's 'Iron Law of Wages' or in the far more elegant but
essentially identical equations of 'Marginal Utility'.

Economics, right through the nineteenth century, could
treat capital on the one hand and labour on the other as
being determined by the 'real' economy, the economy of
goods and services, and thus having no autonomy and no
dynamics of their own.

KEYNES AS A SYMPTOM

In this perspective, the development of monetary economics
culminating in the work of Keynes in the early thirties, be-
spoke a major structural change: the emergence of the capital and investment dimension of the economy into a true
market system in which substantial numbers of people have
choices. For Keynes – and even more for such post-Key-
nesians as Milton Friedman today – the capital and investment dimension is the 'real' economy with goods and
services reflecting money and credit, as in earlier economics,
capital and investment were seen as reflecting goods and
services.

When Keynes published his great works in the early
thirties capital and investment were still very much a
'speciality mass-market' of a small minority, though one
very much bigger than it had been only a few decades earlier. When the New York Stock Exchange announced
around 1945 that it aimed at 'mass ownership of shares', it
had in mind raising the proportion of share owners from
some 1 per cent to 3 or 4 per cent of the American population. The figure now stands at 80 per cent or higher. We
have not 'nationalized' capital, but we have 'socialized' it in
number of Americans own the 'means of production' today
this country. The instrument through which the largest

are financial intermediaries – mutual funds and pension funds above all. They are the real 'capitalists'. These institutions are, so to speak, the 'professional buyers' for the great mass of financial consumers. They are meant when the Securities Exchange Commission and the Stock Exchange talk of 'sophisticated investors'. And they owned, at the end of 1969, between 45 and 50 per cent of the equity capital of American business. As a result, financial ownership in this country is now distributed roughly in the same degree of equality – or inequality – in which consumption of goods and services was distributed in the early twenties in the first great 'mass-consumption' boom. The wealthy, that is, the top 20 per cent of the population, probably still own or control more than 40 per cent of the equity in American business. The poor, the bottom 10 per cent of the population, do not of course own any equity capital at all. The middle group, comprising some 70 per cent of the population, owns directly or through its intermediaries about half of the financial assets. (The rest is held outside the US.)

An example of this development and of its speed is the pension fund of the American college teachers, the Teachers Insurance and Annuity Association. It manages the retirement funds for 300,000 people – for the great majority of the college teachers in the private colleges and universities and increasingly for teachers in state and municipal institutions as well. Founded in the early twenties, it took Teachers fifty years to build up a pension fund of about $2,500 million in conventional annuities, invested mostly in bonds, mortgages, and other traditional life insurance investments. But less than twenty years ago, in 1952, Teachers added a 'College Retirement Equity Fund', that is, a common stock investment trust, and began to offer it to its participating college teachers. Today this fund manages a portfolio of common stock of well over $1,000 million – at which, incidentally, it is still among the medium-sized rather than the large portfolio managers. And almost all the participants in the conventional fixed-payment annuity pension fund have also become common stock investors through the College Retirement Equity Fund.

What is rarely understood is that this is not just a quantitative expansion of the pool of investors. This is a qualitative change in their character. They are not 'capitalists'. They are 'investors'. Their main stake in the economy is not through their investments but through their job and the income therefrom. What they can invest in the economy is, so to speak, 'extra'. They are not dependent on it. And therefore they can afford to take risks with the money. In fact, the most rational economic behaviour for this group is to be a 'speculator', that is, to invest for capital gains rather than for income and security. The middle income group, earning between $3,000 and $20,000 a year, is perhaps most conscious of the tax burden of our steeply progressive income tax and least capable to ease it through tax loopholes and tax dodges, precisely because its income is wages and salaries. Additional income from investments, therefore, holds out little incentive to the group. 'Growth', that is the opportunity for capital appreciation, is worth almost twice as much for the group, in terms of real income, as additional income would be. And this group, which is in effect today's majority stockholder is, therefore, singularly receptive to the promise of 'asset management' and to 'maximization of the value of the stockholders' investment' – and perfectly willing to accept considerable risk in order to attain capital gain and 'asset maximization'.

At first sight, this would not seem to apply to one large segment of these new investors, the pension funds. Traditionally, pension funds have the most conservative investors, if only because they predictably need an income in the future to pay off their pensioners. But today's pension fund, especially the pension fund in industry, has been set up in such a manner that the one and only thing that is predictable is that the income needed in the future cannot be obtained from the contributions paid in the present, but must be supplemented by appreciable capital gains. In the first place, the typical American pension plan bases a man's pension on his income during the last five years of working life – and in a period of steadily rising wages, this means that contributions to a pension fund based on present average wages will not be adequate for future pension needs. In addition, pensions increasingly are being adjusted retroactively for changes in the cost of living or in the wage level of the men still at work. In a period of rising wages and inflationary prices, future pension liability must, therefore, greatly exceed anything that present contributions can provide. Pension funds, in order to live up to the responsibilities under employment and labour contracts, simply have to invest for capital gains. The greater the inflationary pressure in the economy becomes, the more will 'speculative' behaviour appear as the only truly 'conservative' line of action for a pension fund, and what used to be considered 'conservative' behaviour appear as reckless and indeed irresponsible 'speculation'. The only way in which the typical pension fund of today can possibly hope to discharge its obligations is by investing in growth and capital gains: the only way it can possibly be true to its trust is by backing 'asset management'.

The new mass market for capital and investment thus must mean something very different by 'performance' or by 'value' than either the traditional 'capitalist' or the 'professional manager' mean by these words. These new expectations may appear 'speculative' in traditional terms. But they reflect the economic realities of the new financial 'mass-consumer', the employed middle-class. They may be unrealistic; but they are perfectly rational. They reflect the social and economic realities of the employed and educated middle-class.

A MASS-MARKET FOR CAREERS

Perhaps more important in the long run – and far less seen

by the general public as yet – is the emergence of the 'mass-market' in careers for educated knowledge workers, that is, for people with a college education.* Only forty years ago, at the eve of the Great Depression, there were very few careers in which one could really get paid for putting knowledge to work. Essentially these were the old professions, the ministry, teaching, medicine, and the law, to which, in the early years of the century, engineering had been added. The Yale graduates who were hired by Wall Street houses in the twenties to be bond salesmen were not hired for their knowledge; they were hired for their connections.

The supply of men and women with advanced education and prepared for knowledge work has increased almost twenty-fold since 1920. But the supply of job and career opportunities for them has increased even faster. In the last ten years the career choices for knowledge people have seemed to be practically limitless. In fact, that the young people today have to make choices of this kind – and without any real information – is surely an important contributing factor to the unrest on the college campus. The young people are literally overwhelmed by all the opportunities that clamour 'take me'.

The emergence of genuine choice for careers and jobs is so novel that there is no economic theory of a genuine 'job market' so far. But there is the first sign that the old assumptions are being discarded by the economists. For the last ten years the 'Phillips curve' has found increasing application in economic analysis. Named after an English economist who developed it, this curve relates inflation and employment. It attempts to identify the minimum unemployment needed in a given country to avoid inflationary pressures. It assumes, in other words, unlike any earlier economic theorem, that a shortage of men rather than a shortage of jobs is the 'norm' of an economy and that the labour market, far from being

* See on this also the discussion of 'The Knowledge Society' in my book *The Age of Discontinuity* (London: Heinemann, 1969; Pan Books 1971).

the corrollary of the market of goods and services and of the market for money and capital, is in itself a major force moulding the economy and shaping its other two major dimensions. But this is only a beginning. Of a true economic theory of the market for work, jobs, and careers, let alone of anything comparable to Keynes's grand synthesis, there is so far not even the first sign.

Seventy years ago it was still true even in this country – as it is still true for the masses in the underdeveloped world – that most people had no choice of occupation. Even where jobs were plentiful rather than scarce, the job available to a young man and his job from there on throughout his life, was largely determined by his father's occupation and his family's economic position. For the great mass of people this simply meant that son followed father – and in most cases, of course, that son followed father behind the plough. A few very gifted or very lucky or very enterprising ones could break out of this pattern – and in that respect, of course, American society has always had more mobility than any other. But even in American society, such mobility was the exception.

Today no matter how unequally educational opportunities are distributed, the majority of the young have access to a college education, and with it, access to mobility and meaningful career choice.

Again this is even more a qualitative than a quantitative shift. It is a shift from 'looking for a job', to 'expecting a career', from 'making a living' to 'wanting to make a contribution'. The first employee indoctrination brochures, written by the early personnel men in the boom years of the mid-twenties when labour was scarce, usually started out with the question: 'What does the job demand of you?' Today's recruitment brochures usually start out with the question: 'What can you expect from the XYZ Company?' Where it was assumed, even at the peak of an earlier boom, that men were hunting for jobs, it is now assumed that jobs are hunting for men and that, therefore, they have increasingly to satisfy the values, demands, expectations, and aspirations of the knowledge worker. And, of course, the young knowledge worker is also the typical 'investor' of the new mass-capital market. This explains in large measure what to so many observers, especially the older businessmen, appears as total contradition, indeed as glaring hypocrisy, in his behaviour. He loudly proclaims his 'idealism' and his demand for a 'career that makes a contribution'. But in the next breath he asks the company recruiter: 'and what stock options do I get and how much are they worth?' But given his realities, there is no contradiction in these two expectations to the young knowledge worker – or at least not more than most people can comfortably live with.

We have been told repeatedly during the last few years that the academician no longer owes 'loyalty' to his college but instead to his 'profession' or 'discipline'. But this is true of all other knowledge workers today. They have shifted from focus on the 'job' to focus on the 'career'. The young academician is only the most visible of the lot, or perhaps only the one most visible to other academicians who write books.

But to see the full impact of this change, we best go outside the United States to Japan where mobility has always been taken for granted, way beyond its actual incidence.* For in Japan, especially for professional and managerial people, a job has long meant 'lifetime employment'. The young man, graduating from college was, so to speak, 'adopted' into a 'clan', whether government ministry, business enterprise, or university, where he then stayed automatically the rest of his life. Both leaving one's employer and being let go by him were as carefully circumscribed as is divorce in the Roman Catholic Canon Law. One could leave for only one reason: to take over the business of one's old or ailing father. One could be let go

* Job mobility in Japan is further considered in Chapters 8, 9 and 10.

only for very serious misbehaviour or actual crime. These are still the official rules. But they are no longer being observed by the young, educated Japanese. They do indeed expect the organization they join to owe them 'lifetime employment'. But they themselves demand increasingly the right to move – with proper punctilio, of course. Increasingly they expect, which is even more of an innovation, a 'career ladder' appropriate to their education and qualifications rather than advancement by seniority. Sony was the first Japanese company to realize this. Skilfully blending Japanese traditions and the new values of the young knowledge worker, it combines the security of 'lifetime employment' for those who want it with an open hiring policy for those who want to leave their old employers. It also combines pay and title by seniority with job assignments and career ladders according to qualifications and personal choice. This is probably the real 'secret' of Sony's rapid growth and its success against determined resistance to the brash newcomer by the whole force of the Japanese 'establishment'. It may well be an example from which we, in the West, can learn a good deal.

THE FIRST RESPONSES
The structural changes in the economy, at home and abroad, can be understood as first responses to the wants and values of these new mass-markets in investment and careers.

The 'diversification mergers' were defensive responses aimed at shoring up an eroding competitive position in these two new mass-markets. In essence they hardly differ from the similarly defensive mergers of the twenties, except that what forced formerly independent companies to band together at heavy cost in management position and status was growing deterioration and weakness in the capital and careers markets rather than, as in the twenties, in the market for goods and services. Many of the public announcements accompanying these mergers said so very clearly. The merger was undertaken because the combined companies expected to have 'greater ability to raise capital', or 'greater borrowing power', or 'high value for their share-owners' – as well as 'greater career opportunities for our managers', or 'more scope for our young people'. Indeed that a company can finance itself out of 'retained earnings' is, in terms of the rationality of the new markets, a major weakness rather than a strength. It does not mean that a company is 'secure' but that it is 'stagnant'. It may offer income to its owners but not capital growth. It may offer jobs for middle-aged functionaries but not opportunities and careers to young knowledge workers (let alone tempting stock options). Many of the 'diversification mergers' were, of course, only face-lifting; the now merged company is just twice as old, twice as bureaucratic, and twice as 'undynamic' as each of the original businesses were before the merger. But in a good many other cases the 'diversification merger' did, indeed, provide the 'synergism' the merger announcement talked about – but in respect to their performance capacity and ability to compete on the new mass-markets rather than in the markets for goods and services.

By contrast the 'conglomerate' created by the 'take-over merger' is an offensive response to the realities and demands of the new 'mass-markets'. 'Asset management' is simply another term for the design of a 'product' that fits the values and demands of the new investors and of their new investing institutions. For 'asset management' aims at increasing the value of a business by sloughing off the obsolete and unproductive old parts, and adding on to it new parts capable of rapid growth. In effect, the men who built the conglomerates by 'take-over' tactics and financial manipulation presented themselves to the new investor as experts in obtaining the largest capital gain in the shortest period, and above all, as to generating continuing capital gain and asset growth. These men understood that the new investors believe they can afford to take risks and indeed want to take them. The conglomerate builders understood that 'profitability' which used to mean 'return on capital' has come to mean 'price–earnings ratio' for the new investors, at least for the time being.

At the same time, the 'take-over merger' is also 'packaged' for the careers market, though by no means to the same extent. It offers a small number of people opportunities at high risk for great gain, through stock options, for instance. It appealed to a good many young people who in their present position within established, old solid companies, had a 'job' rather than a 'career', let alone a chance to become an entrepreneur themselves.

Equally, indeed more than equally, the new entrepreneurs with their new 'growth' businesses also represent a response to the demands and values of these two new mass-markets. They appealed to two quite different 'consumers' in the new capital market, with different preferences and values. They first sold to the 'sophisticated investor', that is, to the manager of the funds of the new financial consumers, the promise of rapid growth and with it of great appreciation of values. But many of them also realized that old-established large businesses with limited growth opportunities within their scope can afford to pay very high prices for 'glamour', that is, for adding smaller businesses with high-growth potential – it gives them marketability in the new mass-markets. The new entrepreneurs, in many cases, therefore, based their whole strategy on selling out to a 'giant' as soon as their new venture had become profitable.

Above all, the new entrepreneurs represent a response to the new mass-market for careers. They did not, as a rule, go after new graduates – they let somebody else train them and weed them out. They staffed their key positions – franchise owners, executives, editors, research managers, investment specialists, and so on – largely with men who had not found in their first jobs, whether in industry, in government or in the university, the career opportunities that appealed to them. Indeed these new businesses would not have been possible had there not been a large and growing number of men whose demands for career opportunities the existing secure, safe, and even well-paid jobs with the old employers could not satisfy.

The multinational corporation, and the off-shore investment trust are proof that these two new mass-markets are not confined to America but, in varying degrees, are common to all developed countries. The US-based multinational corporation which uses European capital to buy up European businesses packages investment for the new foreign investor just as the 'diversification merger' or the 'take-over merger' packaged investment for the new American investor. It gives the European investor a chance for capital gain. It gives him marketability of his investment where capital markets for most European securities in European countries are restricted to the point of being illiquid; and perhaps most importantly it gives him public disclosure of performance and results, first imposed on US corporations by the securities legislation of the thirties – and thus the information for financial and economic analysis on which 'sophisticated investors' and especially fiduciaries for other people's money must and do insist. It is no accident that the European and even the Japanese companies that have been going 'multinational' have immediately had to adopt standards of disclosure which while still inadequate by American criteria are 'indecent exposure' in a European, let alone a Japanese, business setting.

But, above all, the multinationals exploited the new 'career markets' world-wide. Where, in Europe especially, business still looks upon jobs as favours to be handed out, i.e. still acts on the assumption that even general managers are 'hired hands' of whom there is an unlimited supply, the multinationals had to recruit and had to start out with the assumption that they had to create careers attractive to highly educated young men who had plenty of career choices. On this their success rests in large measure. In many cases the multinationals have become within a decade the industry leader in many countries – not by acquisition but by developing new businesses from scratch. This, it is now generally accepted, is a managerial rather than a technological or financial achievement – but this means, specifically, ability to attract good young people, to hold them, and to allow them to go to work productively.

III

Take-overs, conglomerate-building, even new 'growth' ventures, have lost their bloom and their attraction. They became the first victims of the stock market collapse of 1969–70. Actually it was the investors' disenchantment with these darlings of the boom that set off the stock market slide in the first place.

The disenchantment was bound to happen – and this is not hindsight. It was quite clear from the very beginning that the investors who supported take-overs and went in for the new and untried 'growth' ventures were naïve to the point of being gullible (as well as greedy) rather than 'sophisticated'. It is plain silly to believe, as they did, that anything, and particularly a business, can grow forever at a high growth rate. If there is one thing certain it is that any growth curve will flatten out, and that it will flatten out the faster the steeper its initial rise. If there is one thing predictable in the case of a young and rapidly growing venture, it is a severe crisis – caused by the very growth of the business and the resulting strain on management's knowledge and ability to control. The faster a new business grows, the more severe will its 'adolescent identity crisis' be. Until this crisis has been weathered – and that often requires changes at the highest management level – no one really knows whether the business is viable, let alone whether it can resume its growth.

Some of the conglomerates – though by no means all of them – have actually done quite well; some of the 'asset managers' really managed assets and did succeed in making ailing businesses sound again and tired old businesses again able to venture, to innovate, and to perform. A large number – perhaps the majority – of the new 'growth' ventures met and successfully overcame their 'growth crisis'. But a faith in magic is not maintained by statistical averages. And the faith in the conglomerate, in the creation of productive wealth by financial manipulation and 'take-overs', and in 'growth' ventures that will succeed simply because they are in the currently fashionable industry, was magic rather than 'sophistication'. It could not survive even the slightest shadow of doubt, let alone real setbacks.

As a result of this loss of faith, many of the conglomerates – all those that depended primarily on the 'financial leverage' of a continuous rise in the price of their stocks – are in deep trouble. The most spectacular performer of a few years back, Ling-Temco-Vought, has actually had to sell off some of its earlier acquisitions and others will surely have to do the same. 'Deconglomeration' may be the 'in' word in the next few years. The most spectacular of the multinational 'asset managers', Bernard Cornfeld's Investors Overseas Service, despite its almost $2,500 million in assets, ran into very heavy weather in early 1970, as investors in its numerous affiliates and subsidiaries began to lose faith.

Even the multinational manufacturing companies, though mostly strong, powerful, solidly built companies with a strong base in their home market, face difficult times. Resistance against them on the part of national governments is growing rapidly, with the US Government – Anti-Trust, the Congress, the Internal Revenue – perhaps the most nationalist of major countries today.

THE 'INVENTORY CRISIS' IN THE CAREERS MARKET*

The mass-market for careers will, at the same time, also go through a period of readjustment, will indeed face its own first 'cyclical readjustment' – not because of economic conditions, not because of any cutback in governmental funds, but because of demography. The *supply* of college graduates is, obviously, heavily dependent on the number of babies born twenty-two years earlier. The *demand* in one important market-segment, teaching, is, however, heavily dependent on the number of babies born six to seventeen years earlier. Or to put it differently, young people have to be students and have to have teachers *before* they can themselves become available as teachers. If, therefore, there is a sudden sharp upturn in the number of babies born, there will be, a decade later, a sharp increase in demand over supply with a resultant 'inflationary pressure' on the career market. And if there is a sharp downturn in babies born, there will be, a decade later, 'deflationary pressures'. In fact, demographics (to which economists pay normally no attention) are the true dynamics of the 'career market'.

The demographic pressures on the American career market are just about to reverse themselves. Ten years ago the available new college graduates were still 'babies' of the

---

* In preparing this book for the British reader I have met only one problem of terminology. There are no strictly equivalent terms for educational institutions on both sides of the Atlantic so that amending the text in a routine mechanical fashion might be misleading. A way out, which I hope will prove helpful, is to quote the age ranges of the American students involved. They are: 'elementary school' 6–12 years; 'junior high' 12–15; 'high school' 15–18 ('junior high' and 'high school' are termed 'secondary school'); 'junior' or 'community' college 19–20; 'college' is 19–22. The American 'private school' would be called 'boarding school' in Britain. 'Public schools', which evoke images of Eton and Harrow in England, are nothing of the sort in America: in the US a 'public' school is one accountable to a local authority. The nearest English term I can think of is 'grant-aided'. With this footnote in mind I feel sure the British reader will readily follow my remarks in context.

very low birth years of the late thirties. But since the post-World War II 'baby boom' had exploded in 1946 and kept growing thereafter for ten years, the demand for teachers was, in 1960, at record height with a resulting excess of demand over supply, especially for women graduates, that created severe 'inflationary pressures'. Now, however, and for the next ten years, the situation will be the reverse: the supply will come from the very high birth years 1946–1957 – with the babies of 1957, the peak year, furnishing the graduating college class of 1980. The demand will come from the years after 1957 when the number of births at first remained even for a few years, and then, after 1961, began to fall quite sharply. Elementary school enrolment, in other words, is already going down significantly. Junior high school and high-school enrolment will start to go down in 1972 or 1973; college enrolment may well go down from 1977 or 1978; even to keep enrolment at its present levels would require a significant increase in the percentage of youngsters going to college. The careers market of the last ten years was heavily influenced by one of the sharpest jumps in the number of births ever recorded – almost 60 per cent from the 2·3 million babies born in 1937 to the 4·3 million born in 1957. The career market of the seventies will be heavily influenced by a – much less sharp but still almost unprecedented – drop in the number of babies born between 1957 and 1967 – a drop by one-fifth from 4·3 to 3·5 million.

In some ways this is good news. For it means that other segments of the economy will not be as grossly under-supplied with educated people as they have been these last ten years – health care is the most important example. So in the first place, the total pressure on the career market will go down. Where there were several jobs hunting for a graduate these last ten years – when the number of graduates was still held back by the low baby figures of the thirties and early forties – graduates and jobs will more nearly be in balance the next ten years – even if there is a boom in the economy.

Graduates will have to learn again to hunt for jobs. Above all, however, there is what in the goods-and-services economy is called an 'inventory imbalance'. Teaching, having had the greatest and most crying shortage, has been heavily staffed with young people. This is true not only in elementary and high school but in college teaching as well (even though colleges, unlike elementary and high schools, can 'stretch' the teaching supply by having large classes supplemented by 'teaching assistants' – where public schools have class-size limits imposed on them by law). William Baumol of Princeton, the leading economist of American higher education, points out that in the sixties American colleges hired five new and young teachers for every old teacher who retired or died. As a result, there will be a sharp drop in the proportion of teachers who, in the next ten and twenty years reach retirement age or die – while the total number of students will no longer go up, at least not sharply. Baumol foresees that the colleges will have to hire only three new teachers for every one who retires and dies in the seventies, and only one for each vacancy in the eighties. But in the lower schools the imbalance will be even greater – Geoffrey H. Moore, the Commissioner of Labor Statistics, and Conrad Teauber, Associate Director of the Census Bureau (as reported in *Public Interest*, Spring 1970, page 132) calculate that there will be 4·2 million women graduates between now and 1980 who will, on the basis of past experience, look for a teaching job – and only 2·4 million openings for teachers in elementary and high schools.

The present college students – undergraduate and graduate – are heavily, indeed preponderantly, oriented towards teaching – which is, of course, what the liberal arts degree concretely prepares for. They are not training for the jobs that will be there to be filled: health-care technology; professional and managerial jobs in local government (where most of the educated personnel came in during the Depression or the early forties and is nearing, if not reaching retirement age); and jobs in business, especially the highly technical 'systems' jobs needed for work on environment and ecology. The students today complain that college tries to fashion them for jobs in the 'military-industrial complex'. They would have a much stronger case complaining that they are being grossly misled – especially by the young faculty which, understandably, thinks that the last ten years were 'normal' (whereas they were unbelievably 'abnormal') – into preparing themselves for jobs that will not be available.

The shocked surprise in the spring of 1970, when the graduating class suddenly found out that they had to go out and look for jobs may thus have been the first sign of a typical 'inventory crisis' – which always takes everybody by surprise. Whatever the economic climate, the next few years will be years of sharp readjustment in the 'careers market'. The 'career' boom of the sixties is as much a thing of the past as the stock market boom in 'take-overs', 'conglomerates', and 'growth ventures'.

THE NEW 'ASSET MANAGERS'

But the new mass-markets will remain the realities of the economy – in the US as well as in all other developed countries. Indeed, more difficult times, times in which sleight of hand and manipulation are not readily mistaken for performances, will only make greater demands on the development and management of institutions to serve these new markets, their customers, and their producers.

The 'fiduciaries' – investment trusts, bank-managed funds, and pension funds – will continue to grow as the dominant forces in the markets for capital and investment. Their importance is going to increase rather than decrease if the economy no longer can count on automatic inflation. For then the difference between the 'sound' and the 'unsound' investment, between the 'growth' company and the stagnant or decaying one, between the well-managed business and the one run by chief clerks, really counts. And

then the investor who, employed himself and working for a
living, has neither time nor knowledge to pick investments
for himself, needs an 'informed buyer' far more than in
boom times. He then has to insist on getting as his investment manager the 'sophisticated investor' which so far, in a
great many cases, has only been promised to him.

It is surely symptomatic that, when Investors Overseas
Services ran into trouble in May 1970, the Rothschilds were
offering to take over the floundering investment giant. For
the Rothschilds have a unique record for turning into a permanent major institution a financial innovation when, as
the Rothschilds had predicted from the first, the founder
over-reaches himself. This knack, demonstrated again and
again in the 170 years of their history, is probably one explanation of the longevity record the Rothschilds hold as a
major financial power – outlasting by a good many years
such earlier money dynasties as Medici and Fuggers – not to
mention the one-generation mayflies of finance – the
Morgans, for instance – which America has so far
spawned.

'Asset management' may be altogether more needed than
before and become far more productive in periods of stable,
let alone of declining, business. Then it is even more important, for the health of the economy as well as for the welfare
of employees, communities, and shareholders that a
company's assets be employed most productively. Then it is
even more important that managements which because of
sloth, lack of imagination, or lack of competence, under-
manage or mismanage the assets in their keeping, be re-
placed by managements that can restore a company's
capacity to perform.

This new 'asset management' would, however, not build
'conglomerates', that is, heterogeneous business empires.
Rather one can predict it will re-deploy resources – abandon
unproductive activities, for instance; it will bring in competent management, and it will then turn back a sound

company to public ownership. Indeed some such new 'asset managers' have already begun to appear – some buying a floundering and under-managed company with the intention of re-selling it eventually as a sound and profitable business, some working for the present owners on a fee or bonus basis.

Altogether the trends that characterized the financial markets of the sixties are likely to become more rather than less dominant – even though actual forms may well change. The market is likely to be increasingly a market of 'investors' rather than of 'capitalists', and that means of people primarily interested in 'asset growth' rather than in income. It will also, predictably, become an increasingly competitive market the more informed the buyers become. It is already in all probability more competitive – and certainly far less concentrated than the market for many goods and services. Companies needing money, and that means eventually every company, will therefore have to work on making themselves 'marketable' to this new 'mass-market'. It is most unlikely that concern for financial performance and financial marketability will decrease in the next ten or fifteen years. No matter what the New Left says (indeed no matter what economic doctrine the country accepts) concern for profit will predictably not go down during the next ten years, nor will concern with capital gains. The most we can expect is that a stable dollar and control of inflation may lessen the need of the fiduciaries, and especially of the pension funds, for continuing growth in the paying value of their assets.

MAKING THE CAREERS MARKET WORK

In respect to the second of the new mass-markets, the one for careers, a period of 'inventory adjustment' will create a need for institutions adequate to serve the market. The market needs institutions which will play a role analogous to that of the 'fiduciaries' in the mass-market for capital and investment, i.e. intermediaries who are the 'informed buyers' for the 'mass consumer', the educated people look-ing for career opportunities, but also the 'informed buyer' for the 'mass producers', the employing organizations.

These will have to be 'market institutions'. The career and work dimension, especially as far as educated people look-ing for careers in knowledge work are concerned, is in-capable of being 'planned'. Indeed the Soviet attempt to 'plan' for individual careers and to direct young people ac-cordingly has been the most dismal failure of Russian plan-ning – far greater than the failure in agriculture even. In the first place, the lead time needed to 'develop the resource', that is, to train and educate for specific careers, is far longer than the time span for which we can project future needs which, in general, runs to no more than six to ten years. In addition, 'planning' here runs up against a simple law of mathematics: the impossibility of predicting the unique event (e.g. the toss of any single coin) from a large-number probability (e.g. the distribution of 1,000 tosses of a coin). And individual careers are 'unique events' far more even than tosses of a coin. Finally, of course, 'planning' careers means coercion and regimentation of the individual – and there is, fortunately, little reason to believe that our young educated people would enjoy this for their entire lives any more than they have traditionally enjoyed such 'planning' for the, after all limited, period of military service.

Yet we need to be able to provide information, guidance, and placement. This is particularly important as eight to twelve years hence we may well face another 'demographic shift' – higher birth years are almost inevitable as the babies of the 'baby boom' who now throng our college campuses marry and have children themselves. Beginning in the late seventies the number of children in school will thus start to rise again. But, judging by past experience, this will be pre-cisely the moment when the present guides of young people, especially faculties, will have adjusted their thinking to the changes in the opposite direction that are taking place now.

There are the beginnings of such institutions. The last fifteen or twenty years have seen the emergence of the 'head-hunter', or 'executive recruiter' (to give him his official name), the firm which finds executives in mid-career for new jobs. These firms are most active in business, of course. But there are some who find academic administrators, some specializing in clergymen to fill vacant pulpits, and others working exclusively as 'head hunters' for hospital administrators. There are also of course the college recruiters of the major companies – something which was literally un-heard of thirty years ago but which today is considered as much of a necessity in a large business as a research lab-oratory or a sales department. And there are a few firms which actually give career advice to the individual, and es-pecially to the mature individual who wonders whether he is in the right career path or whether he should change. Yet these are only first beginnings, comparable to the first in-vestment trusts as they developed forty years ago. They indi-cate what we need rather than themselves satisfy the need. Whether tomorrow's institutions in this new market will be 'profit' or 'not for profit', no one can predict – it may also not greatly matter. But the new 'fiduciaries' who are the 'informed buyers' in the careers market are likely to be a major 'growth industry' of the seventies.

Altogether the market for careers, in the long run, will become increasingly competitive. It will be increasingly im-portant for the 'consumer', the educated knowledge worker, to be able to make informed choices. It will be increasingly important for any institution to be able to attract the kind of people it wants and needs and to offer them what they need and look to. It will increasingly be important for any insti-tution, business or non-business, to be able to 'market' its job opportunities. It will, therefore, increasingly be necess-ary for organizations to match the available job and career opportunities to the needs, demands, and wants of the cus-tomers. Perhaps one can sum this up by saying that, during the last fifteen years, there has been great emphasis on 'manager development' aimed largely at making managers better capable to serve their organizations, whether business, government, or hospital. In the future, we are likely to balance this with growing emphasis on 'organization development' aimed at making organizations capable of satisfying the aspirations of their 'career customers', the knowledge workers.

IV

The new mass-markets will predictably generate new problems of public policy. Three in particular are already clearly visible – and for none do we have an answer; we have not even tackled our homework yet for any of them.

THE NON-OWNING 'CAPITALISTS'

The most *novel* one of these problems will be the role and responsibility of the new financial powers, the 'fiduciaries' of the financial mass-consumer who are the real 'owners' of today.

Majority ownership of America's (and Europe's) businesses will increasingly be in the hands of people who are neither owners nor managers, but trustees. What should their role be? It can be argued, in fact it has been argued by some of the most thoughtful fund managers, that being trustees they cannot and must not interfere in management. If they do not like a management, they sell their shares in the company; but they have no authority from anyone to exercise control. But if these institutions do not exercise control, who does – or can? Management either is uncontrolled and uncontrollable, or the policing function falls to the 'take-over' entrepreneur. Clearly neither solution is acceptable. Yet no new one is in sight.

But the problem can also no longer be avoided. Indeed it has been raised – though, as is the rule with new problems,

in the least expected form. 'Nader's raiders' – the young
lawyers who work under and with Ralph Nader of auto-
motive-safety fame – raised it when they asked, in the spring
of 1970, that foundations, endowments, and other trustees
withhold their proxies from General Motors management
and vote their shares instead for a series of changes in the
company's Board, its policies, and its management which
'Nader's raiders' hold to be in the public interest. Almost at
the same time, though of course in a totally unrelated development, the Anti-Trust Division of the Department of
Justice filed suit against a very large fiduciary manager, the
Continental Illinois Bank in Chicago. What the Anti-Trust
Division charged was that the Bank's practice – and every
major bank engages in it – of having different officers of the
bank sit on the boards of directors of competing companies
was in violation of anti-trust even though these directors did
not represent 'ownership' but the shares held by the bank in
trust for very large numbers of individual beneficiaries.
That, in effect, Anti-Trust attacks, as illegal, precisely the
same exercise of control, and the same interference the absence of which 'Nader's raiders' castigate, does not affect the
importance and seriousness of the issue, nor the fact that
nothing in our economic experience is much help deciding
it. But it will have to be tackled – and soon. It will, indeed
should, become a major issue of public policy for a good
many years.

THE MULTINATIONAL COMPANY
VERSUS THE NATIONAL STATE

The most *important* problem in its impact will be that of the
multinational business.

Professor Perlmutter's prediction that, in another fifteen
or twenty years, the world's manufacturing production will
be in the hands of 300 mammoth multinational companies,
while widely quoted, represents an extreme rather than the
most probable trend. But it is not rash to predict that within

every developed non-Communist country a fifth or a quarter of total manufacturing output will be produced by companies that are 'multinational' in their operations. Indeed, this is reality rather than forecast in ten of these countries (the US, Great Britain, Canada, Germany, Italy, Holland, Belgium, Switzerland, Norway, and Sweden), is fast becoming reality in another – Japan – and is not yet accomplished fact in only two (France and Brazil).*

This means that in the developed countries a very big part of the economy is subject to decisions made beyond the reach of the national government. But it also means, conversely, that governmental decisions in most developed countries – France and Canada being the only important exceptions – have impact far beyond the country's own borders through the impact they have on the multinational headquartered in that country. US anti-trust, US tax laws, US restrictions on trade with Communist powers are held by US Government authorities to bind the subsidiaries and affiliates of US-based companies everywhere. No other country is quite so openly nationalistic. But other governments too, especially those of the big countries such as France, Germany, and Japan, like to look upon 'their' multinationals as instruments of their own economic policies in the world, while at the same time, bitterly resenting that the subsidiaries of 'foreign' multinationals on their soil

* Of these, incidentally, the US, Holland, Switzerland, and Sweden are 'headquarters countries'. (These are countries in which local concerns domiciled in the country and run from it control far more business abroad than foreign concerns, domiciled elsewhere, control of the country's own business.) In Germany ownership of industry by companies based abroad – mainly US, Dutch, and Swiss – and ownership of businesses abroad by German companies roughly balance. In Japan where the 'joint-venture' predominated (i.e. a partly foreign-owned company doing business in Japan in partnership with a Japanese company), ownership or co-ownership of businesses abroad by Japanese companies is growing so fast that Japan may soon also be in 'ownership balance'. Great Britain, Canada, Italy, Belgium, France, and Brazil are far more 'owned' than 'owning'.

are, in some measure, beyond their complete control.

This is not a problem of 'capitalism'. Indeed the same ambivalence characterizes the economic relations within the Soviet bloc. Quite clearly the multinationals which the Russians have been trying to build throughout Eastern Europe are primarily resisted for political reasons. They remove a part of the Polish, Czech, or East German economy from the decision and control of the Polish, Czech, or East German governments. Multinationals, whether 'capitalist' or 'Communist', put economic rationality ahead of political sovereignty.

De Gaulle's opposition to the 'multinationals' was therefore not 'anti-American'. He not only opposed non-American multinational attempts, e.g. that of the Italian Fiat company to merge with Citroen, France's ailing automobile manufacturer, as vigorously as he opposed the Americans' coming in. He, above all, forbade French companies to become multinational themselves and to move beyond France. Indeed de Gaulle's insistence on the congruence of political and economic sovereignty is completely consistent and the only rational policy for the problem worked out so far anywhere by anyone.

It was only a total, resounding failure. A larger part of the advanced sectors of French industry – computers or pharmaceuticals, for instance – is controlled by foreign multinationals than in any of the large developed countries other than Canada. French capital, however, is more heavily invested in multinationals than the capital of any other of the 'majors'. But the investment is not in French-based multinationals making their decisions in Paris – for there are none, thanks to de Gaulle – the shares are in foreign-based, i.e. American, Swiss, Dutch, and Swedish multinationals. And at the same time, there is no country where so many of the ablest young executives, researchers, and managers work for foreign-based companies. What defeated de Gaulle, in other words, were the pressures and preferences of the two new mass-markets, especially perhaps that of the new 'consumers' of the career market, the young, educated knowledge people.

Yet de Gaulle with his usual clarity at least saw the problem. The multinational corporation is by far our most effective economic instrument today, and probably the one organ of economic development that actually develops. It is the one non-nationalist institution in a world shaken by nationalist delirium. But is not a political institution itself and must not be allowed to become one. Yet it puts economic decisions beyond the effective reach of the political process and its decision-makers, the national governments. This may well be exactly what we need to de-fang the nationalist monster. But national governments and their organs, whether legislative or executive, are unlikely to see it this way. And how we accommodate this tension between economic rationality and political sovereignty in the next few years will have a tremendous impact on both the economy and the working of government all around the world.

WHEN CONCENTRATION IS COMPETITION
But the most *difficult* problems posed by the emergence of the new markets and the new entrepreneurs are those of concentration and competition. In the other two areas we have to find new answers. In respect to concentration and competition, we have to unlearn old ones. And that is far more difficult, especially as the old ones have been held with almost religious fervour and have almost become sacred chants for large groups of economists, politicians, lawyers, and businessmen.

Two concepts have guided our approaches to the problems of concentration and competition for many years: 'concentration of manufacturing assets' and 'concentration of market power'. The measurements developed for these two aspects of economic concentration are widely accepted as giving us in conjunction both an X-ray photograph of the bony structure of our economy and reliable guides to diagnosis and treatment. But the first measurement is becoming unreliable, the second one misleading.

For a long time, maybe from 1910 on until 1960, 'concentration of manufacturing assets' remained fairly constant. But according to the anti-trusters it took a tremendous jump upward in the last twenty years. In 1950 the 200 largest 'manufacturing companies' controlled 40 per cent of the country's manufacturing assets. In 1970, we are being told, the top 200 'manufacturing companies' control 60 per cent – the biggest increase in economic concentration ever recorded in this or any other country.

The funny thing, however, is that this tremendous concentration has not been accompanied by any increase in concentration in economic power in any single market for goods, that is, in any single market in which manufacturing companies operate. In most of these markets, concentration has probably gone down during the last twenty years. In market after market, new companies have challenged the big old companies and have taken away from them a piece here or a piece there of their traditional business. This is true whether we speak of book publishing or of pharmaceuticals, of building materials, or of retail sales.

'Manufacturing assets' no longer define the concentration in the American producing economy. What is counted in this rubric includes assets shown in the balance sheets of American-domiciled businesses wherever the assets may actually be, whether within or without the United States. In 1950 these assets were almost exclusively within the United States. Today, however, most major American companies are multinational with at least 20 to 30 per cent of their production and assets outside of the United States. One-quarter of these 60 per cent, that is, 15 percentage points should be subtracted right away from the official figure which would bring the rate of concentration in US manufacturing down to 45 per cent.

At the same time, however, what counted as 'manufacturing companies' in 1950 were largely companies that were actually manufacturing. To be sure, General Motors even then owned one of the largest finance companies, the General Motors Acceptance Corporation; but its assets were a very small fraction of total GM. Today, as a result of 'diversification' and 'take-over' mergers, a very substantial number of companies which are still counted as 'manufacturing' actually have very large assets, some the majority, outside of manufacturing, in service businesses and above all in finance. And in finance, 'assets' are not really assets but essentially 'liabilities', that is, money borrowed to be lent out immediately. Whenever a manufacturing company merged with a financial company, it acquired on its balance sheet very much larger financial assets than its own 'manufacturing assets' had been, even though in terms of profitability, let alone of economic power, the manufacturing company may well have been the bigger one. These financial assets are, however, from then on considered 'manufacturing assets' in the figures. When Control Data acquired Commercial Credit on 31 December 1967, it had manufacturing assets of $470 million. Commercial Credit had assets of $3,000 million. The total of both is, however, now considered 'manufacturing assets' since Control Data was legally the acquiring company. If the biggest of all attempted 'take-overs' had gone through, that is if Leasco, a computer service company, had succeeded in taking over Chemical Bank – New York Trust Company, Leasco assets of less than $800 million would have been augmented by Chemical Bank assets of $9,000 million, with the combined total of almost $10,000 million, however, all counted as 'manufacturing assets'. We have therefore to deflate the official figure for 'manufacturing assets' by at least another 10 percentage points to take out assets that should not have been counted as 'manufacturing assets' at all. In other words, in terms of true 'manufacturing assets' in the US, the

200 largest companies today almost certainly have a smaller share of manufacturing industry than they had twenty years ago.

This would bring the two sets of figures – manufacturing assets and concentration of market power – back into alignment. Yet, clearly, the conclusion that there has been no 'concentration' is not plausible. For while there has been neither greater concentration of US manufactured assets nor greater market-concentration, the diversification and take-over mergers – and the multinational expansion – have clearly produced a considerable concentration in decision-making power. They have led to the emergence of very large businesses, acting in many areas and countries but nonetheless incorporated in one legal entity and directed by one top management.

The result, however, is often increased competition, even in the goods and services economy. And there is almost always increased competition – indeed deconcentration – in the capital and investment economy and in the work and careers economy.

The Control Data–Commercial Credit merger increased concentration in neither the computer nor the instalment-paper market. On the contrary, it made their market more competitive by strengthening what had been the 'underdogs' in both. An even more telling example is the acquisition a few years back of Folger, a rather small regional coffee blender, by Procter & Gamble. This clearly added to Procter & Gamble's bigness. Since P & G is also a leader in processed foods through its various brands of shortening, the new acquisition also added, albeit not greatly, to its market share in that industry and thereby to industrial concentration. But with the resources of Procter & Gamble behind it, Folger could reach out for national distribution. Since the national coffee market had, for years, been dominated by a very few brands in a typical 'oligopoly' pattern,

Folger's acquisition by Procter & Gamble therefore also meant significant deconcentration in one important market. What then were the 'real' consequences – concentration or deconcentration?

We may well be drifting towards a situation in which leadership and concentration in one market – that of goods, of capital or careers – is the 'countervailing force' for competition and deconcentration in one or both of the other markets. Surely, it is not without relevance that the most common criticism of 'multinationals', whether the Americans in Europe or the Europeans and Japanese in the US, has been that their size enables them to indulge in 'excessive competition'.

The pressures towards this kind of concentration, which is so very different from what the term has implied traditionally, will increase rather than decrease. Technology is pushing in that direction, especially in the materials and chemicals industries. Technology is forcing DuPont, traditionally primarily a producer of chemicals for the textile industry, e.g. synthetic fibres, to go into pharmaceuticals on the one hand and composite materials including new combination metals on the other hand. Technology has already forced, twenty years ago, two big can companies, producers of a single product, the tin can, to become manufacturers of 'packaging' which includes plastics, glass, paper products, and so on. And this, in turn, forced the largest manufacturer of paper-based packing, Container Corporation of America, as said above, to merge with a retail and mail order chain, Montgomery Ward, to obtain enough financial and management muscle to stand up to the new packaging giants. Another powerful force forcing business towards concentration will be concern with the environment. Purity of heart by itself will not clean up the environment, whether we talk of air, water, the open spaces or the city. It will require massive systems effort in every area, that is, companies that can mobilize major technological and economic resources across a wide variety of skills, disciplines, technologies, and markets.

But above all, the pressures of the new mass-markets, the mass-market for capital and investment and the mass-market for jobs and careers, should push for continuous concentration, along the new lines, that is, along the line of diversification in industry terms and diversification in geographic terms.

We will, therefore, have to think through what kind of 'diversification' is desirable, productive, and rational, and what is simply financial manipulation and empire-building. What kind makes the economy more open, more flexible, more competitive, and what kind furthers concentration and monopoly? Which one creates enterprises that are more manageable and perform better, and which one creates managerial monstrosities?

What we should want is reasonably clear. We want diversification rather than diffusion. We want federalism rather than either centralized tyranny or dispersion. We want 'asset management' rather than financial manipulation. But into which of these categories a given structure falls, is by no means clear. Indeed it is not even clear to the anti-trusters who are sharply split between those who accept and indeed welcome 'conglomerates' as leading to increased competition, and those who bitterly oppose them as producing increased concentration. This issue predictably will be one of the main concerns of the next ten years, in the United States as well as abroad. That there is no 'right' decision is not so important – there rarely is for problems of this kind. But that the old and accepted concepts and measurements are no longer appropriate, is going to make the going rough. And that we will have to learn to 'trade off', that is, to balance concentration in one economic dimension with competition in another, not only goes against the grain of decision-makers, whether economists or politicians, businessmen or bureaucrats; they all, understandably, resent and resist such complexity.

The economic developments of the last ten years signify more than a change in economic structure. They changed the structure of society. They changed economic reality. This will require new thinking and the sloughing-off of a great many traditional concepts, ideas, and policies in respect to 'monopoly', 'concentration', and 'competition', for instance, and in respect to the relationship between world economy and nation–state. It will require the development both of new theoretical understanding and new policy concepts. For so far we have no economic theory that embraces or even connects the three dimensions of the economy and thus integrates the new 'mass-markets' of capital and investment and of jobs and careers with the old mass-market of goods and services, prices, and productivity. The specific developments that characterized the sixties may well have been temporary phenomena, never to recur. The developments, of which they were the first expression and the visible symptom, have only begun.

[This essay was originally published as 'The New Markets and the New Capitalism'.]

2. The Unfashionable Kierkegaard

[From *Sewanee Review*, Autumn 1949]

This essay, written twenty years ago, also uses a symptom to identify a basic shift. The symptom was the sudden re-emergence of a forgotten thinker into the spotlight. When I first began to be interested in the late 1920s in Kierkegaard (1813–55), one had to learn Danish to read him; few of his works had been translated into any other language. Suddenly he became almost a household word. And this, it seemed to me then, indicated a shift in the awareness, the sensitivity, the world view of the West, rather than a literary fashion. What lay behind the fashion, what it could tell us about basic needs of modern man and basic trends in the modern world, is the underlying question of this essay, a question answered by trying to understand what Kierkegaard really meant and what he really had to say to us in what we have now come to call 'post-industrial society'.

I

The Kierkegaard boom of the last few years is showing the first signs of fatigue. For Kierkegaard's sake I hope it will burst soon. The Kierkegaard of the literary boom is a fellow wit and fellow modern, distinguished from the other members of the smart set mainly by his having lived a hundred years earlier. But this Kierkegaard of the psychologists, existentialists, and assorted ex-Marxists bears hardly any resemblance to the real Kierkegaard who cared nothing for psychology or dialectics (save to show them to be inadequate and irrelevant) but concerned himself solely with religious experience. And it is this real Kierkegaard who is meaningful for the modern world in its agony. We have neither Saint nor Poet to make whole the shards of our experience; in Kierkegaard we have at least a prophet.

Like all religious thinkers, Kierkegaard places in the centre the question: How is human existence possible?

All through the nineteenth century this question – which before had been the core of Western thought – was not only highly unfashionable; it seemed senseless and irrelevant. The era was dominated by a radically different question: How is society possible? Rousseau asked it, Hegel asked it, the classical economists asked it. Marx answered it one way, liberal Protestantism another way. But in whatever form it is asked, it must always lead to an answer which denies that human existence is possible except in society.

Rousseau formulated this answer for the whole era of progress: whatever human existence there is; whatever freedom, rights, and duties the individual has; whatever meaning there is in individual life – all is determined by society according to society's objective need of survival. The individual, in other words, is not autonomous. He is determined by society. He is free only in matters that do not matter. He has rights only because society concedes them. He has a will only if he wills what society needs. His life has meaning only in so far as it relates to the social meaning, and as it fulfils itself in fulfilling the objective goal of society. There is, in short, no human existence; there is only social existence. There is no individual; there is only the citizen.

It is hardly possible to exaggerate the differences between Rousseau's 'General Will', Hegel's concept of history as the unfolding of ideas, and the Marxian theory of the

individual's determination through his objectively given class
situation. But they all gave the same answer to the question
of human existence: there is no such thing, there is no such
question! Ideas and citizens exist, but no human beings.
What is possible is merely the realization of ideas in and
through society.

For if you start with the question 'How is society possible?' without asking at the same time 'How is human
existence possible?' you arrive inevitably at a negative concept of individual existence and of freedom: individual freedom is then what does not disturb society. Thus freedom
becomes something that has no function and no autonomous existence of its own. It becomes a convenience, a
matter of political strategy, or a demagogue's catch phrase.
It is nothing vital.

To define freedom as that which has no function is, however, to deny the existence of freedom. For nothing survives
in society save it have a function. But the nineteenth century
believed itself far too secure in the possession of freedom to
realize this. Prevailing opinions failed to see that to deny the
relevance of the question 'How is human existence possible?' is to deny the relevance of human freedom. It actually saw in the question 'How is society possible?' a key to
the gospel of freedom – largely because it aimed at social
equality. And the break of the old fetters of inequality appeared equivalent to the establishment of freedom.

We now have learned that the nineteenth century was mistaken. Nazism and Communism are an expensive education
– a more expensive education, perhaps, than we can afford;
but at least we are learning that we cannot obtain freedom if
we confine ourselves to the question 'How is society possible?' It may be true that human existence in freedom is not
possible; which is, indeed, asserted by Hitler and the Communists as well as, less openly, by all those well-meaning
'social engineers' who believe in social psychology, propaganda, re-education, or administration, as a means of

moulding and forming the individual. But at least the question 'How is human existence possible?' can no longer be regarded as irrelevant. For those who profess to believe in freedom there is no more relevant inquiry.

I am not trying to say that Kierkegaard was the only thinker during the nineteenth century who saw the direction in which Rousseau was leading the Western world. There were the Romanticists, some of whom, especially in France, sensed what was coming. There was the futile and suicidal revolt of Nietzsche – a Samson whose gigantic power pulled down nothing but himself. There was above all Balzac, who analysed a society in which human existence was no longer possible, and who drew an Inferno more terrible than Dante's in that there is not even a Purgatory above it. But although they all asked 'How is human existence possible?' none but Kierkegaard answered.

II

Kierkegaard's answer is simple: human existence is possible only in tension – in tension between man's simultaneous life as an individual in the spirit and as a citizen in society. Kierkegaard expressed the fundamental tension in a good many ways throughout his writings – most clearly and centrally when he described the tension as the consequence of man's simultaneous existence in eternity and in time. He took his formulation from St Augustine; it is the intellectual climax of the *Confessions*. But Kierkegaard gave to the antithesis a meaning that goes far beyond St Augustine's speculation in dialectical logic.

Existence in time is existence as a citizen in this world. In time, we eat and drink and sleep, fight for conquest or for our lives, raise children and societies, succeed or fail. But in time we also die. And in time there is nothing left of us after our death. In time we do not, therefore, exist as individuals. We are only members of a species, links in a chain of generations. The species has an autonomous life in time, specific characteristics, an autonomous goal; but the member has no life, no characteristics, no aim outside the species. He exists only in and through the species. The chain has a beginning and an end, but each link serves only to tie the links of the past to the links of the future; outside the chain it is scrap iron. The wheel of time keeps on turning, but the cogs are replaceable and interchangeable. The individual's death does not end the species or society, but it ends his life in time. Human existence is not possible in time, only society is possible in time.

In eternity, however, in the realm of the spirit, 'in the sight of God', to use one of Kierkegaard's favourite terms, it is society which does not exist, which is not possible. In eternity only the individual does exist. In eternity each individual is unique; he alone, all alone, without neighbours and friends, without wife and children, faces the spirit in himself In time, in the sphere of society, no man begins at the beginning and ends at the end; each of us receives from those before us the inheritance of the ages, carries it for a tiny instant, to hand it on to those after him. But in the spirit, each man is beginning and end. Nothing his fathers have experienced can be of any help to him. In awful loneliness, in complete, unique singleness, he faces himself as if there were nothing in the entire universe but him and the spirit in himself. Human existence is thus existence on two levels – existence in tension.

It is impossible even to approximate eternity by piling up time; mere time, even infinitely more time, will still only be time. And it is also impossible to reach time by subdividing eternity; eternity is inseparable and immeasurable. Yet it is only as simultaneous existence on both planes, existence in the spirit and existence in society, that human existence is possible. St Augustine had said that time is within eternity, created by eternity, suspended in it. But Kierkegaard knew that the two are on different planes, antithetic and incompatible with each other. And he knew it not only by logic and by introspection, but by looking at the realities of nineteenth-century life.

It is this answer that constitutes the essential paradox of religious experience. To say that human existence is possible only in the tension between existence in eternity and existence in time is to say that human existence is only possible if it is impossible: what existence requires on the one level is forbidden by existence on the other. For example, existence in society requires that the society's objective need for survival determine the functions and the actions of the citizen. But existence in the spirit is possible only if there is no law and no rule except that of the person, alone with himself and with his God. Because man must exist in society, there can be no freedom except in matters that do not matter; but because man must exist in the spirit, there can be no social rule, no social constraint in matters that do matter. In society, man can exist only as a social being – as husband, father, child, neighbour, fellow-citizen. In the spirit, man can exist only personally – alone, isolated, completely walled in by his own consciousness.

Existence in society requires that man accept as real the sphere of social values and beliefs, rewards and punishments. But existence in the spirit, 'in the sight of God', requires that man regard all social values and beliefs as pure deception, as vanity, as untrue, invalid and unreal. Kierkegaard quotes from Luke xiv, 26: 'If any man come to me, and hate not his father and mother, and wife and children, and brethren and sisters, yea and his own life also, he cannot be my disciple.' The Gospel of Love does not say: *love* these *less* than you love me; it says *hate*.

To say that human existence is possible only as simultaneous existence in time and in eternity is thus to say that it is possible only as one crushed between two irreconcilable ethical absolutes. And that means (if it be more than the mockery of cruel gods): human existence is possible only as

existence in tragedy. It is existence in fear and trembling; in
dread and anxiety; and, above all, in despair.

III

This seems a very gloomy and pessimistic view of human
existence, and one hardly worth having. To the nineteenth
century it appeared as a pathological aberration. But let us
see where the optimism of the nineteenth century leads to.
For it is the analysis of this optimism and the prediction of
its ultimate outcome that gave Kierkegaard's work its
vision.

It was the very essence of all nineteenth-century creeds
that eternity can and will be reached in time; that truth can
be established in society and through majority decision; that
permanence can be obtained through change. This is the
belief in inevitable progress, representative of the nineteenth
century and its very own contribution to human thought.
You may take the creed of progress in its most naïve and
therefore most engaging form – the confidence that man
automatically and through his very sojourn in time becomes
better, more nearly perfect, more closely approaches the
divine. You may take the creed in its more sophisticated
form – the dialectic schemes of Hegel and Marx in which
truth unfolds itself in the synthesis between thesis and antithesis, each synthesis becoming in turn the thesis of a new
dialectical integration on a higher and more nearly perfect
level. Or you may take the creed in the pseudo-scientific
garb of the theory of evolution through natural selection. In
each form it has the same substance: a fervent belief that by
piling up time we shall attain eternity; by piling up matter we
shall become spirit; by piling up change we shall become
permanent; by piling up trial and error we shall find truth.
For Kierkegaard, the problem of the final value was one of
uncompromising conflict between contradictory qualities.
For the nineteeth century, the problem was one of quantity.

Where Kierkegaard conceives the human situation as essentially tragic, the nineteenth century overflowed with optimism. Not since the year 1000, when all Europe expected the Second Coming, has there been a generation which saw itself so close to the fulfilment of time as did the men of the nineteenth century. Certainly there were impurities in the existing fabric of society. But the liberal confidently expected them to be burnt away within a generation or, at the most, within a century by the daily strengthening light of reason. Progress was automatic. And though the forces of darkness and superstition might seem to gain at times, that was only a momentary illusion. 'It is always darkest just before the dawn' is a truly liberal maxim (and one, incidentally, as false in its literal as in its metaphorical sense). The apogee of this naïve optimism was the book which the famous German biologist, Ernst Haeckel, wrote just before the turn of the century – the one which predicted that all the remaining questions would be finally and decisively answered within a generation by Darwinian biology and Newtonian physics. It is perhaps the best commentary on the fate of the nineteenth-century creed that Haeckel's *Weltraetsel* sold by the millions in the generation of our grandfathers (and still hides out on old bookshelves) at the very moment when the universe of Darwinian biology and Newtonian physics was completely disintegrating.

To those whom the optimism of liberalism or Darwinism failed to satisfy, Marx offered the more complicated but also infinitely more profound vision of a millennium that had to come precisely because the world was so corrupt and so imperfect. His was a truly apocalyptic message in which the impossible, the attainment of the permanent perfection of the classless society, is promised precisely because it is impossible. In Marx the nineteenth-century optimism admits defeat – only to use defeat as a proof of certain victory.

In this creed of imminent perfection, in which every progress in time meant progress towards eternity, permanence, and truth, there was no room for tragedy (the conflict of two absolute forces, of two absolute laws). There was not even room for catastrophe. Everywhere in the nineteenth-century tradition the tragic is exorcized, catastrophe suppressed. A good example is the attempt – quite popular these last few years – to explain so cataclysmic a phenomenon as Hitlerism in terms of 'faulty psychological adjustment', that is, as something that has nothing to do with the spirit but is exclusively a matter of techniques. Or, in a totally different sphere, compare Shakespeare's *Antony and Cleopatra* with Flaubert's *Madame Bovary*, and see how the essentially tragic 'eros' becomes pure 'sex' – psychology, physiology, even passion, but no longer a tragic, i.e. an insoluble, conflict. Or one might, as one of the triumphs of the attempt to suppress catastrophe, take the early Communist explanation of Nazism as 'just a necessary stage in the inevitable victory of the proletariat'. There you have in purest form the official creed that whatever happens in time must be good, however evil it is. Neither catastrophe nor tragedy can exist.

There has never been a century of Western history so far removed from an awareness of the tragic as the one that bequeathed to us two world wars. Not quite two hundred years ago – in 1755 to be exact – the death of 15,000 people in the Lisbon earthquake was enough to bring down the tottering structure of traditional Christian belief in Europe. The contemporaries could not make sense of it, they could not reconcile this horror with the concept of an all-merciful God, they could not see any answer to a paradox of catastrophe of such magnitude. For years now we have learned daily of vastly greater destruction, of whole peoples being starved or exterminated. And it is far more difficult to comprehend these man-made catastrophes in terms of our modern rationality than it was for the eighteenth century to comprehend the earthquake of Lisbon in the terms of traditional Christianity. Yet our own catastrophes make no impression on the optimism of those thousands of committees that are dedicated to the belief that permanent peace and prosperity will 'inevitably' issue from today's horrors. To be sure, they are aware of the facts and duly outraged by them. But they refuse to see them as catastrophes. They have been trained to deny the existence of tragedy.

IV

Yet however successful the nineteenth century was in suppressing the tragic, there is one fact that could not be suppressed, one fact that remains outside of time: death. It is the one fact that cannot be made general but remains unique, the one fact that cannot be socialized but remains personal. The nineteenth century made every effort to strip death of its individual, unique, and qualitative aspect. It made death an incident in vital statistics, measurable quantitatively, predictable according to the actuarial laws of probability. It tried to get around death by organizing away its consequences. Life insurance is perhaps the most significant institution of nineteenth-century metaphysics; its proposition 'to spread the risks' shows most clearly the nature of the attempt to consider death an incident in human life rather than its termination. And the nineteenth century invented spiritualism – an attempt to control life after death by mechanical means.

Yet death persists. Society might make death taboo, might lay down the rule that it is bad manners to speak of death, might substitute 'hygienic' cremation for those horribly public funerals, and might call grave-diggers morticians. The learned Professor Haeckel might hint broadly that Darwinian biology is just about to make us live permanently; but he did not make good his promise. And so long as death persists, the individual remains with one pole of his existence outside of society and outside of time.

So long as death persists, the optimistic concept of life, the belief that eternity can be reached through time, and that the

individual can fulfil himself in society, must have only one
outcome – despair. Suddenly every man finds himself facing
death; and at this point he is all alone; all individual. If his
existence is purely in society, he is lost – for now this existence becomes meaningless. Kierkegaard diagnosed the
phenomenon and called it the 'despair at not willing to be an
individual'. Superficially, the individual can recover from
this encounter with the problem of existence in eternity; he
may even forget it for a while. But he can never regain his
confidence in his existence in society. Basically he remains in
despair.

Society must make it possible for man to die without despair if it wants him to be able to live exclusively in society.
And it can do so in only one way – by making individual life
meaningless. If you are nothing but a leaf on the tree of the
race, a cell in the body of society, then your death is not
really death; you had better call it a process of collective
regeneration. But then, of course, your life is not a real life
either; it is just a functional process within the life of the
whole, devoid of any meaning except in terms of the whole.
Thus as Kierkegaard foresaw a hundred years ago, an optimism that proclaims human existence as existence in society
leads straight to despair. And this despair can lead only to
totalitarianism. For totalitarianism – and that is the trait
that distinguishes it so sharply from the tyrannies of the past
– is based on the affirmation of the meaninglessness of life
and of the non-existence of the person. Hence the emphasis
in the totalitarian creed is not on how to live, but on how to
die; to make death bearable, individual life had to be made
worthless and meaningless. The optimistic creed, that
started out by making life in this world mean everything, led
straight to the Nazi glorification of self-immolation as the
only act in which man can meaningfully exist. Despair
becomes the essence of life itself.

V

The nineteenth century arrived at the very point the pagan world had reached in the late Roman Empire. And like antiquity, it tried to find a way out by escaping into the purely ethical – by basing virtue on man's reason. The great philosophical systems of German idealism – above all Kant's, but also Hegel's – dominated the age because they identified reason with virtue and the good life. Ethical culture and that brand of liberal Protestantism that sees in Jesus the 'best man that ever lived', with its slogans of the Golden Rule, of the 'categorical imperative', and of the satisfaction of service – these and related ethical formulae became as familiar in the nineteenth century as most of them had been in antiquity. And they failed to provide a basis for human existence in modernity just as they had failed two thousand years before.

In its best representatives, the ethical concept leads indeed to moral integrity and moral greatness. Nineteenth-century humanism – based half on Plutarch, half on Newton – could be a noble thing. (We have only to remember the great men of the last nineteenth-century generation, such as Woodrow Wilson, Masaryk, Jaurès, or Mommsen.) Kierkegaard himself was more attracted by it than he realized. Though fighting every inch of the way, he could never quite free himself from the influence of Hegel; and Socrates, symbol of the ethical life, remained to him the apogee of man's natural history.

But Kierkegaard also saw that the ethical concept, while it may give integrity, courage, and steadfastness, cannot give meaning – neither to life nor to death. All it can give is stoic resignation. Kierkegaard considered this position to be one of even greater despair than the optimistic one; he calls it 'the despair at willing to be an individual'. And only too often the ethical position does not lead to anything as noble and as consistent as the Stoic philosophy, but turns into sugar coating on the pill of totalitarianism. This is, I feel, the position of many an apologist for Soviet Russia; he hopes that man will find individual fulfilment in the ethical attempt at making his neighbour happy; and that this will suffice to offset the reality of totalitarianism. Or the ethical position becomes pure sentimentalism – the position of those who believe that evil can be abolished and harmony established by good intentions.

And in all cases the ethical position is bound to degenerate into relativism. For if virtue is to be found in man, everything that is accepted by man must be virtue. Thus a position that starts out – as did Rousseau and Kant a hundred and seventy-five years ago – to establish man-made ethical absolutes, must end in the complete denial of absolutes and, with it, in the complete denial of the possibility of a truly ethical position. This way there is no escape from despair.

Is then the only conclusion that human existence can be only existence in tragedy and despair? Are the sages of the East right who see the only answer in the destruction of self, in the submersion of man into the Nirvana, the nothingness?

Kierkegaard has another answer: human existence is possible as existence not in despair, as existence not in tragedy – it is possible as existence in faith. The opposite of Sin (to use the traditional term for existence purely in society) is not Virtue; it is Faith.

Faith is the belief that in God the impossible is possible, that in Him time and eternity are one, that both life and death are meaningful. Faith is the knowledge that man is creature – not autonomous, not the master, not the end, not the centre – and yet responsible and free. It is the acceptance of man's essential loneliness, to be overcome by the certainty that God is always with man; even 'unto the hour of our death'.

In my favourite among Kierkegaard's books, a little

volume called *Fear and Trembling* (1843), he raises the question: What distinguished Abraham's willingness to sacrifice his son, Isaac, from ordinary murder? If Abraham had never intended to go through with the sacrifice, but had intended all the time only to make a show of his obedience to God, then Abraham indeed would not have been a murderer, but he would have been something more despicable: a fraud and a cheat. If he had not loved Isaac but had been indifferent, he would have been willing to be a murderer. Yet Abraham was a holy man; God's command was for him an absolute command to be executed without reservation; and we are told that he loved Isaac more than himself. The answer is that Abraham had faith. He believed that in God the impossible would become possible – that he could carry out God's command and yet retain Isaac.

Abraham was the symbol for Kierkegaard himself, and the sacrifice of Isaac the symbol for his own innermost secret, his great and tragic love – a love he had slaughtered although he loved it more than he loved himself. But the autobiographical allusion is only incidental. The story of Abraham is a universal symbol of human existence which is possible only in faith. In faith the individual becomes the universal, ceases to be isolated, becomes meaningful and absolute; hence in faith there is a true ethic. And in faith existence in society becomes meaningful, too, as existence in true charity.

The faith is not what today is so often glibly called a 'mystical experience' – something that can apparently be induced by the proper breathing exercises or by prolonged exposure to Bach (not to mention drugs). It can be attained only through despair, through suffering, through painful and ceaseless struggle. It is not irrational, sentimental, emotional, or spontaneous. It comes as the result of serious thinking and learning, of rigid discipline, of complete sobriety, of humbleness, and of the self's subordination to a higher, an absolute will. The inner knowledge of one's own unification in God – what St Paul called hope and we call saintliness – only a few can attain. But every man is capable of attaining faith. For every man knows despair.

Kierkegaard stands squarely in the great Western tradition of religious experience, the tradition of St Augustine and St Bonaventura, of Luther, St John of the Cross, and Pascal. What sets him apart, and gives him this special urgency today, is his emphasis on the meaning of life in time and society for the man of faith, the Christian. Kierkegaard is 'modern', not because he employs the modern vocabulary of psychology, aesthetics, and dialectics – the ephemeral traits which the Kierkegaard boom ballyhoos – but because he concerns himself with the specific disease of the modern West: the falling apart of human existence, the denial of the simultaneity of life in the spirit and life in the flesh, the denial of the meaningfulness of each for the other.

Instead, we have today a complete divorce, the juxta-position of 'Yogi' and 'Commissar' – the terms are of course Arthur Koestler's – as mutually exclusive possibilities: an either–or between time and eternity, charity and faith, in which one pole of man's dual existence is made the absolute. This amounts to a complete abdication of faith: the 'Com-missar' gives up the entire realm of the spirit for the sake of power and effectiveness; the 'Yogi' assigns human existence in time, that is social life, to the devil, and is willing to see millions lose their lives and their souls if only his own 'I' be saved. Both are impossible positions for any religious man to take, but especially for a Christian who must live in the spirit and yet must maintain that true faith is effective in and through charity (i.e. in and through social responsibility).

But at least both are honest positions, honestly admitting their bankruptcy – in contrast to the attempt at evading the problem by way of the various 'Christian' political parties in Europe, Protestant and Catholic, or the movement for 'Social Christianity' still powerful in this country. For these attempts substitute morality and good intentions for faith and religious experience as mainsprings of action. While sincere and earnest, while supported and sometimes led by good, even by saintly men, they must not only be as ineffectual in politics as the 'Yogi' but must also fail, like the 'Commissar', to give spiritual life; for they compromise both, life in time and life in eternity. That Austrian cleric and Catholic party leader who, in the thirties, came out for Hitler with the argument 'at least he is opposed to mixed bathing', was a ghastly caricature of the Christian moralist in politics; but he caricatured something that is ever present where morality is confused with faith.

Kierkegaard offers no easy way out. Indeed it could be said of him – as of all religious thinkers who focus on experience rather than on reason and dogma – that he greatly over-emphasizes life in the spirit, thus failing to integrate the two poles of human existence into one whole. But he not only saw the task, he also showed in his own life and in his works that there is no escape from the reality of human existence, which is one in tension. It is no accident that the only part of Kierkegaard's tremendous literary output that did not originally appear under a pseudonym but under his own name were the *Edifying Discourses* of the late eighteen-forties. Not that he wanted to conceal his authorship of the other works – the pseudonyms could not have fooled anybody; but the 'edifying' books alone translate faith into social effectiveness and are thus truly religious and not just 'Yogi'. It is also not an accident that Kierkegaard's whole work, his twenty years of seclusion, of writing, thinking, praying, and suffering, were but the preparation for the violent political action to which he dedicated the last months of his life – a furious one-man war on the Established Church of Denmark and its high clergy for confusing morality and tradition with charity and faith.

Though Kierkegaard's faith cannot overcome the awful loneliness, the isolation and dissonance of human existence, it can make it bearable by making it meaningful. The philosophy of the totalitarian creeds enables man to die. It is dangerous to underestimate the strength of such a philosophy; for, in a time of sorrow and suffering, of catastrophe and horror (that is, in our time), it is a great thing to be able to die. Yet it is not enough. Kierkegaard's faith, too, enables man to die; but it also enables him to live.

3. The Romantic Generation

[From *Harper's Magazine*, May 1966]

Inundated as we are today by writings on the 'generation gap', or the 'student rebellion', it may come as a surprise that no one, only five years ago – at least not in the United States – had realized that a profound change was in the making in the world view, the attitude, the values of the young, educated people. Yet, to my knowledge, this essay was the first to voice the suspicions that such a change was under way. My editor even then felt that I was making a mountain out of a molehill – he changed my original title which, if I remember, was 'The Desertion of the Young'. Today, five years later, the young no longer read the books they devoured five years ago – Fromm, Paul Goodman, Ayn Rand are no longer campus heroes, at least not among the 'militants'; even Marcuse has apparently become 'yesterday' to them. Still this does not change the diagnosis. For once the moods of adolescence really seem to foreshadow a shift in the vision of the adults. And even the premonition – only a suspicion then – that the idealism and 'sincerity' of the young people could be exploited demagogically and turned into mindless violence, has sadly been borne out by events.

In many ways this essay is a 'response' to the essay on Kierkegaard which precedes it; 'The Romantic Generation' has raised Kierkegaard's existential questions.

I

'I am Mother O'Rourke,' the voice on the telephone said. 'I
am Dean of Students at a large Catholic women's college.
Mother President and all our faculty very much hope that
you will accept our invitation to talk to our girls on social
issues and their importance. Ten years ago our students
were deeply interested in labour relations, international relations, and in other major social and political problems.
Now they care only for matters of conscience and personal
behaviour, such as civil rights, a "personal philosophy of
life", or the size of their own future family and how to raise
it. That's wonderful, of course, and we are all for it. But
economic and political questions still exist and are far from
solved. The girls surely ought to know something about
them and not just concern themselves all the time with their
little selves and their own conscience.'

A dean trying to con a prospective speaker (especially if
there is no fee) has no more truth in him than a Texas wild-
catter raising sucker money. Yet Mother O'Rourke's call
pulled together for me a lot of observations that have made
me question the accepted picture of an important group of
today's young adults – the men and women between twenty
and twenty-five who are in college or graduate school. This
picture, it seems to me, does not fit at all the influential,
though not very large, group which sets the intellectual
fashions on campuses from San Diego State to the Harvard
Yard.

'Everybody knows' for instance that these educated
young adults have discarded the Protestant Ethic of their
forefathers. And ever since David Riesman's brilliant book
The Lonely Crowd in 1950, it has been almost an axiom that
the young American is increasingly outer-directed. But
when I hung up, after extricating myself from Mother
O'Rourke's invitation, it suddenly dawned on me that many
of the young Americans now in college and graduate school

are searching for an ethic based on personal (if not spiritual) values, rather than on social utility or community mores – what one might call an Ecumenical Ethic. The old ideologies and slogans leave these young adults cold – as does President Johnson's Great Society. But there is a passionate groping for personal commitment to a philosophy of life. Above all, a new inner-directedness is all the rage in this group.

The clearest symptom of this is, perhaps, the books that are the fashion on campus. Undergraduates and graduate students alike read a great deal of what one of them – a teaching assistant in history – aptly calls 'Instant Zen'. They read Erich Fromm. They devour those two apparently incompatible but actually complementary pamphleteers: (1) Paul Goodman (*Growing Up Absurd, Utopian Essays*), a latter-day Thoreau opposed to society and all its work whose Walden Pond is the graduate psychology department; and (2) Ayn Rand (*Fountainhead*, *Atlas Shrugged*, and a new book, just out, *The Virtue of Selfishness*), a Nietzsche of the Employers' Association, preaching the organization superman. And they read Sartre. (Despite their professed interest in Existentialism, they tend to consign Camus to the limbo of 'required reading'; his very compassion, generosity and concern for his fellow-man make him suspect as a 'classic'.)

Ever since adolescence was invented 200 years ago, in Goethe's *Young Werther* (incidentally the first international best-seller), it has always had a literature it claimed for its very own. Salinger's *Catcher in the Rye* – another *Young Werther*, though one living in an affluent society which can afford salvation by psychoanalysis, instead of by suicide as in Goethe's book – was the 'in' book of the young adults ten years ago. Our grandmothers hid in their bosoms tear-stained albums of Swinburne's slightly rancid sensuality. Generations of level-headed, no-nonsense New England girls have got drunk on the low-calorie carbonated syrup of Kahlil Gibran's *The Prophet*. Generations of equally level-headed European boys, diligently preparing to be German engineers or French customs inspectors, have swooned over Stendhal's passionately passionless male Lolitas. When my own generation reached young adulthood around 1930, T. S. Eliot's *The Waste Land* and the early Donne were our Bibles; we missed the H. L. Mencken and Nietzsche fashions by only a few years.

The specific authors and books of the campus fashion thus vary greatly from one generation to the other – and not only in their literary merits. But the whole genre has common characteristics. It is naïvely sentimental, for instance, or saturated with the bitter-sweet sadness the Germans call *Weltschmerz* (and which only the very healthy, vigorous, and hopeful – that is the young – can afford). They tend to wallow in self-pity (in which department *The Sorrows of Young Werther* still holds the unchallenged world record). The idols of every campus generation have always been against everything and *for* nothing. The twenty-year-olds, after all, while mature in body and mind, are still exempted from responsibility – are indeed being encouraged in the pleasant delusion that Daddy will take care of everything, whether they smash a car bumper or an institution.

II

This literature always reflects the mood of its generation. It is the young adult's own, precisely because it says what he feels but is unable to express himself. These books do not talk *to* their reader; they talk *for* him. Even though ephemeral – and, often enough, trash – the books faithfully mirror how the campus generation of the moment sees itself, or at the least how it wants to see itself.

The books of this kind in fashion today are contemptuous of, if not hostile to, society and its demands, values, and rewards. They proclaim that truth can be found only in one's own inner experience, and that the demands of one's own personal conscience are a trustworthy guide to behaviour and action. Sartre is 'in' – as Camus is not – because only the cocoon of his own words and thoughts exists for him.

The 'moderate' among these authors today is clearly Erich Fromm, the neo-Freudian psychoanalyst. He plays in today's campus culture the role that Reinhold Niebuhr played thirty years ago. Niebuhr even then warned against forgetting the person and his spiritual needs. But he was the idol of the young because in those days he preached the 'social gospel' of public responsibility and liberal reform. Fromm today, by contrast, warns against forgetting community and society; but he is accepted because his main stress is on the person and his relationship to himself. Niebuhr asked: What society do you, as a moral man, want? Fromm asks: What kind of person do you want to be? Like the others writers who speak for the young adults – from 'Instant Zen' to Paul Goodman and Ayn Rand – Fromm is self-centred.

There are a good many other symptoms of the new 'inner-directedness'. The vogue of the word 'sincerity' is one. To the older generation this is an embarrassing word: we remember the appeasers and quislings of thirty years ago saying, 'At least Hitler is *sincere*'. But to today's young adult 'sincerity' is again a valid, if not the ultimate, test of behaviour, especially in public life. I listened a year ago to some graduate students, bright and well informed, discussing an all-night teach-in at Columbia University. They were not a bit interested in logic or in the arguments, let alone in the factual assertions of the various speakers. All they wanted to know was, 'Do you think he was sincere?'

A related phenomenon is the current interest in the 'mind drugs' such as LSD. Whatever else they do, the hallucinations they produce are entirely self-centred inner experiences of one's own consciousness, with no outside world, no other person, no relationships in them.

On a mountain hike last summer – a few weeks after Mother O'Rourke's telephone call – a psychologist friend began to talk about the 'management problems' of a Midwestern mental-health centre which trains postgraduate students in sizeable numbers to become psychiatrists, psychologists, and social workers.

'To what do you attribute these management problems,' I interrupted. 'Your growth?'

'We have grown of course very rapidly – four-fold since 1950,' he answered. 'But this is a minor factor. Our big problem is the radical shift in student attitude. The men who came to us ten or fifteen years ago wanted to be scientists. They were research-oriented. They got upset when they found out that in psychology or psychiatry empirical data and scientific theory are not enough. We had to hammer home day after day that the practitioner always deals with a unique human being, his emotions, aspirations, experiences, values – and that the practitioner himself is a human being too.

'The men we get today are scientifically much better trained as a rule. But they tend to be frustrated clergymen who only come to us because there is no ecumenical, non-denominational seminary around. We have to tell them every day that fulfilling oneself, compassion, and love for one's neighbour aren't enough – indeed, will do damage unless supported by empirical facts and buttressed by sound theory. The men we got ten or fifteen years ago were out to find the facts; the men we get today, are out to find themselves.'

III

What explains such a shift from the outer-directed student of the 1950s to the inner-directed student of today?

One cause is certainly the disenchantment of this particular group of young people with the traditional social
issues. However important they may be, such issues are not
very exciting in the 1960s. It is hard for anybody to get up
much emotional steam about the pension demands of the
newspaper unions. And who is the 'wicked imperialist' in
the conflict between India and Pakistan? Indeed, most
social problems have ceased to be 'issues' and have become
'fields of study'. Where they used to call for passion leading
to commitment and action, they now call for hard, plodding
work leading to a PhD thesis. And very few PhD theses have
ever fired the imagination and engrossed the emotions even
of the men who wrote them, let alone of a generation of
young people.

A second factor is that there are so many more graduate
students in pursuit of a higher degree. The emergence and
rapid growth of a distinct graduate-student community
fosters emphasis on 'inner experience', on 'sincerity', and on
the search for a 'personal philosophy'. Many graduate students have an outsized guilt feeling and therefore need an
inner-directed ethic to justify themselves to themselves.

In part, they need a rationalization for their economic
status. Most graduate students, while far from rich, live well
above the poverty line. Their income, however, comes from
fellowships or grants rather than from wages. If there is a
wage-earner in the family it is the wife rather than the husband. As consumers they are part of the affluent society. But
as producers they are outside of it. Some graduate students
are so self-conscious about this that they seriously advocate
the payment of regular wages for going to graduate school.
But many more search for an ethic which would base economic reward on what work means to a man and contributes
to his self-development, rather than on its social utility and
its value to others.

Above all, however, the graduate student needs such an
inner-directed ethic to rationalize his own motives. To be

sure, love of scholarship is the main motivation for some, others are attracted by the rewards which our economy offers the man with advanced specialized training. But a good many graduate students know perfectly well that they decided to stay in school in large part because grants and fellowships made it easy. Often they secretly suspect that they use graduate school as a pleasant way to postpone growing up, with its many commitments and decisions. Others are in graduate school for the sake of the draft exemption – and they cannot help knowing it. When they talk about their reasons for staying on in school – and they talk about them on and on and on – they therefore tend to stress 'self-fulfilment', 'sincerity', 'basic values', and 'personal philosophy of life'.

Though going on to graduate school is fast becoming the correct thing to do in the better colleges, the graduate-school community is quite small – maybe half a million people at any one time, counting the students, their wives, and children. This group however has influence out of all proportion to its size. It is highly concentrated in a very few large universities – such as the University of California at Berkeley, Harvard, MIT, Cal Tech, New York University, Chicago, and Stanford. As a result it tends to dominate the prestige schools, which are of course the pace-setters and fashion makers for the entire academic world, faculty as well as students. Indeed, for the first time – in the Berkeley riots and in a good many of the teach-ins – graduates rather than undergraduate students took the lead.

The great catalyst of the new mood has of course been the civil-rights campaign. It gave the campus generation the Cause it had been waiting for: a cause of conscience. The young people are much closer in their views on civil rights to the abolitionists of a century ago than they are to yesterday's liberals. The oppression of the Negro is to them a sin rather than a wrong. 'We Shall Overcome' has the ring of a gospel hymn rather than that of a *New Republic* editorial.

This explains in large part the tremendous impact the civil-rights movement has had on the mood, vision, and world-view of the campus generation. In addition, civil rights has offered scope for individual initiative and effectiveness, something our society otherwise does not readily grant to men or women in their early twenties. There are the students, white and coloured, who have gone South to teach in the Freedom Schools. There are the white college girls up North who in considerable numbers venture into the meanest Negro-ghettos of the big cities to tutor or counsel, often entirely on their own.

Yet developments in this country alone cannot explain the shift in mood. It is by no means an American phenomenon. It is indeed going on in all industrially developed countries, regardless of race or political and economic systems. In both Western and Eastern Europe those apostles of inner-directedness, the American Beat poets such as Allen Ginsberg, are extraordinarily popular. The idol of Russia's university students is Yevgeni Yevtushenko – a poet of the individual conscience, before which society is all but irrelevant. And the one mass movement in any industrial country today that has attracted large numbers of the college generation is the Japanese Soka Gakkai – half religious fundamentalism preaching the absolute primacy of inner experiences, half political fanaticism with 'sincerity' its only slogan.

IV

Fashions – especially adolescent fashions – do not as a rule outlast their generation. There is just a slim chance, however, that the mood of this campus generation will prove to be one of the rare exceptions: a first premonition of a change in the consciousness and vision of modern man.

The present disinterest on campus in social problems may possibly – just barely possibly – be a first hint that the

conventional social issues are increasingly becoming red her-
rings. Terms such as 'management and labour', the
'concentration of economic power', or 'big government' all
assume that there are a few big organizations in a society
which is otherwise relatively power-free. But actually in our
society all social tasks tend to ball together into large and
complex organizations of tremendous power.

The institution that has grown the most in this century is
not in the economic or political sphere at all. It is the university. There is actually more concentration of brainpower in
the twenty largest universities than there ever was a concentration of economic power in the heyday of the Morgans
and the Rockefellers, before the passage of the anti-trust
laws. The hospital has also become big and complex – and
so has the Catholic Diocese in the modern metropolis, the
American Medical Association, the armed forces, the civil
service, and so on. The fact of big, complex organization,
rather than this or that embodiment of it, is now the matter
of central significance. To single out any one institution as
the organization is to make impossible an understanding of
the issue, let alone a solution.

This, I think, is beginning to be felt. Or is it pure coincidence that we recently had two totally unconnected
revolts against organizational power structures which were
never before seen as problem areas: the Berkeley student
riot and the attacks on the Roman bureaucracy of the Catholic Church at the Vatican Council, especially in its first two
sessions before Pope John's death?

The big complex modern organization does indeed present a number of strange problems. In the first place, there is
plenty of evidence that we do not yet really know how to
make it work or how to control it. It tends to be over-admin-
istered but under-managed, tends to mistake procedures and
'proper channels' for direction and energy. The student riots
at Berkeley were greatly aggravated by management malfunctioning and by a ludicrous failure of communications

within a very small top-management group sitting in adjoining offices. Yet Clark Kerr, the university's president, is one of the most accomplished professional managers in the country. Similarly, management malfunctioning and communications failure seem to have greatly aggravated the grievances of the Catholic bishops against the Roman Curia.

Even more important, of course, is the new set of problems which confronts a society of big organizations – their relationship to each other and to the common good; their effective control by government; the effective control of government by the public and its representatives; and the power, authority, and responsibility of these institutional monsters.

Despite everything Paul Goodman – one of the heroes of the campus – has been saying in his all-out attacks on the very idea of organization, we will not do away with it. On the contrary we clearly need more large organizations – for the task of running the modern metropolis, for instance, and for a good many new jobs in the international community such as the policing and traffic control of outer space. But despite everything Miss Ayn Rand – another hero of the campus – has been saying, the problems of the big organization will not disappear if only we give free rein to the superman executive. McNamaras and Hammarskjölds (not to mention the executive-suite Genghis Khans of Miss Rand's *Atlas Shrugged*) are in very short supply.

The problems of the big organization demand new political theory and new social policy. At the moment, indeed, both politics and society require greater skill and greater responsibility precisely because no generally accepted and understood theory is available to statesmen and politicians. The example of Sartre and of some of the more extreme splinter groups of the student leftists show clearly, I submit, how fast in such a situation inner-directedness degenerates into irresponsibility. Yet one can also understand why the

young might conclude that the major tasks in society are
jobs for the professional, the political philosopher, and the
social innovator, for which amateurs, such as they are, need
not apply.

V

But a society of big organizations also raises in new and
acute form the question of the person. What it his relationship to these new leviathans which are at one and the same
time his servants and his master, his opportunity and his
restraint, his tool and his environment? How can the individual maintain his integrity and privacy in such a society?
Is individual freedom necessarily limited to whatever small
air space will be left between the towering organizational
skyscrapers? In such a society of big organizations, the need
becomes more urgent for new answers to the old questions:
'Who am I?' 'What am I?' 'What should I be?' These are
questions the West has tended to consider either as solved or
as unimportant, for the last few hundred years, while it put
its main emphasis on the nature of matter rather than on the
nature of man. But now these questions, the young may
rightly feel, cannot be ignored. They are their own direct,
personal concerns.

The present mood of the present campus generation is not
without serious dangers. It is being exploited by some
dubious people – on the Right and the Left – for political
purposes of their own; but this, while undoubtedly a threat,
may not be the major danger. For the present mood en-
courages irresponsibility. And the emphasis on 'sincerity'
might only too easily degenerate into adulation of that professional specialist in sincerity, the demagogue, or of the
synthetic TV personality. Is it pure accident that California,
the state most strongly influenced by the young adults and
their fashions, is also the one state where TV or movie
success seems increasingly to be accepted as adequate prep-

aration for the job of Governor or US Senator?

The present campus mood is above all drearily futile. Most of the rebels against big organizations will end up – and very soon – as well-paid and fairly successful members of big organizations, whether big university, big government, or big business. They will then predictably impose their own emotional need for security and conformity on their organization, despite all their fine contempt for the Organization Man. The odds are astronomical against Instant Zen's fathering anything but another bull session.

Yet in its return to 'inner-directedness', today's college crowd may, just may, play-act in their school year their homework as tomorrow's adults. The bull session may, for once, be awareness rather than echo. For once today's young-adult fashions may foretell the concerns, and prefigure the intellectual landscape, of tomorrow.

4. A Key to American Politics: Calhoun's Pluralism

[From the *Review of Politics*, October 1948]

This essay and the one following were written twenty years apart, the first in 1948, the second in 1968. They belong together, however. Both deal with the structure and dynamics of the American political process. Both try to identify what makes American government and American politics different from what the European is used to. And both wonder whether the unwritten part of the constitution of the United States is still capable of handling the challenges confronting us.

Actually both pieces can be said to go back to the writer's earliest days in the United States, more than ten years before the first of these essays was written. I first came to the United States in the mid-thirties, charged by a group of British newspapers with interpreting America to their readers. I found myself totally unequal to the task. Reporting was easy; understanding seemed impossible. Clearly the European asked the wrong questions. What the right questions are these two essays try to explain.

The American party system has been under attack almost continuously since it took definite form in the time of Andrew Jackson around 1835. The criticism has always been directed at the same point: America's political pluralism, the distinctively American organization of government by compromise of interests, pressure groups, and sections. And the aim of the critics from Thaddeus Stevens to Henry Wallace has always been to substitute for this 'unprincipled' pluralism a government based as in Europe on 'ideologies' and 'principles'. But never before – at least not since the Civil War years – has the crisis been as acute as in this last decade; for the political problems which dominate our national life today: foreign policy and industrial policy, are precisely the problems which interest and pressure-group compromise is least equipped to handle. And while the crisis symptoms: a left-wing Third Party and the threatened split-off of the Southern Wing, are more alarming in the Democratic Party, the Republicans are hardly much better off. The 1940 boom for the 'idealist' Wilkie and the continued inability to attract a substantial portion of the labour vote, are definite signs that the Republican Party too is under severe *ideological* pressure.

Yet, there is almost no understanding of the problem – precisely because there is so little understanding of the basic principles of American pluralism. Of course, every politician in this country must be able instinctively to work in terms of sectional and interest compromise; and the voter takes it for granted. But there is practically no awareness of the fact that organization on the basis of sectional and interest compromise is both the distinctly American form of political organization and the cornerstone of practically all major political institutions of the modern USA. As acute an observer as Winston Churchill apparently does not understand that Congress works on a basis entirely different from that of Britain's Parliament; neither do nine out of ten Americans and 999 out of 1,000 teachers of those courses in 'Civics'. There is even less understanding that sectional and interest-group pluralism is not just the venal expediency of that stock-villain of American folklore, the 'politician', but that it in itself is a basic ideology, a basic principle – and the one which is the very foundation of our free society and government.*

I

To find an adequate analysis of the principle of government by sectional and interest compromise we have to go back almost a hundred years to John C. Calhoun and to his two political treatises† published after his death in 1852. Absurd, you will say, for it is practically an axiom of American history that Calhoun's political theories, subtle, even profound though they may have been, were reduced to absurdity and irrelevance by the Civil War. Yet, this 'axiom' is nothing but a partisan vote of the Reconstruction Period. Of course, the specific occasion for which Calhoun formulated his theories, the Slavery issue, has been decided; and for the constitutional veto power of the states over national legislation, by means of which Calhoun proposed to formalize the principle of sectional and interest compromise, was substituted in actual practice the much more powerful and much more elastic but extra-constitutional and extra-legal veto power of sections, interests, and pressure groups in Congress and within the parties.‡ But *his basic principle itself: that every major interest in the country, whether re-*

* A perfect illustration was the outraged amazement with which most book reviewers greeted Edward J. Flynn's *You're the Boss* – a simple and straight recital of facts every American should really have known and understood all along.

† A *Disquisition on Government*; and *A Discourse on the Constitution and Government of the United States.*

‡ Calhoun's extreme legalism, his belief that everything had to be spelled out in the written Constitution – a belief he shared with his generation – is one of the major reasons why the importance of his thesis has not been generally recognized. Indeed it is of the very essence of the concept of 'concurrent majority' that it cannot be made official and legal in an effective government – the express veto such as the UN Charter gives to the Great Powers makes government impossible.

gional, economic or religious, is to possess a veto power on political decisions directly affecting it, the principle which Calhoun called – rather obscurely – '*the rule of concurrent majority*', has become the organizing principle of American politics. And it is precisely this principle that is under fire today.

What makes Calhoun so important as the major key to the understanding of American politics, is not just that he saw the importance in American political life of sectional and interest pluralism; other major analysts of our government, Tocqueville, for instance, or Bryce or Wilson, saw that too. But Calhoun, perhaps alone, saw in it more than a rule of expediency, imposed by the country's size and justifiable by results, if at all. He saw in it a basic principle of free government.

> Without this [*the rule of concurrent majority based on interests rather than on principles*] there can be ... no constitution. The assertion is true in reference to all constitutional governments, be their forms what they may: It is, indeed, the negative power which makes the constitution, – and the positive which makes the government. The one is the power of acting; – and the other the power of preventing or arresting action. The two, combined, make constitutional government.
>
> ... it follows, necessarily, that where the numerical majority has the sole control of the government, there can be no constitution ... and hence, the numerical, unmixed with the concurrent majority, necessarily forms, in all cases, absolute government.
>
> ... The principle by which they [governments] are upheld and preserved ... in constitutional governments is *compromise;* – and in absolute governments is *force* ...*

* Quotations from *A Disquisition on Government* (Columbia, S. C., 1852), pages 35 to 37.

And however much the American people may complain
in words about the 'unprincipled' nature of their political
system, by their actions they have always shown that they
too believe that without sectional and interest compromises
there can be no constitutional government. If this is not
grasped, American government and politics must appear
not only as cheap to the point of venality, they must appear
as utterly irrational and unpredictable.

II

Sectional and interest pluralism has moulded all American
political institutions. It is the method – entirely unofficial
and extra-constitutional – through which the organs of
government are made to function, through which leaders are
selected, policies developed, men and groups organized for
the conquest and management of political power. In particular it is the explanation for the most distinctive features
of the American political system: the way in which the Congress operates, the way in which major government departments are set up and run, the qualifications for 'eligibility' as
a candidate for elective office, and the American party structure.

To all foreign observers of Congress two things have
always remained mysterious: the distinction between the
official party label and the 'blocs' which cut across party
lines; and the power and function of the Congressional
Committees. And most Americans though less amazed by
the phenomena are equally baffled.

The 'blocs' – the 'Farm Bloc', the 'Friends of Labor in the
Senate', the 'Business Groups', etc – are simply the expression of the basic tenet of sectional and interest pluralism
that major interests have a veto power on legislation directly
affecting them. For this reason they must cut across party
lines – that is, lines expressing the numerical rather than the
'concurrent' majority. And because these blocs have (*a*)

only a negative veto, and (*b*) only on measures directly affecting them, they cannot in themselves be permanent groupings replacing the parties. They must be loosely organized; and one and the same member of Congress must at different times vote with different blocs. The strength of the 'blocs' does not rest on their numbers but on the basic mores of American politics which grant every major interest group a limited self-determination – as expressed graphically in the near-sanctity of a senatorial 'filibuster'. The power of the 'Farm Bloc' for instance, does not rest on the numerical strength of the rural vote – a minority vote even in the Senate with its disproportionate representation of the thinly populated agricultural states – but on its 'strategic' strength, that is on its being the spokesman for a recognized major interest.

Subordination of a major interest is possible; but only in a 'temporary emergency'. Most of the New Deal measures were, palpably, neither temporary nor emergency measures; yet their sponsors had to present them, and convincingly, as 'temporary emergency measures' because they could be enacted only by over-riding the extra-constitutional veto of the business interests.

Once the excuse of the 'temporary emergency' had fully lost its plausibility, that major interest could no longer be voted down; and the policy collapsed. By 1946, for instance, labour troubles could be resolved only on a basis acceptable to both labour and employer; high wages *and* higher prices. (Even if a numerical majority had been available to legislate against either party – and the business group could probably still have been voted down two and a half years ago – the solution had to be acceptable to both parties.)

The principle of sectional and interest compromise leads directly to the congressional committee system – a system to which there is no parallel anywhere in the world. Congress, especially the House, has largely abdicated to its committees because only in the quiet and secrecy of a committee room can sectional compromise be worked out. The discussion on the floor as well as the recorded vote is far too public and therefore largely for the folks back home. But a committee's business is to arrive at an agreement between all major sectional interests affected; which explains the importance of getting a bill before the 'right' committee. In any but an American legislature the position of each member, once a bill is introduced, is fixed by the stand of his party which, in turn, is decided on grounds that have little to do with the measure itself but are rather dictated by the balance of power within the government and by party programmes. Hence it makes usually little difference which committee discusses a bill or whether it goes before a committee at all. In the United States, however, a bill's assignment to a specific committee decides which interest groups are to be recognized as affected by the measure and therefore entitled to a part in writing it ('who is to have standing before the committee'), for each committee represents a specific constellation of interests. In many cases this first decision therefore decides the fate of a proposed measure, especially as the compromise worked out by the committee is generally accepted once it reaches the floor, especially in the House.

It is not only Congress but every individual member of Congress himself who is expected to operate according to the 'rule of concurrent majority'. He is considered both a representative of the American people and responsible to the national interest and a delegate of his constituents and responsible to their particular interests. Wherever the immediate interests of his constituents are not in question, he is to be a statesman; wherever their conscience or their pocketbooks are affected, he is to be a business agent. This is in sharp contrast to the theory on which any parliamentary government is based – a theory developed almost two hundred years ago in Edmund Burke's famous speech to the voters at Bristol – according to which a member of Parliament represents the commonweal rather than his constituents. Hence in all parliamentary countries, the representative can be a stranger to his constituency – in the extreme, as it was practised in Weimar Germany, there is one long national list of candidates who run in all constituencies – whereas the Congressman in this country must be a resident of his constituency. And while an American Senator considers it a compliment and an asset to be called 'Cotton Ed Smith', the Speaker of the House of Commons not so long ago severely reprimanded a member for calling another member – an official of the miners' union – a 'representative of the coal miners'.

The principle of sectional and interest pluralism also explains why this is the only nation where Cabinet members are charged by law with the representation of special interests – labour, agriculture, commerce. In every other country an agency of the government – any agency of the government – is solemnly sworn to guard the public interests against 'the interests'. In this country the concept of a government department as the representative of a special interest group is carried down to smaller agencies and even to divisions and branches of a department. This was particularly noticeable during the war in such fights as that between the Office of Price Administration – representing the consumer – and the War Production Board representing the producer, or, within WPB between the Procurement branches speaking for the war industries and the Civilian Requirements Branch speaking for the industries producing for the 'home front'.

The mystery of 'eligibility' – the criteria which decide who will make a promising candidate for public office – which has baffled so many foreign and American observers, Bryce for instance – also traces back to the 'rule of the concurrent majority'. Eligibility simply means that a candidate must not be unacceptable to any major interest, religious or regional group within the electorate; it is primarily a negative qualification. Eligibility operates on all levels and

applies to all elective offices. It has been brilliantly analysed in
'Boss' Flynn's *You're the Boss*. His classical example is the
selection of Harry Truman as Democratic vice-presidential
candidate in 1944. Truman was 'eligible' rather than Wallace, Byrnes or Douglas precisely because he was unknown;
because he was neither Easterner nor Westerner nor South-
erner, because he was neither New Deal nor Conservative,
etc, in short because he had no one trait strong enough to
offend anybody anywhere.

But the central institution based on sectional pluralism is
the American party. Completely extra-constitutional, the
wonder and the despair of every foreign observer who
cannot fit it into any of his concepts of political life, the
American party (rather than the states) has become the instrument to realize Calhoun's 'rule of the concurrent majority'.

In stark contrast to the parties of Europe, the American
party has no programme and no purpose except to organize
divergent groups for the common pursuit and conquest of
power. Its unity is one of action, not of beliefs. Its only rule
is to attract – or at least not to repel – the largest possible
number of groups. It must, by definition, be acceptable
equally to the right and the left, the rich and the poor, the
farmer and the worker, the Protestant and the Catholic, the
native and the foreign-born. It must be able to rally Mr
Rankin* of Mississippi and Mr Marcantonio† of New York
– or Senator Flanders** and Colonel McCormick‡ –
behind the same presidential candidate and same 'plat-
form'.

* The ultra 'white supremacist' of the thirties and forties in the
House of Representatives.
† The farthest left member of the House in the same period – and a
Democrat like Rankin.
** Then the leader of the Liberal Republicans and a leading inter-
nationalist Senator from New Hampshire.
‡ Publisher of the *Chicago Tribune* and an extreme isolationist and
right-winger – somewhat to the right of Barry Goldwater.

As soon as it cannot appeal at least to a minority in every major group (as soon, in other words, as it provokes the veto of one section, interest or class) a party is in danger of disintegration. Whenever a party loses its ability to fuse sectional pressures and class interests into one national policy – both parties just before the Civil War, the Republican Party before its reorganization by the great party boss of the 1890s, Mark Hanna, both parties again today – the party system (and with it the American political system altogether) is in crisis.

It is, consequently, not that Calhoun was repudiated by the Civil War which is the key to the understanding of American politics but that he has become triumphant since.

The apparent victors, the 'Radical Republicans', Thaddeus Stevens, Seward, Chief Justice Chase, who dominated American politics, and especially the Congress, in the years at the end of the Civil War, were out to destroy not only slavery and states rights but the 'rule of the concurrent majority' itself. And the early Republican Party – before the Civil War and in the Reconstruction Period – was indeed determined to substitute principle for interest as the lodestar of American political life. But in the end it was the political thought of convinced pluralists such as Abraham Lincoln and Andrew Johnson rather than the ideologies of the Free Soilers and Abolitionists, the radical ideologies of mid-nineteenth century America, which moulded the Republican Party. And ever since, the major developments of American politics have been based on Calhoun's principle. To this the United States owes the strength as well as the weaknesses of its political system.

III

The weaknesses of sectional and interest compromise are far more obvious than its virtues; they have been hammered home for a hundred years. Francis Lieber, who brought the dominant German political theories of the early nineteenth century to this country, attacked pluralism in Calhoun's own state of South Carolina a century ago. Twenty years later Walter Bagehot contrasted, impressively, General Grant's impotent administration with those of Gladstone and Disraeli to show the superiority of ideological party organization. The most thorough and most uncompromising criticism came from Woodrow Wilson; and every single one of the Professor's points was amply borne out by his later experience as President. Time has not made these weaknesses any less dangerous.

There is, first of all, the inability of a political system based on the 'rule of the concurrent majority' to resolve conflicts of principles. All a pluralist system can do is to deny that 'ideological' conflicts (as they are called nowadays) do exist. Those conflicts, a pluralist must assert are fundamentally either struggles for naked power or friction between interest groups which could be solved if only the quarrelling parties sat down around a conference table. Perhaps, the most perfect, because most naïve, expression of this belief remains the late General Patton's remark that the Nazis were, after all, not so very different from Republicans or Democrats. (Calhoun, while less naïve, was just unable to understand the reality of 'ideological' conflict in and around the slavery problem.)

In nine cases out of ten the refusal to acknowledge the existence of ideological conflict is beneficial. It prevents fights for power, or clashes of interests, from flaring into religious wars where irreconcilable principles collide (a catastrophe against which Europe's ideological politics have almost no defence). It promotes compromise where compromise is possible. But in a genuine clash of principles – and, whatever the pluralists say, there *are* such clashes – the 'rule of concurrent majority' breaks down; it did, in Calhoun's generation, before the profound reality of the slavery issue. A legitimate ideological conflict is actually aggravated by the pluralists' refusal to accept its reality: the compromisers who thought the slavery issue could be settled by the meeting of good intentions, or by the payment of money, may have done more than the Abolitionists to make the Civil War inevitable.

A weakness of sectional and interest pluralism just as serious is that it amounts to a principle of inaction. The popular assertion 'it's better to make the wrong decision than to do nothing at all', is, of course, fallacious; but no nation, however unlimited its resources, can have a very effective policy if its government is based on a principle that orders it to do nothing important except unanimously. Moreover, pluralism increased exorbitantly the weight of well-organized small interest groups, especially when they lobby *against* a decision. Congress can far too easily be high-pressured into emasculating a bill by the expedient of omitting its pertinent provisions; only with much greater difficulty can Congress be moved to positive action. This explains, to a large extent, the eclipse of Congress during the last hundred years, both in popular respect and in its actual momentum as policy-making organ of government. Congress, which the Founding Fathers had intended to be the central organ of government – a role which it fulfilled up to Andrew Jackson – became the compound representative of sections and interests and, consequently, progressively incapable of national leadership.

Pluralism gives full weight – more than full weight – to sections and interests; but who is to represent the national welfare? Ever since the days of Calhoun, the advocates of pluralism have tried to dodge this question by contending that the national interest is equal to the sum of all particular interests, and that it therefore does not need a special organ of representation. But this most specious argument is contradicted by the most elementary observation. In practice, pluralism tends to resolve sectional and class conflicts at the

expense of the national interest which is represented by
nobody in particular, by no section and no organization.

These weaknesses had already become painfully obvious
while Calhoun was alive and active – during the decade after
Andrew Jackson, the first President of pluralism. Within a
few years after Calhoun's death, the inability of the new
system to comprehend and to resolve an ideological conflict
– ultimately its inability to represent and to guard the
national interest – had brought catastrophe. For a hundred
years and more, American political thought has therefore
revolved around attempts to counteract if not to overcome
these weaknesses. Three major developments of American
constitutional life were the result: the growth of the functions and powers of the President and his emergence as a
'leader' rather than as the executive agent of the Congress;
the rise of the Supreme Court, with its 'rule of law', to the
position of arbiter of policy; the development of a unifying
ideology – the 'American Creed'.

Of these the most important – and the least noticed – is
the 'American Creed'. In fact I know of no writer of major
importance since Tocqueville who has given much attention
to it. Yet even the term 'un-American' cannot be translated
successfully into any other language, least of all into 'English' English. In no other country could the identity of the
nation with a certain set of ideas be assumed – at least not
under a free government. This unique cohesion on principles shows, for instance, in the refusal of the American
voter to accept Socialists and Communists as 'normal'
parties, simply because both groups refuse to accept the assumption of a common American ideology. It shows, for
another example, in the indigenous structure of the American labour movement with its emphasis on interest pressure rather than on a political philosophy. And this is also
the only free Western country in which 'democracy' (or
rather 'American democracy') could be taught in schools –
the only democratic country which believes that a correct

social philosophy could or should be part of public education.

In Europe, a universal creed would be considered incompatible with a free society. Before the advent of totalitarianism, no European country had ever known anything comparable to the flag salute with which the American school child begins the school day.* For in Europe all political activity is based on ideological factions; consequently, to introduce a uniform ideology in a European country is to stamp out *all* opposition. In the United States ideological homogeneity is the very basis of political diversity. It makes possible the almost unlimited freedom of interest groups, religious groups, pressure groups, etc; and in this way it is the very base of free government. (It also explains why the preservation of civil liberties has been so much more important a problem in this country – as compared to England or France, for instance.) The assumption of ideological unity gives the United States the minimum of cohesion without which its political system simply could not have worked.

IV

But is even the 'American dream' enough to make a system based on the 'rule of the concurrent majority' work today? Can pluralism handle the two major problems of American politics – the formulation of a foreign policy, and the political organization of an industrial society† – any more successfully than it could handle the slavery issue? Or is the American political system as much in crisis as it was in the

---

* The perhaps most profound discussion of the American ideological cohesion can be found in the two decisions of the Supreme Court on the compulsory flag salute, and in the two dissents therefrom, which deserve high rating among American state papers.
† (Footnote 1971) Or, even more, the race issue?

last years of Calhoun's life – and for pretty much the same reasons?

A foreign policy can never be evolved by adding particular interests – regional, economic or racial – or by compromising among them; it must supersede them. If Calhoun's contention that the national interest will automatically be served by serving the interests of the parts is wrong anywhere, it is probably wrong in the field of foreign affairs.

A foreign policy and a party system seem to be compatible only if the parties are organized on programmatic grounds, that is on principles. For if not based on general principles, a foreign policy will become a series of improvisations without rhyme or reason. In a free society, in which parties compete for votes and power, the formulation of a foreign policy may thus force the parties into ideological attitudes which will sooner or later be reflected in their domestic policies too.

This was clearly realized in the early years of the Republic when foreign policy was vital to a new nation, clinging precariously to a long seaboard without hinterland, engaged in a radical experiment with new political institutions, surrounded by the Great Powers of that time, England, France, and Spain, all of them actually or potentially hostile. This awareness of foreign policy largely explains why the party system of the Founding Fathers – especially of Hamilton – was an ideological one; it also explains why the one positive foreign-policy concept this country developed during the entire nineteenth century – the Monroe Doctrine – was formulated by the last two politically active survivors of the founding generation, Monroe and John Quincy Adams. No matter how little Calhoun himself realized it, his doctrine would have been impossible without the French Revolution and the Napoleonic Wars which, during the most critical period of American integration, kept its potential European enemies busy. By 1820, the country had become too strong, had taken in too much territory, to be easily attacked; and it was still not strong enough, and far too much absorbed in the development of its own interior, to play a part in international affairs. Hence Calhoun, and all America with him, could push foreign policy out of their minds – so much so that this is the only country in which it is possible to write a comprehensive work on an important historical period without as much as a mention of foreign affairs, as Arthur M. Schlesinger, Jr managed to do in his *The Age of Jackson.*

But today foreign policy is again as vital for the survival of the nation as it ever was during the administrations of Washington and Jefferson. And it has to be a foreign *policy,* that is, a making of decisions; hence neither 'isolationism' nor 'internationalism' will do. (For 'internationalism' – the search for formulae which will provide automatic decisions, even in advance – is also a refusal to have a foreign policy; it may well have done this country, and the world, as much harm as 'isolationism' – perhaps more.) To survive as the strongest of the Great Powers, the United States might even have to accept permanently the supremacy of foreign policies over domestic affairs, however much this may go against basic American convictions, and indeed against the American grain. But no foreign policy can be evolved by the compromise of sectional interests or economic pressures; yet neither party, as today constituted, could develop a foreign policy based on definite principles.

The other great national need is to resolve the political problems of an industrial society. An industrial society is by nature ultra-pluralistic, because it develops class and interest groups that are far stronger, and far more tightly organized, than any interest group in a pre-industrial age. A few big corporations, a few big unions, may be the actually decisive forces in an industrial society. And these groups can put decisive pressure on society: they can throttle social and economic life.

The problem does not lie in 'asocial behaviour' of this or

that group but in the nature of industrial society which bears much closer resemblance to feudalism than to the trading nineteenth century. Its political problems are very similar to those which feudalism had to solve – and failed to solve. It is in perpetual danger of disintegration into virtually autonomous fiefs, principalities, 'free cities', 'robber baronies', and 'exempt bishoprics' – the authority and the interest of the nation trampled underfoot, autonomous groups uniting to control the central power in their own interest or disregarding government in fighting each other in the civil conflict of class warfare. And the alternative to such a collapse into anarchy or civil war – the suppression of classes and interest groups by an all-powerful government – is hardly more attractive.

An industrial society cannot function without an organ able to superimpose the national interest on economic or class interests. More than a mere arbiter is needed. The establishment of the 'rules of civilized industrial warfare', as was done by both the Wagner Act and the Taft-Hartley Act, tries to avoid the need for policies by equalizing the strength of the conflicting sections; but that can lead only to deadlock, to collusion against the national interest or, worse still, to the attempt to make the national authority serve the interest of one side against the other. In other words, an industrial society cannot fully accept Calhoun's assumption that the national good will evolve from the satisfaction of particular interests. An industrial society without national policy will become both anarchic and despotic.

Small wonder that there has been increasing demand for a radical change which would substitute ideological parties and programmatic policies for the pluralist parties and the 'rule of the concurrent majority' of the American tradition. Henry Wallace's Third-Party Movement, while the most publicized, may well be the least significant development; for third parties are, after all, nothing new in our political history. But for the first time in a hundred years there is a flood of books – and by serious students of American government – advocating radical constitutional reform. However much Senator Fulbright, Henry Hazlitt, and Thomas Fineletter disagree on details, they are one in demanding the elimination – or at least the limitation – of the 'rule of the concurrent majority', and its replacement by an ideological system functioning along parliamentary lines. More significant even may be Walter Reuther's new unionism with its blend of traditional pressure tactics and working-class, that is ideological, programmes and aims.*

V

Yet all these critics and reformers not only fail to ask themselves whether an ideological system of politics would really be any better equipped to cope with the great problems of today – and neither the foreign nor the industrial policy of England, that most successful of all ideologically organized countries, look any too successful right now; the critics also never stop to consider the unique strength of our traditional system.

Our traditional system makes sure that there is always a legitimate government in the country; and to provide such a government is the first job of any political system – a duty which a great many of the political systems known to man have never discharged.

It minimizes conflicts by utilizing, rather than suppressing, conflicting forces. It makes it almost impossible for the major parties to become entirely irresponsible: neither party can afford to draw strength from the kind of demagogic opposition, without governmental responsibility, which perpetually nurtures fascist and communist parties abroad. Hence, while the two national parties are willing to

* (Footnote 1971) In this sense the 'New Politics' of the Kennedys, or of the 'New Left' since 1968, are only continuation of the old search for an ideological basis in American politics.

embrace any movement or any group within the country that commands sufficient following, they in turn force every group to bring its demands and programmes into agreement with the beliefs, traditions, and prejudices of the people.

Above all, our system of sectional and interest compromise is one of the only two ways known to man in which a free government and a free society can survive – and the only one at all adapted to the conditions of American life and acceptable to the American people.

The central problem in a free government is that of factions, as we have known since Plato and Aristotle. Logically, a free government and factions are incompatible. But whatever the cause – vanity and pride, lust for power, virtue or wickedness, greed or the desire to help others – factionalism is inherent in human nature and in human society. For 2,000 years the best minds in politics have tried to devise a factionless society – through education (Plato), through elimination of property (Thomas More), through concentration on the life of the spirit outside of worldly ambition (the political tradition of Lutheranism). The last great attempt to save freedom by abolishing faction was Rousseau's. But to create the factionless free society is as hopeless as to set up perpetual motion. From Plato to Rousseau, political thought has ended up by demanding that factions be suppressed, that is, that freedom, to be preserved, be abolished.

The Anglo-American political tradition alone has succeeded in breaking out of this vicious circle. Going back to Hooker and Locke, building on the rich tradition of free government in the cities of the late middle ages, Anglo-American political realism discovered that if factions cannot be suppressed, they must be utilized to make a free government both freer and stronger. This one basic concept distinguishes Anglo-American political theory and practice from continental European politics, and accounts for the singular success of free and popular governments in both countries. Elsewhere in the western world the choice has always been between extreme factionalism which makes government impotent if not impossible and inevitably leads to civil war, and autocracy which justifies the suppression of liberty with the need for effective and orderly government. Nineteenth-century France with its six revolutions, or near revolutions, stands for one, the totalitarian governments of our time for the other alternative of continental politics.

But – and this is the real discovery on which the Anglo-American achievement rests – factions can be used constructively only if they are encompassed within a frame of unity. A free government on the basis of sectional interest groups is possible only when there is no ideological split within the country. This is the American solution. Another conceivable solution is to channel the driving forces, the vectors of society, into ideological factions which obtain their cohesion from a programme for the whole of society, and from a creed. But that presupposes an unquestioned ruling class with a common outlook on life, with uniform mores and a traditional, if not inherent, economic security. Given that sort of ruling class, the antagonist in an ideological system can be expected to be a 'loyal opposition', that is, to accept the rules of the game and to see himself as a partner rather than as a potential challenger to civil war. But a ruling class accepted by the people as a whole, and feeling itself responsible to the people as a whole, cannot be created by fiat or overnight. In antiquity only Rome, in modern times only England, achieved it. On the Continent, all attempts to create a genuine ruling class have failed dismally.

In this country, the ruling-class solution was envisaged by Alexander Hamilton and seemed close to realization under the presidents of the 'Virginia Dynasty', the Virginia gentlemen and whigs who, for a quarter-century, from George Washington to James Madison, provided America's presidents and set its political tone. Hamilton arrived at his concept with inescapable consistency; for he was absorbed by the search for a foreign policy and for the proper organization of an industrial society – precisely the two problems which, as we have seen, pluralism is least equipped to resolve. But even if Hamilton had not made the fatal mistake of identifying wealth with rulership, the American people could not have accepted his thesis. A ruling class was incompatible with mass immigration and with the explosive territorial expansion of nineteenth-century America. It was even more incompatible with the American concept of equality. And there is no reason to believe that contemporary America is any more willing to accept Hamilton's concept, Professor Galbraith's idea of the academic *élite* notwithstanding. This country as a free country has no alternative, it seems, to the 'rule of the concurrent majority', no alternative to sectional pluralism as the device through which factions can be made politically effective.

It will be very difficult, indeed, to resolve the problems of foreign and of industrial policy on the pluralist basis and within the interest-group system, though not provably more difficult than these problems would be on another, ideological, basis. It will be all the harder as the two problems are closely interrelated; for the effectiveness of any American foreign policy depends, in the last analysis, on our ability to show the world a successful and working model of an industrial society. But if we succeed at all, it will be with the traditional system, horse-trading, log-rolling, and politicking all included. An old saying has it that this country lives simultaneously in a world of Jeffersonian beliefs and in one of Hamiltonian realities. Out of these two, Calhoun's concept of 'the rule of the concurrent majority' alone can make one viable whole. The need for a formulated foreign policy and for a national policy of industrial order is real – but not more so than the need for a real understanding of this fundamental American fact: the pluralism of sectional and interest compromise is the warp of America's political fabric – it cannot be plucked out without unravelling the whole.

5. On the 'Economic Basis' of American Politics

[From *The Public Interest*, Winter 1968]

I

Why is there not one single American among the 'great economists'? From its earliest days this country has had more economists than any other country. It has led in the development of the tools of economic analysis. Economists are everywhere – in government, in business, in the universities, in the labour unions. In no other country, indeed, is a knowledge of economics considered part of ordinary education; in the United States, however, we have for many years been trying to combat 'economic illiteracy' in the secondary schools. And certainly there is no country in which popular interest in economics is greater, and in which economic issues are more prominent.

Yet we conspicuously lack the Great Economist, the economist who changes our ideas about economics and gives us new approaches to the interpretation and direction of economic events.

Or, rather: the great economists America has produced are not known as such, are not recognized as such. Alexander Hamilton (1757–1804) and Henry Clay (1777–1852) certainly deserve being considered very great economists: Hamilton, at the very dawn of systematic economics, created a basic theory of economic development which has not been much improved since; Henry Clay's 'American System' is the fount and origin of all welfare economics. Yet their very names are rarely mentioned in histories of economic thought, whereas the German Friedrich List, who repeated what Clay had taught him, usually occupies a prominent place in these books.

Of course, neither Hamilton nor Clay really wanted to be known as an economist. Their own ambitions were elsewhere: Hamilton on becoming the Commanding General of a victorious United States Army, Clay on being elected President. To both men, their economics were totally incidental to their politics, and a tool thereof. For both Hamilton and Clay, economic policy was clearly a means to a political end. And when their economic views are discussed, they are correctly treated as part of their political theories and political strategies.

The explanation for this state of affairs would seem to be this: economics is too important to American politics to be left to the American economist. Economics has a political role to fulfil that transcends its own subject matter. For well over two hundred years it has been the unifying impulse in this country's political process. Since colonial days, 'economic interests' have been used systematically to create political forces and political alignments, and above all to unite regional and sectional groups behind one leader and one programme. The names of these economic interests have changed; but whether we speak of the 'manufacturing interest', the 'farming interest', or the 'silver bloc', the idea itself has not changed. Similarly, for well over two centuries, economic issues – such as the tariff, the currency, or free soil* – have been used to overcome and neutralize

---

* 'Free soil' was political shorthand for forty years for the demand that the empty lands to the west of the frontier of settlement be reserved, free of charge, for smallholder settlers – finally realized in 1860.

ideological cleavages and conflicts that otherwise might have
torn apart the nation. During all of our history, fundamental
rifts in the country have been bridged by polarizing politics
on economic issues; these are issues on which a compromise,
distributing dollars and cents, is always possible. The classical example is, of course, the compromise over the 'Tariff of
Abomination'* between the South and Andrew Jackson
that postponed the conflict over slavery for thirty years. All
along it has been good American political manners to talk
dollars and cents when we really mean political decisions.
The way in which Robert McNamara, as Secretary of De-
fense in both the Kennedy and Johnson administrations,
used budgetary control radically to alter strategic concepts
and military organization is another good example.

Perhaps most revealing is the way in which we have used
the economic sphere to think through and work out basic
issues of the relation of government to society. Big business
is far more powerful in France or Germany, for instance,
than it is in the United States. But only in the United States
has the relationship between 'Government and business'
come to be considered the key issue for a fundamental discussion of the role and power of government in society.
Indeed, our public discussions for a century now have led
many a naïve foreign observer to conclude that in the
United States there are no noteworthy social institutions
other than business institutions.

THE GREAT THEMES OF AMERICAN HISTORY
The result of this peculiar role of economic issues and economic controversy in the American political process is most

* The term of the free-traders, mostly agriculturalists of the South
and West, for the proposal, made in 1830, for heavy protective
duties on imports of manufactured goods that would effectively
have closed the American market to foreign imports and given the
New England industrialists a tight monopoly.

paradoxical. On the one hand, economics in this country appears to be far more prominent and far more important in the political life than in any other country. American history seems to be dominated, at first sight, by economic conflict. Indeed it is possible to overlook the fact that the great themes of American history have all along been moral and constitutional: slavery, the industrial versus the agrarian society, and federalism in the nineteenth century; racial equality, the role and function of the central government, and America's place in an international society in this century. In sharp contrast to countries whose politics have an ideological organization and pattern, such as all European countries, these great themes are barely mentioned in day-to-day, year-to-year American politics, where the slogans are primarily economic. It is, therefore, only too easy to mistake the appearance for reality. It is thus possible to argue, as a whole school of historians did, that the Civil War was an 'unnecessary conflict' and could have been avoided by paying a few hundred million dollars to the slave owners. It is possible, as Arthur M. Schlesinger, Jr, did in his brilliant *The Age of Jackson*, to overlook completely that the central theme and the crowning achievement of the Jackson administration was to establish the sovereignty of the national government over all regional or sectional interests; instead, Mr Schlesinger made economic and class interests paramount. It is even possible, as Charles Beard (active from 1890 to 1940) did in a long life as a historian, to see the whole of our history as determined by, and subordinated to, economic interest. But Beard lived long enough to find out that any attempt to predict the course of American history and American political behaviour from economics is bound to misfire.

Every American politician must indeed know how to use economic measures for political ends. If he aspires to a national role, he must be a master of finding and creating economic alignments that unify diverse groups across the nation. Even John C. Calhoun*, the most nearly 'metaphysical' of our political thinkers, spent the last two decades of his life in an abortive attempt to bridge the moral gulf of slavery between South and West by means of their common economic interest as farmers.

So it is that, despite its appearance of centrality, economics in the American experience is actually a subordinate means to predominantly non-economic ends. Our values are not economic values, nor is our economics autonomous. Politics even decides what economic issues are allowed to appear on the stage of American history. For, to be 'available' as a political vehicle an economic issue must fit into our political logic. It must mobilize national energies and must unify large masses across regions for joint political action and for the conquest of the central political power that is the presidency.

This explains the absence of the Great Economist. Such a man must assume the autonomy of the economic sphere in human life. He must assume the reality of economic values. If he is interested at all in politics (as few of them were), he must treat politics as a handmaiden of economics and as a tool for achieving economic purposes. These assumptions make no sense to the American experience. What flourishes in this country, therefore, are economic technicians of skill and renown, economic analysts, and expert fashioners of economic tools. We have political economists and economic politicians galore. But the climate is most uncongenial to the Great Economist. Such a man must assume an autonomous economic reality, of which the political issues are merely a reflection. In our American experience, however, economics is the conventional shorthand and the *lingua franca* for issues and decisions which are not economic, but political and moral. One might indeed formulate a basic rule of American politics to read: *If at all possible, express a political*

* Whose work was examined in the preceding essay, Chapter 4.

*issue and design a political alignment as an economic issue
and an economic alignment.*

II

The insight that economic interests can be used as the hinge
of politics is commonly traced to the famous Number 10 of
the Federalist Papers (1787–88) in which James Madison
(following Harrington's *Oceana* and John Locke) concluded
that power follows property. But, when Madison wrote,
American political life had already, for a century, been ha-
bitually organized around economic issues and in economic
alignments, Madison only codified what had been fairly general American experience during the colonial period.

Colonial legislatures had indeed no alternative if they
wanted to be effective at all. The matters that now occupy a
legislature – public order and law, the administration of justice or education – may have been of very great interest to
them, but were normally not within their reach. They had,
perforce, to be left to the individual local communities, the
towns and counties. In colonial America, distances were too
great, population too sparsely settled for any central authority to be effective. If the local community would not look
after its own internal affairs, nobody else could. The major
burning issue for the colonial legislature was relations with
the mother country. And those turned on economic problems and economic questions: taxes and tariffs, coinage and
credit, and so on. It was in these matters, above all, that the
colony's Royal Governor was interested; for in eighteenth-
century theory and practice, an overseas colony was an
economic asset. Of course such recurrent disturbances as
Indian risings or the endemic war with the French occupied a
good deal of the time and attention of the colonial politician. But his main job was to represent the colonist before
and against the economic power represented and exerted by
the Governor. His very *raison d'être* was economic. And

only by identifying and organizing economic interests could the eighteenth-century colonial politician create unity in the electorate he represented – an electorate which, as the century wore on, became increasingly diversified in its other characteristics (religious beliefs, ethnic origins, and so on). There never was much need to do for the eighteenth-century politician, in the state houses of Boston, Philadelphia, and Williamsburg what Sir Lewis Namier had to do in our century for his English counterpart: to seek out and identify his economic affiliations and interests. That was the one fact about the politician in colonial America that was always clear, evident, and known to everybody.

But to Madison – and to all the brillant politicians who, in the first quarter-century of United States history, established the political conventions and the political processes for the infant country – should be given credit for one fundamental insight: economic interests could be used to *unify*. They could be used to overcome the pernicious 'factions', the cleavage of society into ideological camps divided by their basic beliefs, which the founding fathers rightly feared as incompatible with nationhood and political stability.

THE USES OF ECONOMIC CONFLICT

This is a political view of economics, a view which explains economic events in terms of human behaviour. This, more than anything else, distinguishes the traditional American approach to economics from the approach of the economist. The economist understands the behaviour of commodities. And if he is naïve (as our present-day neo-Keynesians tend to be), he believes that human beings behave as commodities do. But even at his most profound and sceptical, he is likely to consider ordinary human behaviour as economically non-rational behaviour. In fact, the economist has, all along, been either suspicious or at the least contemptuous of the politician who, so it seems to him, subordinates the clear logic of economic rationality to the murky unreason of human emotions and vanities. From this starting point, the classical economists essentially arrived at a denial of politics. To them there was a pre-established harmony in the economic self-regulation automatically producing the optimum for all groups and classes in society. Marx himself was no less contemptuous of the politician: no longer accepting the classical doctrine of harmony, but instead accepting the reality of economic conflict, he deduced therefrom the inevitability, beyond any politician's contriving, of class war and revolution.

The political economists of the American tradition never for one moment believed in pre-established economic harmony. Economic conflict was much too obvious for that. It had, after all, characterized relations between the infant colonies and the mother country, culminating finally in a violent upheaval of the political order in the Revolution. But at the same time, they saw in economic conflict their means to prevent the more dangerous ideological conflict. And they saw in economic conflict the means to establish order – *not* harmony, which they did not expect on this earth. Above all, they saw that economic conflict was the one clash within the body politic that could be managed. It could be managed because economic interests are divisible whereas political or religious beliefs are not. One can always split an economic difference in two – and while half a loaf is better than no bread, half a child, as King Solomon long ago perceived, is no good at all. The same goes for half a religion, half a philosophy, or half a political principle.

Above all, their experience, unique at that time and quite at variance with what 'common sense' would have taught elsewhere, had convinced the founding fathers that, unlike all other cleavages, economic conflicts tend to become less acute with time. They may not be self-healing, but they are capable of amelioration. If the fight is over 'who gets how much', then one can satisfy both sides if the amount available for distribution increases. And their experience as colonists on the virgin continent had taught them that the economic pie is indeed capable of being increased by human action, rather than being fixed forever.

They may not have consciously thought this through. But Alexander Hamilton started out from the assumption that it is possible to increase the economic resources available. This assumption explains in large part why his countrymen, no matter how much they distrusted his politics, took to his economics at once, but also why he never attained full respectability as an economist. For the economist traditionally – until well past World War II – took it for granted that economic resources are given and limited, so that the problem is their most effective distribution in a system of equilibrium. In this respect Keynes, however much he otherwise might have differed from his predecessors, was as traditional as anyone. It was not until the most recent decades, until the advent of 'economic development' as a goal of economic policy – with President Truman's 'Point Four' declaration of the early 1950s being the crucial date – that proper economists accepted the purposeful creation of dynamic disequilibrium as possible and meaningful.

To the American – no matter how faithfully he repeated the teachings of the economist, no matter how faithfully he himself taught them in the classrooms of his colleges – it was obvious that in his country the economic resources had been proven to be capable of almost infinite expansion through human and, in large measure, political action. He may have agreed with the economist that this was purely the result of the rarest of accidents: the existence on this continent of vast areas of empty soil, ready for the plough, ready to be appropriated and to be converted into an economic resource. But very early we find in the actual political behaviour of the American strong evidence that, deep down, he knew differently. He knew what Hamilton had known in the last decade of the eighteenth century: that there is an economic dynamic and that economic resources are the creation of man rather than of Providence. This underlies quite clearly such bold measures as the Morrill Act of 1865 which, in creating the 'land-grant colleges' (the original foundation of most American State Universities, such as the University of Michigan and the University of California), clearly assumed that the application of knowledge creates economic value and productive capacity well beyond that given in the existing resources. It underlay, from the beginning, all American trade-union movements. American 'business unionism' assumes, not only that the economic pie can be made greater, but above all that the fight over the division of the pie is by itself likely to produce a larger pie – that, in other words, economic conflict by itself leads to economic growth and therefore, at the same time, to political and social unity.

III

There can be little doubt that the American concept of 'economic interest' as an effective and unifying political force has served this country exceedingly well.

In fact, it is questionable whether there could have been an American nation without it. With the wisdom of hindsight, we have come to see in the frontier a source of strength. But, in reality, the experience of the frontier must have been an almost unbearable strain – as witness all other countries that have undergone a similar experience. It was not only the kind of strain on the physical resources and on the political energies which rapid, turbulent expansion produces. Above all, it was a strain on the unity of a country in which the new tidal wave of immigrants of different social background, national origin, and religious allegiance always arrived long before the preceding wave of immigrants had been absorbed. In such a country, growing at a frenetic speed, ideological, philosophical, or religious cleavages might have been fatal.

One should not forget that the immigrants, by and large, had themselves no tradition of self-government or even of political activity; it was not, after all, the respectable or well-to-do who arrived in the holds of the immigrant ships. And yet these vast heterogeneous masses had to become a nation under one government and with one set of basic values practically overnight – or else the American experiment would have floundered. If economic interests had not been available as the political organizer, it would either have been necessary to impose the most rigid authority on the population or else pluralism would have organized itself *against* the nation and its unity – with every imported tradition of religion and culture, every imported political value and belief, the focus of an ideology alien, if not hostile, to American nationhood (as is so clearly the case in Latin America).

The great phenomenon of the nineteenth century is not, after all, the rise of the American economy. It is the creation of the American nation. For a nation, as we are now finding out the world over, is not something one can easily create. It is, on the contrary, usually the fruit of long experience and of historical forces operating over many centuries. Neither the nations of Europe nor Japan were created overnight. That nationhood is difficult and takes a very long time to create is proven by the fact that, outside of these old nations – and of the United States – very few, if any, nations have yet come into being. In all of Latin America, for instance, despite centuries of political identity, only Mexico and, to a lesser extent, Brazil, can be said to be 'nations' – and, in both, nationhood has come only in this century. But the United States achieved nationhood in a few short decades, or, at the most, within a century. This it owes to a very large extent to the tradition which used economic interests and their clashes and conflicts as the foundation for political issues, political alignments, and political conflicts. This has enabled the United States to tolerate, if not to encourage, pluralism in all other spheres, to survive the fiercest of civil wars, and to attain a unity of allegiance and of basic commitments which represent as strong a common bond and communion as centuries of common history, common language, and common experiences have given to any of the older nations.

THE BIAS TOWARDS 'BI-PARTISANSHIP'

But the convention of economic interests has not only tended to prevent ideological issues from arising. It has forced the American political system into a non-partisan approach to non-economic problems.

A non-economic issue threatens the existing political alignments. It is not easily encompassed within the American political system. As was argued in Chapter 4, the American politician shuns ideological stands, for the simple reason that they are certain to alienate a large proportion of a constituency brought together and held together by economic interests. Any non-economic ideological stand would have at once, for instance, exploded the alliance between the lily-white, fundamentalist Protestant, and proudly Anglo-Saxon South and the cosmopolitan, largely Catholic or Jewish, working class in the big cities on which the Democratic party was based for so long. The only thing that could hold them together – and could thereby get a Democratic politician into federal office – was their economic opposition to the manufacturing interest.

This built into the American political process a powerful incentive to handle non-economic issues on a 'bi-partisan' basis, that is, to remove them essentially from party politics. Indeed, the greatest praise in our political system is reserved for the 'patriot' who turns a potentially disruptive non-economic issue into bi-partisan consensus. It is for this act of patriotism at the expense, legend has it, of his presidential chances, that American history primarily remembers Henry Clay. And a century later, Arthur Vandenberg earned himself a permanent place in the American political pantheon by similarly making American foreign policy after World War II 'bi-partisan' – thereby again sacrificing whatever chance for the presidential nomination of his party he might ever have had. A great many voters repudiated Barry Goldwater in 1964, not because they disagreed with his views, but because his decision to take a partisan stand on non-economic issues seemed to them a greater threat to the Republic than a wrong, but bi-partisan consensus on the issues. And, in the context of the American political process, they were right.

Foreign affairs, religion, education, civil rights, and a host of other areas which, in any other country, are the bread and meat of party politics and political organization are, therefore, as much as possible, treated as 'bi-partisan' in the American political system. This does not mean that they are not controversial. It means that the system, as long as it works, uses them to bring together otherwise warring factions rather than to create new factions on each side of the controversy. In fact, we much prefer not even to tackle such issues unless there is available for them a broad coalition cutting across our conventional political alignments. Again and again, initiative in such an issue is left, as if by passive agreement, to the one body within the American political system that is outside the established party alignment, the Supreme Court. That in both the great constitutional issues of the recent years, civil rights and reapportionment of voting districts, a Supreme Court decision took the place of political action in these politically crucial areas was in full accord with the tradition that goes back to John Marshall's long tenure (1801–35) as Chief Justice of the United States. For a Supreme Court decision is the 'law of the land' and thus establishes its own consensus.

THE LIMITATIONS OF 'CONSENSUS'

There are obvious and real limitations to the effectiveness of the convention of economic issues in American politics. Not every non-economic – that is, ideological, political, or moral – issue can be either made to appear as economic or organized as 'bi-partisan'. Indeed the most important issues and decisions in the life of a nation cannot be handled in this fashion. The great example is slavery, of course, for in this country slavery did not primarily serve an economic function (as it did, for instance, in the plantation economy of Brazil). At least by the second quarter of the nineteenth century, the main function of slavery was to endow the 'poor white' in the South with a feeling of human superiority no matter how wretched his physical or moral condition. Even if slavery in its origin and spread was an economic institution, by the time it became an issue, that is, after 1820 or so, the main beneficiary was no longer the slave-owner but rather the non-owner who derived the psychic benefits of a slave society without having to carry the increasing economic burden of maintaining the slaves. In other words, the Abolitionists, as we now know, were right: slavery in this country was a sin rather than a crime. And for this reason the abolition of slavery by itself, without true civil rights for the blacks, settled so very little.

And for this reason too, slavery could not be camouflaged as an economic issue, no matter how hard the politicians of the early nineteenth century tried. Moreover, as a truly 'irreconcilable' issue, that is, as a spiritual and moral one, there could be no 'consensus' on it – even though the Supreme Court of the time tried to establish it in the Dred Scott decision of 1857 which tried to protect a Southern slave-owner's property rights in a slave even in a Northern state where slavery was forbidden. Nor could the existing political organization handle such a non-economic issue – and probably the political system of no country, no matter how organized, could have handled it. On the issue of slavery, then, the American political system floundered and sank into Civil War, almost destroying the country with it.

But even in less crucial and less sensitive areas, the American political system is not geared to handling the non-economic issue. This is particularly true whenever foreign policy cannot be organized on the basis of 'consensus' and 'bi-partisanship'. Any such failure leaves deep and long-lasting scars. For any such failure endangers national cohesion. This was true of the War of 1812. It was true of the bitter foreign policy conflict that preceded our entry into World War I. But for the Japanese attack on Pearl Harbor, the rift over foreign policy in the years before World War II might similarly have proven incapable of being organized within the American political system and might have torn apart American national unity. Today, Vietnam poses a similar threat.

But then there is also always a danger that our politicians may forget that the economic issue is a convention and fall into the error of believing that economics really controls politics. In domestic affairs, the danger is not very great. It is a very stupid politician who will not intuitively realize the limitations, as well as the uses, of the convention. Certainly, no strong president – Jackson, Lincoln, the two Roosevelts, or Truman, for example – ever believed that economic interests and economic policy were by themselves sufficient, or that they necessarily prevailed. But in foreign affairs we have made this mistake again and again – and have paid dearly in every case. Again and again we have fallen for the illusion of 'economic sanctions' as an effective tool in foreign affairs. And again and again we have found that they are ineffective. This holds true for the belief of the South that 'King Cotton' would force the North to its knees and constrain Europe to ally itself with the Confederacy, but also for the balancing belief of the North that the Confederacy could be defeated by economic blockade. And we now also know, from the diaries of pro-Western Japanese leaders, that the economic sanctions which the United States and Great Britain imposed on Japan in 1940 and 1941 only strengthened the war party and deprived the moderates of all influence – just as the blockade of Germany in World War I emasculated the moderates in the German government and made the military extremists all-powerful. Ironically, we now also know that economic sanctions did not even work in the one case in which they seemed to have been successful – the case which probably explains the blind American belief in this policy: the 'economic sanctions' of the American colonists against the first British attempt to tax them, a decade before the American Revolution. Recent historical research has made it reasonably certain that the British cabinet used the American boycott as an excuse for a retreat from a policy which had proven exceedingly unpopular among powerful backers at home, and not primarily for economic reasons.

The convention of economics as the ground of political action and organization is, in other words, just a tool. Like every tool, it has to be used with judgement. And like every tool, it has limitations. Whoever mistakes the convention for reality pays the heavy penalty one always has to pay for deceiving oneself.

But while not perfect, not infallible, and not a panacea by any means, the convention has served the American people remarkably well.

IV

The question, however, is not really how well the convention has served in the past. It is: is it still useful, still serviceable? Can the common, ordinary, political business of the American people still be ordered by the traditional rule to formulate issues, as far as possible, as economic issues, and to define alignments to the greatest extent possible as economic alignments?

It is just barely possible that this traditional convention of domestic American politics has a major future role to play in foreign and international affairs. But at the same time, it may be at the end of its usefulness at home.

Every one of the many new countries that has come into existence in the last two decades has yet to become a nation. Every one is less well equipped for this task, by history and tradition, than was the infant American Republic two hundred years ago. In every one, the cleavages between tribes, between religions, between races run deep – and will have to be bridged fast if the country is to survive. No one of them could survive a conflict of ideologies. In this situation, a good many of them, if not all, will predictably take recourse in the elimination of politics – the vain promise of every dictatorship. Equally predictably, this will only worsen the conflicts and make them even less tractable. Predictably also, some of them at least will seek escape in braggart nationalism, if not in conquest abroad. This, too, history amply teaches, will not succeed. Only an approach to politics which allows conflicts to be productive, and to create unity across the dividing line of tribe, religion, tradition, or race would seem to fit the needs of the new countries. In the traditional American approach, which makes politics turn on economic interests and economic issues, the new countries might well find what they need, ready-made and well tested.

Indeed, this approach might become increasingly more important for the international community altogether. The world today is threatened by a danger even greater than that of class war in the nineteenth century. It is threatened by the danger of a world-wide race war of the poor and largely coloured majority against the largely white minority of the rich. At the same time, this is an infinitely smaller world than was that of the eighteenth century, a world in which everybody is everybody else's neighbour and in which, therefore, there is no alternative to living together. In such a world, a political concept which allows for productive conflict, but which also organizes unity beyond the ideologies and traditions which divide, might be of the greatest importance.

We are obviously very far from any such accomplishment; the 'Alliance for Progress' in President Kennedy's original version was probably the closest to it. But, in retrospect, the development efforts of the 1950s and 1960s may well one day appear as the first uncertain and faltering steps towards a new, non-ideological, and yet unifying concept of international order, different alike in its flexibility and effectiveness from the world anarchy of sovereign states which has become a hopeless anachronism, and a world government which, if at all feasible, could today be only a world-wide tyranny.

THE NEED FOR INNOVATION

But at the same time, it seems likely that in domestic politics the traditional economic convention has come to the end of its usefulness. It is not that we are dissatisfied with it or that we hanker after ideological politics. It's just that the problems and challenges of American life no longer can be cast easily, if at all, into an economic mould. The civil-rights issue in all likelihood is typical of the issues that will be central to American politics from now on: the problems of the metropolis; the structure, values, and relationships of a society increasingly organized in large and powerful institutions; or the role, function, and limitations of science and technology. These questions cannot be converted into economic issues. Nor, despite President Johnson's recent attempts at 'consensus', are they likely to admit of 'bi-partisanship'. Bi-partisanship is effective when the answers are known, at least in broad outline. But great political innovations, such as we need, are rarely the children of compromise.

And yet these are also issues which the traditional ideological alignments, the alignments of European politics, cannot tackle. To do as so many foreign and domestic critics of the American political system have urged us to do for well over a century – to organize our political life on the basis of 'liberal' and 'conservative', or 'right' and 'left' – would only add to the confusion. What is 'liberal' in respect to the government of the metropolis? Or in respect to the relationship between the individual and the large organizations on which he depends for effectiveness, but on which he must not depend if he wants to be free? And what does it mean to be a 'conservative' on these issues? There is obviously going to be violent disagreement in respect to these issues – in fact, there is need for such disagreement and for a diversity of approaches to their solution. But ideological alignments are bound to be as irrelevant to these issues as the traditional alignment by economic interests. The 'New Left' is thus bound to be sterile and to be condemned to total frustration.

If, indeed, the world will permit us the luxury of domestic affairs in the next half century or so, we will not only have to face up to new issues. We shall have to devise a new approach to domestic politics altogether. This signifies a greater upheaval in our political life, a greater strain on political sanity and stability, than the new issues themselves could possibly mean and a greater opportunity for creative political thought and effective political leadership than this country has known since the days of the founding fathers.

In seizing this opportunity, we may well have to abandon the traditional reliance on economic interests and economic issues as symbols of political intercourse and as means of political organization. I hope that we will not give up with them the principle underlying them: the mobilization of conflict to create unity, and the appeal to interest against the fanaticism of ideological faction. It is not only a civilized concept; it is a principle that makes politics productive for the common good. It has served the American people well – so well that doing without the Great Economist seems a very small price indeed.

6. Martyrs Unlimited

[From *Harper's Magazine*, July 1964]

Today one would no longer, as this essay did in 1964, treat America's wallowing in self-pity as a laughing matter. It has become a nation-wide affliction; what was merely absurdity a few years ago is becoming obsession.

I

There is not one occupation, trade or profession in this country that is not misunderstood, neglected, underrated, unloved, and rejected. No group that is not steadily slipping in popular esteem and in ability to attract the young. It is heartrending how much suffering each trade and profession endures – patiently if not exactly in silence.

It is not at all surprising that the undertakers demanded equal time on television to rebut what they felt was a preposterous attack on them and their business methods. What is surprising is that the other trades have not yet rebelled so vocally against the crushing contempt in which all are held by a cruel American public. So far they confine themselves to speeches at their conventions, articles in their journals, resolutions, and public relations campaigns. But more drastic means are needed to restore all our professions and occupations to their rightful place in public esteem.

Take the military, for instance. At first glance it might

seem to have little to complain about. We have more generals and admirals on the payroll than ever before in peacetime. A professional soldier was recently President of the United States for eight years, and he remained to his death an immensely popular hero whose word of approbation was the coveted prize of all republican aspirants to the office. Dozens of other generals and admirals are public figures, commanding more respect and wielding greater influence than military men usually do even in war. I can't think, for example, of any precedent for Admiral Rickover's triple role of educational oracle, one-man lobby, and production czar. Retired officers are in civilian jobs everywhere, as corporation executives, as trade-association secretaries, as university presidents, and as diplomats. The service academies have so many applicants that they can impose the admission standards of the Ivy League colleges. And with half of the federal budget going to defence there should be no lack of money to pay these public servants handsomely.

But, alas, appearances are completely deceptive. Every issue of every service journal (not to mention newspaper columns by military pundits) contains harrowing tales of the sufferings of the military man: of his rude neglect by civilian authority which, as Senator Goldwater (who is also a major general in the Air Force) complained last March, 'turns the profession of arms into a second-class craft'; of the shortage of company presidencies for the major generals who, at age 54, look for their first jobs in business; of the callow indifference of the youngsters who prefer civilian pay as mechanics to the joys of the second hitch as corporals.

II

Other groups suffer just as much. The Civil Service, whatever its growth in numbers and pay, smarts under the public contempt for the 'bureaucrat' who 'never met a payroll'. The labour leader is snubbed and slighted by business and held up to contempt as a grafter and to ridicule as a clod by the press. The businessman, in turn, is all but submerged by a rising tide of socialism. Nobody knows how little profit he makes – and that little is snatched out of his hand by the grasping tax collector.

The academician is beset by the all-but-universal 'anti-intellectualism' of the American people (as shown, for instance, by their sending their children to college in ever larger numbers). Even though the professor clearly knows how to do it better – doesn't he teach it after all? – politicians rather than professors still run the government, writers produce the best-sellers, businessmen manage companies, and administrators the schools. And nobody ever listens to the professor – even though more academicians are being asked to speak on more subjects to more and larger audiences than ever before in this gab-happy nation.

Every smaller occupational group within the big ones suffers similarly. The Army gangs up on the Air Force and both on the Navy. The English teachers scream loudly about the science faculties getting all the lush government grants and consulting fees and all the new buildings. Yet the scientists are far from happy. They are deeply worried by their 'image'. The public apparently pictures the scientist as a 'barbarian' (according to Rockefeller Institute's René Dubos) or as a 'white-coated witch doctor' (according to Professor Dupree of the University of California). The public image of the scientist is 'cold, objective, impersonal', Margaret Mead reported in a constantly quoted survey a few years back. The public completely fails to see, let alone to appreciate, that this monster is kind to children and puppies, is a loving husband, and (judging by his behaviour in faculty meetings) often as spontaneously emotional as Juliet. In every other issue of *Science* there is an editorial or a letter to the editor bemoaning this horrible misunderstanding. How it could have arisen is indeed hard to see, considering that the rest of *Science* is full (as of course it should be) of such heart-throbs as 'New Papovavirus Contaminating Shope Papillomata'.

Big business is conspicuously misunderstood. Every survey shows that the public refuses to recognize DuPont or Westinghouse – or any other of the big technological companies – as just folks and simple, friendly neighbours. Instead the public perversely appreciates only their technological leadership or their product quality. This is such gross injury to the corporate psyche as to call for a massive programme of 'public education'.

III

As a result of this public cruelty not one career attracts high-calibre youngsters any more. Indeed the figures show conclusively that 'youngsters of high ability' just go nowhere at all. At a sales executives' meeting I recently attended, the results of a survey were disclosed to the horrified members. Only one out of every twenty high-ranking college sophomores gave 'selling' as his career preference. Most of the students, when asked to characterize the successful salesman used such terms of near-contempt as 'aggressive', 'values money', or 'persuades people to buy'. As the speaker forcefully pointed out, this can only end in the destruction of the American economy (which is, after all, based on selling) and of the individual initiative that underlies our free society.

What is true of selling is just as true of dentistry and other careers. Two-thirds of the dentists do not want their children to become dentists, one survey shows. Other surveys give similarly alarming figures for lawyer and banker, plumber and nurse. Science as a career 'has very little attraction for young Americans today', concluded Margaret Mead in the survey cited earlier. 'The best young men go into government rather than into business', every conference of personnel vice-presidents is told. The Government agencies, on

the other hand, have figures that prove conclusively that the
good young men don't seek government jobs but go into
business instead. The engineers complain that the ablest of
the young fall for the glamour of pure science; the teachers,
that the ablest of the young want to go into research; the
researchers, that the ablest of the young lust for the
fleshpots of industry. I am sure that portentous reports are
presented at the board meetings of the Mafia warning that
the ablest young Sicilians no longer want to make a career in
dope-peddling.

The saddest case is undoubtedly that of the doctors. They
are damned if they do and damned if they don't. Far from
being honoured because they have become men of science,
they feel they have lost the respect which patients gave to
yesterday's 'family doctor' with his warm human sympathy.
Indeed, as an American Medical Association Survey
brought out, a full third of the public believes that the doctor
today makes too much money and compares unfavourably
with old Dr Jones, who was willing to be paid in turnips
when cash was scarce. The same perverse public, however,
also wants 'socialized medicine' – which would completely
destroy the present warm and personal relationship between
patient and doctor. No wonder that the ablest young men
don't apply to medical school!

IV

In cold fact, however, these tales are self-delusion. No one
occupation or profession is persecuted, misunderstood, or
rejected in this country. The figures presented at all the wail-
ing conventions may be valid – but the conclusions drawn
from them are pure hogwash.

No one career *should* get all the bright boys or even most
of them. We would not want all the top graduates to go into
selling – what would we do with them there? It is perfectly
true that boys find their heroes in President Kennedy, Gen-

eral Eisenhower, and the astronauts rather than in the independent small businessman (as an otherwise sane young company president in Cincinnati complained to me in all seriousness). But it is just plain silly to conclude therefrom, as he did, that no one respects a businessman or appreciates his contribution. It is perfectly true that the role of the physician and the practice of medicine have changed radically these last fifty years. But if anything deters college graduates from going to medical school, it is the difficulty of getting in, the long years and high expense of the training, and the mechanical memorizing required by so many medical courses, especially in the early years. The position of the military man in society is indeed a problematic one – but only because we never before had a military establishment of such size, importance, and prominence in peacetime. And if the able young academician spurns teaching, it is because the entire faculty pushes him into research, where the promotions are.

Does the appliance company that is respected for its technical competence rather than loved for its folksiness really have much to complain about? The housewife, after all, does not buy the dishwasher for 'togetherness'. What distinguishes the scientists, as they themselves have been telling us for centuries, is the impersonal objectivity drilled into them in their training. And does the depositor really want his bank to be a 'friend' or a 'helping hand'? This is the role of the Community Chest. I'd rather be sure that the man who loans out *my* good money to a perfect stranger checks up on his collateral.

In sum: we do not suffer from a national outbreak of disrespect. We suffer from an indulgence in self-pity of epidemic proportions. Like the heroine in a Victorian penny-dreadful, our occupational and professional groups do not feel proper unless they have had a good self-righteous cry over their sad plight.

There is rich comedy in this – in the solemn nonsense of

the learned surveys, in the pretentious jargon of the image-coiffeur, in the brazen publicity-chasing of the press release that deplores 'vulgar publicity'. A good deal of it is almost as funny as the lachrymose bragging of those rascals, the Dauphin and the Duke, on Huckleberry Finn's raft. Not even Mark Twain could have improved on the complaint of the morticians' president that his members are deprived of the basic right of every American to brag about a sale.

There is perhaps even some small social benefit in all this breast-beating. Once in a while, a group will be persuaded to do something about its own behaviour rather than just complain about being maligned. Some county medical associations, especially in California, have tackled the thorny job of enforcing professional standards on member physicians who grossly exploit health insurance. Concern for the 'image', not just fear of local ordinances, has led several companies into cleaning up air and water pollution long before the environment became a 'cause' – for instance, the anti-smog campaign Monsanto spear-headed in the early 1950s in St Louis. Philip H. Abelson, the powerful editor of *Science* and himself a writer of rare clarity, campaigns vigorously against the obscurantist and inept style of so much scientific writing – which is surely the greatest barrier to public understanding of science and the scientist. And quite a few of the young (and often very able) officers who know that they will be retired as majors or colonels before they reach 50 are quietly finding out what skills to acquire to prepare themselves for civilian jobs. A few days ago, for example, I received a letter from a colonel totally unknown to me who, at the age of 47, expects to be retired from the Army in a few years and wants to prepare himself to be a computer programmer in industry.

V

But the occasional benefits are outweighed by the dangers of
our wallowing in collective self-pity.

It is only a short step from self-pity to the conspiracy
delusion. And we have gone dangerously far down the road
to national paranoia. Some quite normal businessmen give
money to the Birchers or to the radio and TV programme of
H. L. Hunt's 'Facts Forum' with their lurid tales of insidious
communist conspiracy in high and low places. These men
know perfectly well that former President Eisenhower or
former Chief Justice Warren were middle-of-the-roaders.
Yet being told every day how business is being maligned and
downgraded all around, they begin to wonder: there must be
some sort of conspiracy somewhere. In turn, quite a few
college professors believe in a sinister 'military-industrial
complex' with tentacles everywhere which conspire against
freedom and world peace. (By the way, all our recent Presidents, the whole Supreme Court, and most of our public
figures manage the amazing feat of belonging to both the
'communist' and the 'fascist' military-industrial conspiracies at once.)

Businessmen these days work closely with consultants
from the academic world. Yet many are ready to believe
that the college faculty is a nest of 'fellow-travellers' plotting
the downfall of the Republic and poisoning the minds of the
young against free enterprise. But there are also the self-
consciously shrill 'liberals' – in Houston or Milwaukee or
elsewhere – with good jobs or thriving businesses who feel
that they live in as much danger of life and limb as a mission-
ary in cannibal country – if the reports they publish 'back
home in the East' can be trusted.* And there is the Parent-
Teacher Association board of a Los Angeles progressive

* Having spent most of the last fourteen summers in Colorado I can
reassure 'my liberal' friends in New Jersey: the natives 'out there'
are friendly.

school which pulls the shades tight lest the wicked reactionaries spy on its meetings.

There are real conspiracies in this frightened and frightening world. All the more reason not to encourage delusions of conspiracy. Every time an occupational or professional group pities itself as misunderstood and maligned, it feeds delusion. President Johnson was right when, at a US Chamber of Commerce meeting, he advised the American businessman to shed his 'martyr complex'.

Luckily, the sane and responsible people – they are the vast majority in every occupation and profession – finally go into action when paranoia becomes rampant in their own group. The counter-attack that in the end stopped the late Senator McCarthy's witch-hunt was first launched by the top management of the Ford Motor Company. Ford's general counsel, William T. Gossett, was the first well-known lawyer and the first senior corporation executive to attack McCarthy as a public menace – in a Bar Association speech delivered in McCarthy's stronghold, Dallas, in October 1951, long before the Senator reached his crest. Two years later – a year before McCarthy's fall – Gossett's campaign for civil liberties, decency, and justice reached its climax in the Notre Dame *Law Review* in an anti-McCarthy issue which Gossett edited and largely wrote. This is widely credited with depriving McCarthy of the crucial support from the Bar, the Catholic hierarchy, and the professional corporation executives. Similarly today a number of highly respected academic liberals are becoming convinced that the 'military-industrial conspiracy' story could become dangerous to national welfare and are quietly tackling it.

But self-pity is too dangerous to be indulged in until it has become psychopathic. The sane and responsible people in each group better make up their minds to stop the self-pity peddlers. Whenever they are being told how maligned, misunderstood, unloved their own group is, they might ask: 'How badly are we really doing – in jobs and opportunities,

in money and in influence?' In the twenty years of un-
paralleled prosperity since World War II, practically every
single occupation and profession in America has done very
well indeed. One can of course always find someone who has
done even better. But the groups that complain the loudest
of being injured and unappreciated are precisely those that
have done the best: the academicians, the physicians, the
military, and business.

VI

The most important point to stress is, however, much
simpler. Americans as a people accept all work as honour-
able and respectable – for everyone. They do not look down
upon any occupation, or person, as inherently inferior. They
may laugh at him a little, but they respect the scholar who
buries himself in ancient Assyria as well as the salesman
hustling on the highways to make a dollar. But because our
society accords respect to all occupations, it grants superiority only to the individual for personal performance and accomplishment. As it denies 'class', it recognizes no
inherently superior calling, be it the intellectual or the
businessman, the politician, the soldier, or the undertaker.
And if – as seems only too likely – the complaint of 'disrespect' by a profession or occupation really means that the
group wants deference as superior to the rest of us, it does
not deserve sympathy or support. It deserves a loud, vulgar
raspberry.

7. Henry Ford: Success and Failure

[From *Harper's Magazine*, July 1947]

Businessmen make poor symbols. There are the Medici or the Rothschilds, of course; and there is Krupp. But no businessman in history, whether banker, trader, or manufacturer, has ever had the charismatic stature which Henry Ford had throughout the world fifty years ago. No other has perhaps also had as great an impact on the way we live and on the problems we face, as Ford who put the world on wheels by fathering mass-production, the assembly line, and with it today's industrial worker. This Henry Ford, the Henry Ford of deed and legend, died with the crash of 1929. The old man who lived on, almost another twenty years, was no more than a shadow. Yet the name still possessed magic – indeed it still possesses it today in the most unlikely places. Medici, Rothschild, even Krupp are not names Japanese know, except for specialists in European history; the name 'Ford' every Japanese schoolboy immediately identifies.

What is it that made this man – not a particularly interesting one at that – into a culture hero of our century?

I

Henry Ford's hold on America's imagination – indeed on the imagination of the world's masses – was not due to his fabulous financial success. And it can only partly be explained by the overwhelming impact of the automobile on our way of life. For Henry Ford was less the symbol and embodiment of new wealth and of the automobile age than the symbol and embodiment of our new industrial mass-production civilization.

He perfectly represented its success in technology and economics; he also perfectly represented its political failure so far, its failure to build an industrial order, an industrial society. The central problem of our age is defined in the contrast between the functional grandeur of the River Rouge plant, with its spotless mechanical perfection, and the formlessness and tension of the social jungle that is Detroit. And the two together comprise Henry Ford's legacy.

Both his success and his failure can be traced to his being thoroughly representative of that most native and most dominant of all American traditions, the one which in Populism found its major political expression. Indeed, Henry Ford was both the last Populist and perhaps the greatest one. He owed all his basic convictions to Bryan: pacifism, isolationism, hatred of monopoly, and of 'Wall Street' and of 'international bankers', firm belief in a sinister international conspiracy, and so forth. He also made true the great dream of the political crusaders of 1896: that industrial production might be made to serve the common man. This dream had obsessed the American people since Brook Farm and Robert Owen's New Lanark, half a century before Bryan.

The Populists had believed that a Jeffersonian millennium would result automatically from eliminating 'monopoly' and the 'money power' and the 'satanic mills' of crude industrialism – as these terms were understood in the nineteenth century. Ford fulfilled the dream. He succeeded without benefit of monopoly, he defied the big bankers, he gave his factories a clean and airy efficiency which would

have delighted nineteenth-century reformers. But in
fulfilling the dream he dispelled it. And in the place of the
old enemies which he vanquished we have today, in the industrial system which Ford did so much to develop, new
problems to face: the long-term depression, and the political
and social problems of industrial citizenship in the big
plant. Henry Ford's solution of the industrial problems with
which the nineteenth century had wrestled unsuccessfully
constituted his success, his achievement. His inability to
solve the problems of the new industrial system, his inability
to see even that there were such problems, was the measure
of his final and tragic failure.

It may seem paradoxical to interpret Henry Ford's importance in terms of a concept – especially a political concept
such as Populism. He himself had nothing but contempt for
concepts and ideas, and prided himself on being neither a
theoretician nor a politican but a 'practical man'. And the
main criticism which has been levelled against him and
against everything he stood for – the criticism embodied in,
for instance, Charlie Chaplin's *Modern Times* – has been
that he made mechanical perfection an end in itself. But
even his contribution to technology was not really a technical but a conceptual one – superb production man and
engineer though he was. For he invented nothing, no new
technique, no new machine, not even a new gadget. What he
supplied was *the idea of mass-production itself* – organization of man, machines, and materials into one productive
whole.

In economics, too, Ford discovered no new facts; the data
showing the effect of volume production on costs had all
been collected and analysed. But Ford was the first manufacturer to understand that these data disproved the traditional theory that restricted production and a high profit
margin – that is, monopoly – provided the most profitable
form of industrial production. He demonstrated that one

could raise wages, cut prices, produce in tremendous volume, and still make millions.

Above all Ford himself regarded his technical and economic achievements primarily as means to a social end. He had a definite political and social philosophy to which he adhered to the point of doctrinaire absurdity. Concern with the social effects of his actions determined every one of his steps and decisions throughout his entire life. It underlay the break with his early partners who wanted to produce a luxury car for the rich rather than follow Ford's harebrained idea of a cheap utility car for the masses. It motivated the radical wage policy of the early Ford who in 1914 fixed his minimum wage at the then utopian figure of $5.00 a day for unskilled labour. It showed in Ford's lifelong militant pacifism, of which the tragicomic Peace Ship episode of 1915–16 was only one manifestation. It showed in his isolationism, in his hostility to Wall Street, and in the raucous pamphleteering of the Dearborn *Independent* in the twenties. This social philosophy explains the millions he poured into 'chemurgy' or into utopian village communities of self-sufficient, sturdy, yeoman farmers. It was responsible for his belief in decentralization, and for this nostalgic attempt to recreate the atmosphere of an earlier and simpler America in a museum community – right next door to the River Rouge plant.

It might almost be said that Henry Ford's life work, despite these moves of his, brought about the opposite kind of world from the one he hoped for and believed in. Thus Ford, the pacifist, built up one of the world's greatest armament plants and helped to make possible the mechanized warfare of our age. Ford, the isolationist, more than any other man has made it impossible for this country to stay out of international politics and international wars: for he made this country the most powerful industrial nation on earth. Ford, the agrarian decentralist, left as his life's work the River Rouge plant, the most highly centralized and most completely mechanized concentration of industrial power in the world. The enemy of finance-capital and bank credit, he made instalment buying a national habit. An orthodox Jeffersonian, he has come to stand for the extreme application of the assembly-line principle, with its subordination of the individual to the machine. And the very workers at the Ford Motor Company whose mass-production was to give economic security and full industrial citizenship to all, are today organized in the most class-conscious union in America.

Yet it would be wrong to argue from the failure of Ford's social ideas that they never were anything but 'eccentric hobbies', as the obituaries rather condescendingly called them. The tragic irony with which his every move turned against him in the end does not alter the fact that his was the first, and so far the only, systematic attempt to solve the social and political problems of an industrial civilization. There is also little doubt that Ford himself believed – certainly until 1941 when the Ford workers voted for the CIO, and perhaps even afterwards – that he had actually found the answer for which the American people had been searching for almost a century: the realization of the Jeffersonian society of independent equals through industrial technology and economic abundance.

Nor was he alone in this appraisal of the meaning of his work. It was shared by the American people as a whole in the years immediately following the First World War – witness Wilson's urging in 1918 that Ford run for the Senate, and the powerful 'Ford for President' boom of 1923. The view was also held abroad, especially in the Europe of the early twenties and in Lenin's Russia – perhaps even more generally there than here. Indeed, it was the performance of Henry Ford's America which in 1918 and 1919 gave substance to Wilson's promise of the millennium of peace, democracy, and abundance, and which established America's moral and political authority in those years. And

the Ford spell remained potent long after Wilson's promise
had faded under the cold light of the international realities
of the nineteen-twenties.

The post-war world of today is at least as much under the
spell of Franklin D. Roosevelt's name as an earlier generation was under that of Wilson. But Henry Ford today no
longer symbolizes an America that has successfully solved
the basic social problems of an industrial world. He stands
instead for the lack of a solution. And that surely accounts
in large measure for the difference between 1919 and 1947 in
the acceptance and the effectiveness of America's moral and
economic leadership.

II

Henry Ford took the conveyor belt and the assembly line
from the meat-packing industry where they had been in general use as early as 1880. The interchangeability of pre-
cision-made parts was an even older principle; it went back
to the rifle plant which Eli Whitney built in Bridgeport for
the War of 1812. The idea of breaking down a skilled job
into the constituent elementary motions, so that it could be
performed by unskilled men working in series, had been
thoroughly explored – by Taylor among others – and had
been widely used in American industry twenty years before
Ford came on the scene, as for example by Singer Sewing
Machine and National Cash Register. Yet we associate all
these principles with Henry Ford, and rightly so. For each of
them had been employed only as an auxiliary to the traditional manufacturing process. It was Ford who first combined them and evolved out of them consciously and
deliberately a new concept of industrial production, a new
technology. It is this new concept of mass-production which
in scarcely more than one generation has given us a new
industrial civilization.

To Ford the importance of this new principle lay in its

impact upon society – as the means for producing an abundance of cheap goods with the minimum of human effort and toil. Mass-production itself, however, he considered as something purely technical, as simply a new method of organizing *mechanical* forces. Ford disciples, heirs, and imitators, the engineers and production men who today run our big industries, are certainly as convinced as their master that mass-production is a mechanical technique; many use it as if it were a mere gadget. And Charlie Chaplin took the same view when, in *Modern Times*, he caricatured our modern industrial civilization.

But if mass-production were indeed only a technique, and primarily mechanical – if it were different in degree but not in kind from pulley, lever, or wheel – it could be applied only to mechanical tasks similar to the ones for which it was first developed. But long before the recent war, mass-production principles were used for such jobs as the sorting and filing of orders in a mail-order house or the diagnosis of patients in the Mayo Clinic. Henry Luce even used it successfully to organize writers – traditionally regarded as extreme individualists – for the mass-production of interchangeable 'formula-writing'. And during the war we applied mass-production principles to thousands of new products and processes and to such problems as the selection and training of men in the armed services. In all these uses the mechanisms of the assembly line are purely subordinate if indeed applied at all. In other words, mass-production is not, fundamentally, a mechanical principle but *a principle of social organization*. It does not coordinate machines or the flow of parts; it organizes men and their work.

Ford's importance lies precisely in the fact that his principle of mass-production substitutes the coordination of human beings for the coordination of inanimate parts and of mechanical forces on which industry was originally based. When we talk of the Industrial Revolution, we think at once of Watt's steam engine. It is true that there was a lot more to the Industrial Revolution than new machines; but the steam engine is a good symbol for it because the essence of early industry was the new organization of mechanical forces. Mass-production is based, however, on the organization of human beings and of human work – something radically different from anything that was developed in the early days of industry. Indeed it has brought about a new Industrial Revolution. The assembly line is a symbol for a new principle of social organization, a new relationship between men who work together in a common task, if not for a common purpose.

On what basis does this mass-production principle organize men? What kind of society does it either assume or create? It assumes or creates a society in which things are produced by the cooperation of individuals, not by a single individual. By himself the individual in modern mass-production industry is completely unproductive and ineffectual. But the organized group produces more, better, and more effectively than any individual or any number of individuals working by themselves ever could. In this society the whole – the organized group – is clearly not only more than, but different from, the sum of its parts.

Proof of this is what happens when a man loses his place in the organized group, or his access to the productive organism; when, in other words, he becomes unemployed. Under modern mass-production conditions, the man who has lost his job is not just out of luck economically; in fact, in a rich country such as ours, the direct economic consequences of unemployment can be minimized almost to the vanishing point. But he is incapable of producing anything, of being effective in society; in short, he is incapable of being a citizen, he is cast out. For he derives his productiveness, his function in the community, his citizenship – at least his effective rather than purely formal citizenship – from his position in the group effort, in the team, in the productive organism.

It is this social effect of unemployment, incidentally, rather than the economic effect, that makes it the major catastrophe it is. That unemployment endangers people's standards of living is, of course, bad enough; but that it endangers their citizenship and self-respect is its real threat and explains our panicky fear of the 'next depression'.

In the society of the modern mass-production plant everyone derives his effectiveness from his position in an organized group effort. From this follow some important consequences. One is that such a society needs a government, a direction, a management responsible to no one special-interest group, to no one individual but to the overall purpose, the over-all maintenance and strengthening of the whole without which no individual, no special-interest group could be effective. It also follows that in such a society there must be rank: a difference of authority and prestige based on the differentiation of functions. But at the same time, in such a society no one individual is less important or more important than another. For while no one individual is irreplaceable – only the organized relationship between individuals is irreplaceable and essential – every single operation, every single function is equally necessary; the whole order would collapse, the entire productive machine would come to a stop, were one to take out one function, one job – just as the whole chain becomes useless if one takes out one link. That is why, in such a society, there should be simultaneously an inequality of subordination and command based on the differentiation of functions, and a basic equality based on membership and citizenship.

This is by no means a new type of social organization; on the contrary, it is a very old one. It was described in the old Roman fable retold in Shakespeare's *Coriolanus* which likened society to the human body, none of whose organs – neither feet, nor hands, nor heart, nor stomach – could exist or work by itself, while yet the body could not properly work without any of them. It was expressed in the medieval metaphors of the order of the spheres and of the chain of being. And even as a practical way of organizing men for economic production, the mass-production principle is not new. Indeed, the first thorough applications of mass-production and the assembly line were not in the Ford plant in Detroit, but hundreds of years earlier and thousands of miles away, in the workshops of the medieval stone masons who built the great cathedrals. In short, mass-production society, of which the assembly line is the symbol, is a hierarchical one.

This shows clearly when we analyse what popularly passes for a clear explanation of the essence of mass-production: the saying that it replaces skilled by unskilled labour. That is pure nonsense, if taken literally. Of course, in mass-production manual skill is eliminated by breaking up each operation into the component simple operations, with each worker performing only one unskilled operation or a series of such. But this presupposes a fantastic skill in analysing and breaking up the operation. The skill that is taken out of the manual operation has to be put back again further up the line, in the form of much greater knowledge, much more careful planning for the job: for there is such a thing as a law of the preservation of skill. And in addition mass-production needs a new skill: that of organizing and leading the human team. Actually 'unskilled' mass-production needs proportionately more and more highly skilled men than 'skilled' production. The skills themselves have changed from those of the craftsman to those of engineer, draughtsman, and foreman; but the number of trained and skilled men in American industry has been growing twice as fast since 1910 as that of unskilled and semi-skilled men.

Above all, the cooperation and coordination which are needed to make possible the elimination of manual skill presuppose an extraordinarily high level of social skill and social understanding, of experience in working together. The difficulties that our war plants had with new labour showed that very graphically. And contrary to popular belief, it is no more difficult to export the old methods of industrial production to a new industrial country, even though those methods require considerable manual skill on the part of the worker, than it is to export mass-production techniques where no manual but a great deal of social skill is required.

What we mean when we say that mass-production is based on unskilled labour is simply that the individual becomes effective and productive only through his contribution to the whole, and not if viewed separately. While no individual does the job, each one is necessary to get the job done. And the job, the end-product of cooperative effort, is more skilled than anything the most skilled person could have produced by himself. As in every hierarchical society, there is no answer in the mass-production plant to the question who does the job; but there is also no answer to the question who does not do the job. For everybody has a part in it.

There are a good many industries today which do not use the mass-production principle. Among them are some of the most efficient ones, for instance, the modern cotton mills (in which one worker may manage a great many looms) and a good many of our chemical industries (in which one worker may perform a number of different functions). Nevertheless, the mass-production industries are representative of our American industry as a whole because they express in the purest form the essence of industrial production, i.e. a principle of social organization. The real Industrial Revolution of our day – the one which Henry Ford led and symbolized – was not a technological one, was not based on this or that machine, this or that technique, but on the hierarchical coor-

dination of human efforts which mass-production realizes in
its purest form.

III

It is understandable that Henry Ford's disciples and imitators failed to see the political and social implications of
mass-production until they were confronted by them in the
form of an aggressive union movement – and very often not
even then. For most of these men were really only concerned
with technical problems, and really believed in mechanical
efficiency as an end in itself. But Henry Ford's own blind-
ness cannot be so simply explained as due to a lack of social
or political concern – not even as due to a lack of social or
political imagination. The real explanation is that Ford was
concerned exclusively with the solution of the *social and
political problems of the pre-Ford, the pre-mass-production
industrial civilization.* And because his answers really did
solve these problems, or at least the more important of
them, it never entered his mind to subject this answer of his
in turn to a social and political analysis. His gaze was firmly
fixed on the industrial reality of his own youth, the industrial reality against which Populism had revolted in vain. He
never even saw what he himself had called into being. As a
high official of his own company once said: 'What Mr Ford
really sees when he looks at River Rouge is the machine
shop in which he started in 1879.'

Though Henry Ford may never have heard of Brook
Farm, of Robert Owen's New Lanark, or of any of the many
other utopian communities that had dotted the Midwest not
so many years before his birth in 1863, they were his intellectual ancestors. He took up where they had left off; and he
succeeded where they had failed. Colonel McCormick's
Chicago Tribune called him an 'anarchist' in the red-hunt-
ing days of 1919 when the term meant more or less what

'Communist' would mean today in the same paper. But in spite of the obvious absurdity of the charge, the jury awarded Ford only six cents in damages when he sued for libel; for he was undeniably a radical. He turned into a stand-patter after 1932, when his life's work had shown itself a failure in its inability to produce the stable and happy society of which he had dreamed. But the Henry Ford of the earlier Model T days was an iconoclast attacking in the name of morality and science the established order of J. P. Morgan and of Mark Hanna's Republican party.

The Utopias of the 1830s and 1840s were in themselves the reaction to a failure: the abortive attempt during Jackson's administration (1828–37) to bring back to America the lost innocence of the Jeffersonian society of self-sufficient independent farmers. The Utopians no longer hoped to be able to do away with the modern division of labour or even with industry. On the contrary, they promised to obtain for mankind the full benefits of industrial productivity, but without its having to pay the price of subjecting itself to the 'money power' or to 'monopoly', or of having to work in the 'satanic mills' of Blake's great and bitter poem. These were to be eliminated by a blend of pious sentiment, community regulations, and social science.

Of all the Utopias only the Mormons survived – and they only by flight from the land of the Gentiles. But though they failed, Brook Farm, New Zion, New Lanark, and all the other attempts at the American industrial Jerusalem left a very deep imprint on the consciousness of the American people. Neither Fourier, whose ideas fathered Brook Farm, nor Robert Owen was an American. Yet it is possible, indeed probable, that the mixture of earnest, semi-religious sentiment and trust in a 'scientific' principle which is so typical of the American 'reformer' or 'radical' has its roots in much older and deeper layers in our history than the Utopias. But it is certain that the Utopias determined the specific form which American radicalism was to take for a whole century. They provided the targets, the battle cries, and the weapons for Populism, for Wilson's New Freedom, and even for much of the early New Deal (such as the 'scientific' gold magic of 1933). They fathered Henry George, Bellamy,* and the anti-trust laws. They moulded the beliefs and the hopes of America's inland empire in the Midwest. But they remained a futile gesture of revolt until Henry Ford came along.

Today we know that in depression and unemployment we have as serious an economic problem as 'monopoly' and the 'money power' ever were. We see very clearly that mass-production creates as many new social and political questions as it answers. Today we realize that as a *final* solution to the problems of an industrial civilization Henry Ford's solution is a failure.

But Ford's mass-production was not aimed at these new dangers but at the traditional devils of American radicalism. And these it actually did exorcize. Ford succeeded in showing that industrial production can be production *for* the masses – instead of production for the benefit of monopolist or banker. Indeed, he showed that the most profitable production is production for the masses. He proved that industrial production could give the workers increasing purchasing power to buy industrial products and to live on a middle-class standard; that was the meaning of his revolutionary $5.00-a-day minimum wage.

Finally – and to him most importantly – he proved that, properly analysed and handled, industrial production would free the workers from arduous toil. Under modern mass-production conditions, the worker is confined to one routine operation requiring neither skill nor brawn nor mental effort. This fact would not have appeared to Henry Ford as a fatal defect but as a supreme achievement; for it meant

* Both writers and radical reformers of the last decades of the nine-teenth century – comparable perhaps in their positions and influence to H. G. Wells in Edwardian England.

that – in contrast to the tradition of the 'satanic mills' – the worker's skill, intelligence, and strength would be fully available for his community life as an independent Jeffersonian citizen outside of the plant and after working hours.

At Brook Farm, too, the 'real life' was supposed to come in the 'communion of the spirits' in the evening after the day's work had been done; but the day's work took so much time and effort that the 'real life' could be lived only by neglecting the work. Mass-production cuts both time and energy required for the day's work so as to give the worker plenty of scope for this 'real life'. No wonder that Ford – the Ford of 1919 – thought he had built the 'New Jerusalem' on a permanent foundation of steel, concrete, and four-lane highways.

IV

It was Ford's personal tragedy to live long enough to see his Utopia crumble. He was forced to abandon his basic economic principle – the principle of the cheapest possible production of the most utilitarian commodity. First he scrapped the Model T. That was in 1927. Then, five years later, he abandoned the Model A and adopted the annual model change which substitutes the appeal of prestige and fashion for the appeal of cheapness and utility. When he did this he became just another automobile manufacturer. Even so his share in the market dropped from nearly half in 1925 to less than twenty per cent in 1940. Even more decisively proven was his failure to give the worker industrial citizenship; in 1941 the Ford workers voted to join the CIO almost three to one.

Up to the hour when the results were announced, the old man is said to have firmly believed that 'his' workers would never vote for a union. All along he had fought off realization of his defeat by pretending to himself that his downfall was being caused by sinister conspiracies rather than by faults in the structure of the community which he had built. This tendency to look for personal devils – itself a legacy from the Utopians – had shown itself quite early in the tirades of the Dearborn *Independent* against international bankers, Wall Street, and the Jews during the nineteen-twenties. It became the basis on which he fought the unions all through the thirties. It also probably explains why Harry Bennett, starting as the plant's chief cop, rose to be the most powerful single individual in the Ford organization of the thirties, and the only one who really seemed to enjoy the old man's confidence. But the union victory – followed shortly by the unionization of the foremen – must have hit Henry Ford as a repudiation of all he had thought he had achieved, and had achieved primarily for the workers. The last years of the old man must have been very bitter ones indeed.

The lesson of Ford's ultimate failure is that we cannot hope to solve the problems of the mass-production society by technological devices or by changing the economics of distribution. These were the two approaches on which all nineteenth-century thought had relied, whether orthodox or rebel. Henry Ford went as far along these lines as it is possible to go.

For the time being, the political results of Ford's achievement were extraordinary. It took the wind out of the sails of the socialist critique of capitalist society. In this country it brought about the change from the fiery political action of Eugene Debs to the politically impotent moralism of Norman Thomas; in continental Europe it converted social democracy from a millennial fighting creed into a respectable but timid bureaucracy. Even more telling was the reaction of Communist Russia to Ford. In the twenties the Russians had to add to the messianic hopes of Karl Marx the promise of achieving eventually in a socialist society what Ford had already achieved in a capitalist one: a chance for the worker to drive to the plant in his own car and to work in collar and tie, and without getting calluses on his hands. And until 1929 – as every meeting of the Third International affirmed – the Communists were completely convinced that Ford's America had actually solved the basic problems of capitalism and had restored it to ascendancy all the world over. Not until the Great Depression were the Communist leaders able to revitalize their creed, by making it appear to do what it cannot do: to solve, by the sheer force of the police state, the new, the post-Ford problems of industrial society as they appeared after 1929.

As we in America confront these problems, the economic ones will not be the most difficult. Indeed the chief economic problem of our time – the prevention of depressions – should be solvable by basically mechanical means: by adapting our employment, fiscal, and budgeting practices to the time span of industrial production – that is, to the business cycle. Much more baffling, and more basic, is the political and social problem with which twentieth-century industrialism confronts us: the problem of developing order and citizenship within the plant, of building a free, self-governing industrial society.

The fact that Henry Ford, after his superb success, failed so signally – that there is today such a grim contrast between his social utopia and our social reality – emphasizes the magnitude of the political tasks before us. But however treacherous the social jungle of our present mass-production society, however great the danger that it will fester into civil war and tyranny, the twentieth-century evils which Henry Ford left to us may well be less formidable than the nineteenth-century evils which he vanquished.

8. The Baffled Young Men of Japan

[From *Harper's Magazine*, January 1961]

Japan has suddenly become 'fashionable'. Discussions of the Japanese 'economic miracle' abound. But they suffer – in my opinion fatally – from a tendency to look at the Japanese economy as if it could be divorced from Japanese society and culture. They suffer from an implicit 'Western' bias which assumes that the economic achievement of Japan is the central, the dynamic, the causative factor in the Japanese 'success story'. My interest in Japan goes back many years before the present 'discovery' of the Japanese economy: and it began with an interest in Japanese culture and art, rather than with an interest in Japanese business. This essay and the following one (Chapter 9), therefore, try to look at the Japanese 'economic miracle' in the context of Japan, rather than in the context of economics. They try to analyse and interpret the development of Japan – surely one of the central events of this century – in terms of the dynamics of Japanese society rather than in terms of investment, capital formation or marketing. They are based on the assumption that it is fallacious to speak of the 'Westernization' of Japan. Rather what we see is something the Japanese have specialized in in their long history, the 'Japanization' of foreign (in this case 'Western') techniques, approaches, goals, and expectations. With Japan rapidly emerging as a leading economy – indeed in the opinion of some observers, as the economy likely to become the world's foremost within a few short decades – an understanding of Japan in Japanese terms, rather than an imposition of Western ideas on so alien and ancient a culture, certainly is badly needed.

The third and latest piece (Chapter 10) – actually the most recent essay in this volume – tries both to explain the Japanese phenomenon and to learn from it. It asks the question I always ask when I run across success in an area where most of us have little or none; what do these people do that the rest of us don't do, and what do they not do that we tend to do?

What ails the young educated people of Japan? To the outsider from the West, they look singularly accomplished and attractive. They will surely be important leaders in tomorrow's world. Yet, for all their achievement and promise, the young post-war Japanese carry the world-wide distemper of their generation, and are endangered by it.

There is for example my friend Ho-Itsu, the young economist of whom I saw a great deal during 1959 and 1960* on my tours of lectures, conferences, and seminars in Japan. In early 1960, at 32, Ho-Itsu was put in charge of all planning and development work for a leading machinery manufacturer, a company with 20,000 employees, operating in the major countries of the East and in South America.

Even in America, 32 would be very young for so big a job; in seniority-bound Japan it is sensational. Yet Ho-Itsu comes from a poor peasant family and owes his entire career to his ability and performance: his admission to Tokyo University (as much of a feat for a boy from a small rural school in Japan as it would be for a boy in a backwoods school in

* (Footnote 1971) And on many subsequent visits, with little or no change in the intervening years.

Mississippi to get a full, four-year scholarship to MIT); his graduate scholarship to America; his advanced degree from Chicago; the two-year trainee job with an American company in St Louis; the job as junior economist with his present company when he got back home five years ago; and his rapid promotion since. Ho-Itsu loves his work with infectious enthusiasm. He is happily married to a charming girl and dotes on his two lively boys. Any Junior Chamber of Commerce would elect him 'Man of the Year' without hesitation. And yet this gay, lively, enthusiastic man, who has every obvious reason to be satisfied if not smug is, just below the surface, a frustrated man who considers himself a failure.

Above all, he is frightened. Why?

A few years hence, the young educated Japanese will be in control of the only non-white and non-Western country that is a fully developed economy, a Great Power, and an educated society. Today, however, the positions of leadership in government, business, army, universities, and labour unions are still held by men who were already halfway up the ladder at the end of World War II. Now in their fifties and sixties, they are pre-war and 'old Japan' in their formative experiences and in their popular support.

The present pro-American conservative government, for instance, rests on the two traditional classes: the farmers, secure in their newly gained land and their lush rice subsidy, and the small tradesmen and shopkeepers. The farmers are still two-fifths of the population; but within ten years they will be only a quarter – less if the flight from the land continues at the present rate. And the small shopkeepers and tradesmen are either being squeezed out or completely made over by Japan's rapid economic advance.

The university leadership, too, is pre-war – still dominated by largely German-trained, nineteenth-century 'old liberal' scholars. And in business, also, today's top

managers are the ablest of the middle-manager of 1945, men
who were selected and trained by the Zaibatsu, the old
family holding-companies.

Within a few years leadership in all these fields will have
to be shared with the educated younger generation – men
like my friend Ho-Itsu still under 35, who have grown to
manhood since Defeat and Occupation. Certainly, within
five to ten years, their support will be the mainstay of any
Japanese government. As in every other major industrial
country, tomorrow's majority in Japan will be the professional middle-class – such as the graduate students with
whom I worked in Tokyo one summer. What they stand for,
believe, and support will be what Japan stands for, believes,
supports. What kind of people are they?

They are, all visitors agree, pure joy. They are everywhere; for Japan is a country of young people and has a
larger proportion of them in colleges and universities than
any other country except the United States. Wherever one
meets them – at a lecture or a folk festival, at an open-air
concert or camping along the trails in the Japanese alps –
they are gay yet quiet, warm, interested; proud to show off
their few bits of English, yet ready to laugh at their mistakes
and to split their sides at the foreigner's attempts to speak
their language. They are poised but natural and friendly as
puppies – much more like our conventional picture of the
'gay Neapolitans' than our (totally false) picture of the
'subtle Oriental' with his reserve and his ceremonial
stiffness. They are also quite confident about their personal
future. They know that a job is waiting for them, that there
are acute shortages of trained people: engineers, teachers,
accountants, chemists, and so on.

And yet, whenever one gets to know these serene young
people a little better, one finds underneath a deep sickness of
the spirit, a feeling that something has gone terribly wrong.
One sees them by the hundreds in the bookstores, reading.
And the bookstores are open and crowded till late at night.

But one also sees them by the hundreds standing, as if hypnotized, in the pinball alleys. And these *pachinko* joints are open twenty-four hours a day – and there are ten times as many as there are bookstores (25,000 in Tokyo alone).

I rarely worked with a more responsive group than the Tokyo students that summer: outgoing, full of questions, and well read. They were surprisingly conservative, especially in economics where they would have been criticized as rather old-fashioned on any 'liberal' campus in America. Two or three hinted rather broadly that I was way too radical for their tastes. Yet the same young people had, only a few days earlier, run with the howling mobs that rioted in the streets with murder in their eyes.

THE UNDERPAID BOSS

But these are students, many older people say, and naturally they are unsettled and easily misled. In a few years they will have forgotten their radical notions. Sure, they say, the Zengakuren, the semi-official student organization (which, by the way, the Occupation imposed on Japan), is Communist-led. But there is no more than a handful of activists whether of the 'main-stream' (Peking) or 'anti-main-stream' (Moscow) persuasion. They have control precisely because the great majority of students are completely uninterested, never go to meetings, and do not vote in student elections.

But much more mature and responsible members of the post-war generation suffer from the same disorder. Ho-Itsu, a staunch anti-Communist, felt just a little envious of the students who can still let themselves go and riot.

'Anti-Americanism' is not the explanation – it is mostly myth anyway. Communism – of the Chinese rather than the Moscow brand – may be the ultimate result. But it is not the cause – the few Communists simply manage, as they did in the June riots of 1960, to exploit frustration. Nor is the cause to be found in that elusive catch-all, the 'Japanese temperament'.

The malaise of the young educated Japanese has more complex roots. It is in part grounded in the confusion of a society in transition, a society built and kept alive by the educated professionals but without a real place for them. It is in part a reaction to success – both an emptiness now that the job of rebuilding a war-shattered country has been done and a fear of the power this success has given to Japan. And finally it is a lack of purpose – and a vague but pervasive feeling that America is failing them in providing a direction, a standard under which the makers of tomorrow can rally.

The first thing Ho-Itsu – or any of his friends – will say when asked what ails him is that he is poorly paid. And so he is. Even Ho-Itsu, who earns three or four times as much as any of his former classmates at Tokyo University, cannot afford a small car. Starting salaries for young educated people are shockingly low, even by Japanese standards. They run between $300 and $500 a year, and stay there until a man is close to 30.

But this is not what really gripes Ho-Itsu and his friends. When he says 'our salaries are too low', he is thinking of the fact that every single one of the seventy-five men who now report to him in the company, makes at least twice, if not three times what he, their boss, makes. They are all older and have been there longer. Altogether what irks the young educated people is that, by any comparison, they are the poorest paid group in Japan's modern economy, despite their scarcity, despite their rapid promotions to bigger responsibilities, despite their success. The real income of the worker, skilled or unskilled, in a modern plant in Japan is at least one-third that of his American counterpart, and his real cost to the employer is a good deal more. The real income of a Japanese top executive, not counting the perquisites, is similarly about one-third that of his American counterpart (unless he is also the owner of the business in which case he may make much more). But the real income of the educated professionals, the young economists, engineers, or teachers, is between one-twentieth and one-tenth of the corresponding American income.

Income is only a symptom. The industrial system depends on the educated professional and makes much of him. Yet he simply does not fit into the Japanese social system (*see* 'Note' on wages and jobs at the end of this essay). This system – though often enough a cloak for exploitation – was the key to Japan's achievement in the nineteenth century. Without it, Western science, technology, and economics would have destroyed a country, which in its own, highly cultured way was as little 'Western' or 'modern' as Tibet. The system also had a lot to do with Japan's comeback after World War II. But today it tends increasingly to stifle, above all, the young educated people.

What the young people need is a little cash today for the down payment on the house – instead they get a promise of future benefits. What they need is challenge – and they get security. What they want is recognition of performance and merit – and they get seniority. What they want is ability to use their knowledge wherever it can be made productive; but instead they are limited, on the whole, to one employer and to the opportunities he offers. The traditional Japanese system is built on mutual obligations between master and subject. The young professional employee is neither.

FIXED IN A FLUID SOCIETY

The traditional system is still considered the norm in Japan, but actually it is changing amazingly fast. The decisive step was the Land Reform which made the farmer, up till then the most immobile and caste-bound group in Japan, into a producer for the market and a proprietor. More and more, there are wage workers on the Western model, employed usually as permanent 'temporary employees'. The small shops with their underpaid craftsmen are disappearing as the young people use education as an escape hatch from the 'traditional' economy.

Ho-Itsu is himself a symbol of change. Thirty years ago he would not have held a top job at his age, no matter how able. Since the war a great many new businesses have grown, starting from nothing, especially in the electronics field. And the people in these do not seem to have heard of the 'old school tie'. Even some old companies now sometimes hire young men who have started with somebody else.

But that the situation is fluid only makes it more confusing. No one knows what the rules are, nor, half the time, what game is being played. Here is an illustration:

Sikoku-san, in his early thirties, is a successful consultant on personnel training. He is working with the biggest companies in the country, making excellent money. He lectures at a big university. He is the kind of son-in-law respectable parents dream of. Yet when his wife and his children go to visit her parents, he does not come along. His father-in-law disapproves too sharply of his being on his own. 'A man of 34,' the father-in-law holds, 'is too young not to have a boss. He needs somebody to tell him when he makes a mistake, he needs somebody to protect him.' The irony of this story is that the father-in-law, dean at one of the big universities, is one of the leading Japanese 'liberals' and 'pro-Westerners' and is famous for his impassioned speeches against 'feudalism'.

The young people themselves are torn. They are in revolt against the 'organization man' of Japanese tradition, against the kind of 'human relations' which underlies Japanese business, Japanese government service, and the whole of Japanese life. But this means a revolt also against the very spirit of their country. Japanese culture, Japanese art, the Japanese language even, are all founded on personal relations of mutuality, not on such impersonal things as goods produced or employment contracts. Even the most dissatisfied of the young educated people therefore shrink from the anarchy and uncertainties of a Japan that would have sloughed off the values and traditions of its past. The best of them – and the best in Japan are amazingly good – know that they have to find a way which preserves the great values of the Japanese traditions, and yet creates a new society appropriate to a highly industrialized country in which the bulk of the work must be done by educated people. They only do not know how this is to be done.

The best – an architect in Kyoto; a sociologist at Tokyo University; an amazingly young department head in a major ministry; a bright, eager co-ed in a law school – see clearly that this task is not for Japan alone but for the entire 'non-white' world. It is a task Japan should be uniquely fitted for. It is so very similar to the achievement of the Japan of a century ago – when, in thirty years, one of the most stagnant, most caste-bound, and poorest of clan societies transformed itself into a modern country. And (contrary to general belief in Japan as well as outside) the job then was not accomplished by copying the West. It was done primarily by original and bold social innovation – such as adapting clan concepts and values to the nineteenth-century Western factory. The confusion of today's Japan should therefore be the opportunity for the young educated people. Japan needs a new generation of leaders similar to those of 1867 who created a new and yet fundamentally 'Japanese' order.

But many, many more of the young people only know that they are baffled, confused, and on very treacherous ground. What is amazing is that so few, until now, have fallen for the strident 'dynamism' and the over-simple, black-and-white certainties of the extremists, either right or left. For the dream merchants promise precisely what the young people are looking for: a goal, a direction, a challenge.

RELUCTANT GIANT

'I don't have any difficulty getting all the good young men I need,' boasted the owner of a bus company from a poor and backward region. 'All I've got to say is: In my part of the country the big job, the job of building the new Japan, has still to be done.'

He neatly pinpointed the second major cause for the restiveness, the sense of emptiness in the young Japanese: the big job of restoring war-torn Japan is done. It set a goal for ability and ambition; and it gave stability to the nation. What is there to take its place?

The Japanese themselves talk of 'rebuilding Japan'. This indicates that even they do not fully see the scope of their achievement; outside of Japan it is not seen at all. Germany 'rebuilt'; the Japanese built anew. Germany regained her pre-war place as the third industrial producer in the world. But Japan, which before the war ranked around tenth, now is the fourth-largest industrial country* (after the US, Russia, and Germany) in total output.

In family income pre-war Japan was one of the less poor of the poor countries. Today she is one of the less rich of the rich – well ahead of Russia and on a par with Northern Italy. Only in North America, in Great Britain, and in Germany are there more TV aerials on village roofs than there are in Japan. And the dollar a day which is considered minimum in Japan for the most menial jobs – sweeping the streets with hand brooms for instance – is three times what Spain, Greece, or Sicily pays for such work.

More striking even is the comparison with China and India. No matter how rapidly either country develops, it could not possibly reach the present industrial production of Japan for another twenty years; this is indeed the official goal of the Chinese planners, whom no one has accused of modesty. It would take another twenty-five years for either India or China to reach the present family income of the

* (Footnote 1971) By now Japan has, of course, overtaken Germany and ranks number three – and may well be about to catch up on the Soviet Union.

Japanese – today family income in India is one-fifth, in China one-eighth of Japan's.

More important even: today's economy rests on industries that barely existed in pre-war Japan: chemicals, precision tools and precision optics, electronics, and so on. It is a great achievement. And though American help and American orders – especially during the Korean war – contributed heavily, it is the result of a tremendous concentration of energy on the part of the Japanese, of effort, of courage and hard work.

And now it is done – the let-down is terrific. It takes several forms. The intellectuals want the fruits of the 'business civilization', but reject its values. Many businessmen are excited by the great challenge of developing the underdeveloped areas; they are making Japan a leader in technical-assistance work throughout Asia. But in many, especially of the younger people, the let-down creates a feeling of futility such as a crack athlete might have when, fully trained for the Olympics, he arrives at the stadium only to be told that the race has been called off.

One reaction, however, is general: the recoil from the power of this new Japan. Suddenly the Japanese have realized that the combination of a hundred million people and the fourth-largest industrial plant makes them a Great Power – the strongest one after the 'Super-powers', and, for years to come, the only truly modern power in Asia.

The power is bound to grow. In another ten years Japan may be the most influential country in the Arabian and Persian Gulfs, simply because she is likely to be the single most important market for Near Eastern petroleum.* The more she helps in developing underdeveloped countries, the greater her influence in these countries. And by 1975 Japan, according to an official and rather conservative forecast, will have doubled her national income and production. She will

* (Footnote 1971) This is now fast becoming fact, at least for South-East Asia.

produce as much per person as West Germany does today –
and have twice Germany's population.

A year or two ago few Japanese realized their country's
power. I met with amazed incredulity when I mentioned it
during my 1959 lecture tour. When I came back for my
second lecture tour in June 1960, I found general awareness
of it. But the Japanese are not happy over it. On the contrary it frightens them out of their wits, especially the
younger ones.

To understand this one must first realize that the Japanese
tended to underrate their strength after the defeat of 1945 as
much as they had overrated it before. They tended to see
themselves as a kind of Asiatic Switzerland, in which our
Occupation policies confirmed them (such as the famous
anti-war clause, the Article 9 of the Constitution). The reaction against the Security Treaty with the United States was
so emotional and so violent because it destroyed this illusion.

THE NEW ASSASSINS

The second thing to understand is that in all Japanese history power has always meant military dictatorship. The
militarist régime of the thirties was only the latest in a series
that goes back a thousand years and more. At that, military
dictatorship in Japan was originally a great political
achievement, with civil war the bitter alternative in a
country of tightly knit, feuding clans. The only difference in
this respect between Japan and Scotland is that the Japanese
succeeded where Robert the Bruce and Montrose failed. As
a result, however, 'power' in Japan means rule by the man
on horseback.

Again it was the Security Treaty which awakened the
Japanese. Seen from America, the crucial clause of the
treaty looked like a major concession. We promised to consult the Japanese government before taking any military
action from bases on Japanese soil. But few Japanese be-

lieve that such a decision could or would be made by a civilian government controlling the military. In Japanese history, the military has always controlled military decision, if not the civilian government altogether. Seen from Japan, this article is therefore a subterfuge to bring the military back into power over the nation's destiny; at least it is the opening wedge.

This is, of course, a gross misunderstanding of the letter as well as of the intent of the Security Treaty. But as soon as the Treaty had passed the Diet, Japan's greatest political danger reappeared: 'government by assassination'. There were first two unsuccessful murder attempts, one in June of 1960 on the life of a Socialist leader, another one in mid-July of the same year on the life of Kishi, the retiring conservative Prime Minister. Then in October 1959, Japan's most popular Socialist, Inejiro Asanuma, was actually killed during a non-partisan rally.

All three assassins were members of very small, semi-secret, right-wing societies dedicated to the restoration of the pre-war military dictatorships. They have altogether only a handful of members and no respectable backing whatever. But, unlike Germany, Japan teaches the history of the last thirty years in her schools. And every young Japanese – let alone every older Japanese – knows that the toboggan ride into dictatorship, war, and defeat began thirty years ago with exactly such small, obscure groups of 'super-patriots' specializing in 'government by assassination'.

It is no consolation to the intelligent and serious of the young Japanese that the right-wing extremists can say, 'The left wing started it'. The left-wingers have, it is true, not murdered anyone of importance – so far (which many Japanese put down to careful calculation by the left's masters in Peking). But the Security Treaty gave the few semi-secret, disciplined fanatics on the left – the Peking inspired 'main-stream' cells in student associations and labour unions – the opportunity to unleash their bully boys. By threats and violence on a large scale they have harassed students who do not join in 'spontaneous' demonstrations, workers (especially on the railroads) who refuse to go out on a political strike, professors who are not sufficiently 'democratic'. They do not always succeed; in August of 1960, for instance, striking coal miners turned on the 'student volunteers' the Communists had sent in to 'help' them, and chased them out of town. But the left-wing fanatics now have what, thirty years ago, was the strength of the right-wingers: protection and encouragement from above. The professors play the role today which the generals played then – they disapprove, of course; but excuse and explain away.

In some part this tolerance of the goons is the result of stark fear. In large part it is opportunism: under the present 'reactionary' régime one does not risk anything by being pro-left, but the Socialists, once in power, might not be so tender. There is also a good deal of the moral confusion of the intellectual which makes him excuse evil because its perpetrators are 'so sincere'. And then there is a great deal of political colour-blindness among Japanese intellectuals, very similar to the affliction of their American colleagues in the late thirties, and similarly exploited by the Communists. But the main reason is certainly the heavy legacy of clan loyalty as the 'higher law' which all Japanese legend preaches and which in today's Japan is probably strongest among the very intellectuals who forever rail against the 'remnants of feudalism'.

Many of the young people, especially students, react to the danger that power will bring dictatorship by the extremists of right or left with a desperate head-in-the-sand manoeuvre. Disabused of their belief that Japan is going to be the 'Switzerland of Asia', they search for someone else to blame. (That Switzerland owes her neutrality both to being the most heavily armed country in the world for its size, and to being vigorously and openly opposed to all dictatorships, the young Japanese neither know nor would believe, by the way.)

There are many more young Japanese who know that Japan can no more escape the reality of power than an elephant can be brushed under the rug. But they are still deeply perturbed. Ho-Itsu spoke for a great many of them when he said: 'Our company will triple its output in the next ten years. One reason is that Japan needs some sort of a navy, if only to protect her coasts. After all, the Russians in Sakhalin are only twenty miles or so away from us. It's a wonderful challenge to build like this. But at the same time I feel like a traitor to all I believe in. The ships are all right. But I am scared stiff of the people who will command them.'

THE MISSION THEY CRAVE

But the real disease that afflicts the young educated Japanese is neither social nor political. The real illness is one of the spirit. They are no longer at home in the Japan of their ancestors. They find it much easier to talk or do business with a Westerner than with a fellow-Asian from an underdeveloped country. Yet they need much more from the West than the horse operas their TV stations run – and they do not find it.

The Japanese crisis is basically an absence of leadership, of direction and purpose, of beliefs, and of example to be followed. There are 'Marxists' in Japan, to be sure. But except for a small number of 'true believers', they are Marxists largely because there is no democratic opposition party to which a young man, bored with the career-politicians' game of musical chairs, can turn. There are 'Nihilists' – 'hooligans who have heard of Sartre', a Japanese friend explained the term. But they matter only as long as their elders excuse them because they are 'sincere'. Much more symptomatic and important than these political manifestations is what the young educated Japanese read today. They do not read politics. They read the same books the 'non-political' young Europeans read in the twenties. Most popular among them are for instance the early novels of the German-Swiss Nobel Prize winner, Hermann Hesse, books dripping with self-pity, in which nature-boy somehow escapes from work, responsibility, and civilization into arty loafing and bucolic sex in the old sawmill. For a people so robust, so energetic, so much in love with work and with the newest gadgets, this kind of literary taste argues considerable emotional instability and confusion.

Eventually only the Japanese can provide the leadership they need. But it cannot, as yet, be found in Japan. The generation gap between the young and the pre-war men at the top, is too great. The 'Professors' (who enjoy in Japan the standing once reserved to the German 'Herr Geheimrat') are incapable of leadership. Their two traditions, one Confucian, one German nineteenth-century, are traditions of scholarly specialization and social irresponsibility. And the young academicians are still years away from power and influence.

Where guidance will be found in the next decade will determine what the new Japan will be – the Japan created by Defeat, Occupation, and Reconstruction. American control of Japan ceased ten years ago. American leadership in Japan has not yet begun.

The Japanese, especially the young ones, expect too much from us. They feel that we have taken them up the mountain top and shown them the promised land – and then cast them out into the wilderness. If Japan goes Communist or Fascist, it will be out of disappointment with America. It will be because individual dignity, free society, and economic growth will appear to have brought material rather than spiritual satisfactions. The deep disease of the young educated Japanese has Japanese causes. But it became acute as the result of the crisis in American values and leadership in the world.

We are rightly conscious of the importance of India's and

China's attempts to develop themselves. But for a good long time to come it will be true, that as goes Japan, the only developed Asian country, so goes Asia. We can also expect the problems of the young educated men to be infinitely more acute in those countries that are only starting their development, in Asia, Africa, and in South America. But if we cannot give the young Japanese, with a century of industrial background, the leadership, the hope, the mission they need and crave, we have little chance elsewhere.

'You asked me,' Ho-Itsu said, at our last talk at the airport a few minutes before my flight was called, 'whether many of our young people are attracted to Communist China. Of course, ancient China means to any educated Japanese what Ancient Greece and Renaissance Italy mean to any educated Westerner. But you aren't fond of a gangster because he happens to have a Greek grandfather, are you? We are not attracted to Communist China. We are attracted to the West. We never expected anything from the Chinese and they promised nothing. We are not therefore going to be disappointed by them. You in the West, however, have been our light – and we worry lest it fail us just when we need light the most.'

NOTE ON WAGES AND JOBS IN JAPAN

The Westerner who applies his ideas of wages and jobs to Japan, finds himself confused. Wages, he is told, are low, but labour costs are high. Yet no Japanese industrialist knows what his labour costs are. The Japanese system is perfectly rational – but quite different from ours.

(1) There are two distinct economies in Japan, with little flow of people from one to the other. One is the 'Western' economy of essentially modern industries making goods pre-Western Japan did not produce. The other is the 'traditionally Japanese' economy of small workshops – at the most fifty people – producing the goods of pre-1867 Japan such as lacquer ware, silk fabrics, or silver. Wages in the

'traditional' economy have been rising fast but are still no more than two-fifths those of the 'Western' economy – with the result that the most highly skilled craftsmen tend to get the lowest wages.

(2) A man does not 'get a job' in Japan. He is, so to speak, adopted into a clan: once on the payroll, always on the payroll. In many cases a young man joins the 'clan' when he enters college. Large companies, government agencies, teaching fields often 'belong' to this or that university and usually do not even consider other graduates. There need therefore be no 'comparable wage' between industries or companies, except for the starting wage – and there is none.

(3) Wage and salary in Japan are an instalment on a lifetime contract of mutual loyalty, not payment for work done. This makes seniority, rather than skill or accomplishment, the basis for wage levels, and raises the overhead in older companies.

For example Sony, the Japanese radio and TV manufacturer, has recently moved to a plant in Ireland, where gradually all Sony products for export all over the world are to be made. This plant buys only transistors in Japan; everything else comes from Western Europe, where prices are lower. Sony is a young company; but most of its suppliers apparently are not – and their costs are therefore high.

(4) Japan knows no hourly or piecework rates; only 'monthly salaries'. Because the lifetime relationship between employer and employee is considered a family tie, the employee also participates in the earnings of the enterprise, over and above the employer's fair share. Hence – most confusing to a foreigner – the bonus system. Actually people do not get twelve monthly salaries; they get between fifteen and twenty-four according to the size of the semi-annual bonus. And wage negotiations usually turn on the number of 'monthly salaries' in the bonus.

(5) The Japanese have always considered wages to be only

peripheral to the relationship between employer and employee, not central. For over a thousand years *all* incomes in Japan were reckoned in terms of the amount of rice one man needs to live on for a year. To this day, cash wages, while becoming increasingly important, are only one part of labour costs and incomes. The only exception is the young educated employee – he is 'above' the workers' benefits but far too young for the perquisites that come with seniority.

Because benefits are the main compensation for most employees, the manufacturer literally does not know what his labour costs really are. For benefits are not fixed as a rule. The employer is expected to pay for all legitimate employee needs ... from hospital bills (including abortions) and support of an employee's widow and children, to home-making courses for girl employees and even dowries and income taxes.

These needs vary tremendously, and so, of course, does the generosity of employers. But even the largest companies pay without clear policy and as the need arises – the stingiest will support the penniless widow of an employee, the most generous will not pay if she has a prosperous brother. The only certain thing about labour costs is therefore that cash wages, even with the bonus, are at best one-half, more often only one-third, of the total.

9. Japan Tries for a Second Miracle

[From *Harper's Magazine*, March 1963]

Japan was almost overrun during my 1962 visit by Western economists, bankers, and industrialists who had come to study the 'Japanese economic miracle'. Arthur Burns, Chairman of the Council of Economic Advisers under Eisenhower, was there in that spring; he was so impressed, according to Washington reports, that he strongly recommended that President Kennedy adopt some of Japan's tax and money policies to spur our laggard economy. A little later the London *Economist* sent a senior editor on a three months' tour; the result was two supplements in the magazine in September 1962, the first of which was called 'The Most Exciting Example'. Dozens of Wall Street analysts poked around Japan looking for 'growth' stocks to recommend to American investors who were disenchanted with their own market. And there were industrialists from all over – from Germany, Italy, France, Canada, the United States, and Australia – searching for products to buy, for Japanese partners for joint-ventures, or for Japanese markets.

The only people who did not talk about the 'Japanese economic miracle' were the Japanese themselves. Their businessmen, economists, labour leaders, and government people fretted instead about the threat to Japan's exports and about 'excessive competition' at home. They talked about the need to retrench and they complained about the growing 'flood of American imports'* that, they said, was about to drive entire Japanese industries to the wall. Most of this was just talking-poor, of course. Any competition in the home market is likely to be considered 'excessive' in Japan, where for thirty years goods had been scarce. Now, however, with four out of five Japanese families having TV sets, customers no longer stand in line, money in hand, to buy whatever the manufacturers turn out.

But poor-talk or not, Japan has fundamental decisions to make on the character and structure of its economy and society and on the nature of its political life – precisely because its economic success has made it the only modern nation outside the West.

The last decade in Japan has proved that the methods, tools, and policies of a free economy can generate very fast economic development on non-Western soil. It has also proved that with a free economy a non-Western nation can achieve an educated population and a high and rising standard of living. In the next few years, however, Japan will have to demonstrate that the social and political values of a free society (1) can generate effective and well-organized political forces, and (2) can resolve the inherited social conflicts of a non-Western culture and tradition. Already a technically advanced and highly educated Great Power – the only non-Western nation to attain this position – Japan now has to prove that it can become the first *society* to be both truly modern and fundamentally non-European.

CAUSE FOR CONFIDENCE ....
What has happened in Japan since the end of the American Occupation in April 1952 is the most extraordinary success story in all economic history.

When the Peace Treaty went into effect and Japan

* (Footnote 1971) Now, of course, it's the Americans complaining about 'the flood of Japanese imports'.

regained her sovereignty, she had just barely worked her way back to her pre-war levels of production and income. This was far above any level that could be called 'under-developed' – as witness Japan's industrial output and technical performance in World War II. But the Japan of 1952, like that of 1941, still rated only as a minor industrial country, perhaps twelfth to fifteenth among the industrial nations. Her dominant industries were those that typify the early stages of industrialization, for instance textiles. Her food shortages were chronic and apparently incurable; the two staples, rice and wheat, were still rationed in the spring of 1952. Even such recovery as Japan had made depended on American orders for the Korean War, and these orders were rapidly drying up. Inflation had been rampant and labour unrest that came close to armed insurrection was endemic. Joseph Dodge, the Detroit banker who had been the Occupation's economic adviser, said what nearly all the experts thought when he predicted in his final report in 1952 that the Japanese economy was headed for collapse.

Now, ten years later, Japan ranks fourth among all nations in total industrial production. Only the United States, the Soviet Union, and West Germany are ahead of her, and she may actually be on the point of overtaking the Germans.* Since 1952 her national income has tripled and her industrial production and industrial exports are five times what they were. This means that Japan has achieved an annual average growth rate of 9 per cent for national income and almost 20 per cent for industrial production and exports. No nation in recorded economic history has ever done this before.

To accomplish this astonishing feat Japan has in a decade managed to make massive breakthroughs on five different and distinct fronts – in new investment, in mass marketing,

* (Footnote 1971) She did a few years later; and by 1975 she may have overtaken the Soviet Union in *total* production – with less than half Russia's population.

in agriculture, in education, and in health. Briefly, this is what she has accomplished:

First: Year after year the Japanese have put more than a quarter of their national income into new investment. It has been this, primarily, that has made possible the rapid spurt in industrial capacity and production.

Second: At the same time the Japanese have created the first genuine mass consumer market outside the Western World. As early as 1962, for example, the Japanese discovered to their amazement that only the United States has more consumer appliances per family than they have; they are better supplied with TV sets, refrigerators, and washing machines than the British or the West Germans (though the automotive revolution is only just beginning). What is more, along with her mass consumer market, Japan has created a mass stock market, a phenomenon known otherwise only in the United States. In pre-war Japan only banks and big industrialists owned shares in industrial companies; today every tenth Japanese family owns some common shares. (That is not to say that the US stock exchange laws would approve of the methods by which these shares are sold.)

Third is the breakthrough in agriculture. Ten years ago half the Japanese population worked on the land, but Japan could not feed herself. Today only a third of the population is still on the land. But though the Japanese now have to feed a far larger population than they did a decade ago, they have now acquired that fashionable national disease, an unmanageable farm surplus.

The *fourth* breakthrough has been in education. Only the United States and Israel have a larger proportion of their young people in higher education than Japan. Every third or fourth young man of twenty is now in college; this stands in marked contrast to Europe where the 'educational revolution' is yet to come.

And, *finally*, in one short decade, life expectancy in Japan has risen from less than fifty years (which was high for a non-Western country) to seventy (which is equal to that of the most advanced countries of the West). Furthermore, Japan has managed to cut its birth rate to the Western level so that alone of all non-Western countries, Japan is not being overwhelmed by a 'population explosion'.

One would expect these achievements to be expensive, but while the Japanese were forging ahead on all these fronts their tax burden has not gone up. It has been Japanese budget practice to anticipate the economic growth for the year ahead, figure out what it will mean in higher revenues, and then cut tax rates enough to hold the tax burden down. (It was this, apparently, that so impressed Dr Arthur Burns.) One might expect such a tax policy to create inflation, but there has been less inflation in Japan than there has been in Europe or America.*

Even more surprising, perhaps, the tremendous economic growth in Japan has been accomplished with very little money from abroad. Since the Marshall Plan began in 1948, America has sent $25,000 million in aid to Europe. In the same period Japan (with 100 million people, or one-third the population of all Europe including Great Britain) got at most $1,000 million. Furthermore, Japan has been extremely wary of foreign investment and there has, consequently, been almost none† – a marked contrast to Europe where the $5,000 million to $8,000 million of direct American investment have provided much of the fuel for the boom of the last few years.

In 1961 the growth rate in Japan actually hit 15 per cent. The government, afraid of inflation, stepped on the brakes – hard – and forced a slow-down. But a Japanese 'slow-down' would be a gallop anywhere else – the economy grew by 5 per cent in 1962 despite credit restrictions and officially

* (Footnote 1971) This is no longer true.
† Except in joint ventures where the foreign partner contributes technical and product knowledge while the Japanese partner manages and controls.

decreed 'austerity'. (The US growth *goal* is a rate of $3\frac{1}{2}$ to 4 per cent a year!*) In 1959 the Japanese government predicted that the economy would double again in the ten years between 1960 and 1970. Last September the Ministry of Finance cut the period back to seven years; the growth from 1960 to 1963 alone had already added 40 per cent to the 1959 economic level.

Japan, of course, has one very special advantage – a very low defence burden. Though growing steadily, the budget for the Japanese 'Self-defence Forces' still takes less than 2 per cent of the country's national income – as against a defence burden of 10 per cent of national income in the US. (Japan and West Germany should be a convincing answer, by the way, to fears of the economic effects of disarmament.) But even after making full allowance for this and a great deal of luck, the Japanese economic achievement is still a real 'economic miracle'.

This sort of accomplishment ought to make the Japanese smug. On the contrary, they are deeply worried. A good many sane and unexcitable Japanese talk seriously today about what they call 'a crisis of self-confidence'. Why?

... AND CAUSE FOR JITTERS

The immediate cause of Japan's jitters is that in her own self-interest she has to open her domestic market to competition from the West and especially from Europe and the United States. Since 1900 when Japan first began to export manufactured goods in quantity, she has been a tough, aggressive competitor in international markets. But her home market has always been insulated – and neither economically nor socially is Japan prepared for competition in it.

Japan is thoroughly mercantilist. It is, indeed, the one example of successful mercantilism which combines

* (Footnote 1971) And we were very proud during the Johnson years to reach it – for a time – though just barely.

governmental direction with entrepreneurial vigour, and aggressive competition abroad with protectionism and imposed price stability at home. To do away with this protectionism at home is going to mean changing drastically both the entire system of industrial hiring and firing, and the long-entrenched but extremely expensive system of distributing goods.

Then why should Japan now, after her economic success, have to let the foreigners come into her domestic market?

Japan's entire post-war expansion has been in the new 'advanced' industries – in machinery, synthetic fibres, and plastics; electronics, optics, and pharmaceuticals; trucks and household appliances. The 'traditional' industries which dominated pre-war Japan are no longer very important in the domestic economy today. Japan depends, for instance, less on cotton-mill employment than does our own Old South. But of her exports almost half are still in 'traditional' goods – textiles, toys, footwear. On these exports depends Japan's ability to buy abroad the raw materials – above all, petroleum and iron ore – without which the 'advanced' industries could not keep going for one day. And exports of 'traditional' goods are shrinking – fast and inexorably. Japan is already out-produced and undersold in the 'traditional' goods by such new, truly low-low-wage areas as Hong Kong, Singapore, the Philippines, or Pakistan. Within a very few years Japan will have to replace 'traditional-goods' exports by 'advanced-goods' exports.* And the only possible buyers of these additional 'advanced-goods' exports are the big markets of the European Common Market and of Great Britain, where Japan today sells practically nothing.

* (Footnote 1971) In fact Japan sees herself threatened now by low-wage imports – of textiles and footwear, for instance – from Hong Kong and Singapore while her own textiles and other labour-intensive products are threatened with denial of access to Western and especially US markets.

The problem of the 'traditional' exports would have
arisen anyhow – no one knew it better than the Japanese.
The emergence of the European Common Market as a great
economic power, however, brought it to a head a full decade
before Japan was ready to face it. Suddenly in the early
1960s the Japanese realized – as we and the British did – that
they must get into the European market fast or risk being
out forever.

There is no economic reason why Japan's 'advanced'
products should not sell as well in Europe as they have been
selling in the much tougher and much more competitive US
market. But the Japanese cannot even ask for access to
Europe unless they offer the Europeans access on equal
terms to their own lush domestic market of 100 million
prosperous customers – which, after the US and Western
Europe, is the world's third-richest market. This, however,
means that the Japanese for the first time will have to be able
to meet industrial competition on their own home
grounds.

To Westerners, who have been used to stories of 'Japanese low costs', Japan would seem to have nothing to worry
about. It is hard for us to believe, for instance, that Italian or
Swiss silks could undersell the Japanese product. Yet
Tokyo's largest silk store offers beautiful European silks 30
per cent or so below the price of comparable Japanese
fabrics, despite a fat Japanese customs duty on such
imports. For Japan's is a high-cost economy, except in its
most advanced industries, and especially in its advanced
export industries. Labour productivity in industries producing for the home market is one-third or so of labour
productivity in the West. And the Japanese customer pays
almost twice as much for distribution as we pay here despite
our vast distances and high transportation costs. These are
costs demanded by the social structure rather than by economic inefficiency and accordingly require social remedies
with all their potential political dangers.

KEPT ON TO DO NOTHING

Let me explain. The Japanese worker is as productive as any worker in the world. He is better educated and better trained than almost any other worker, and he works cheerfully, hard, and for long hours. Yet, in some Japanese factories it takes six times as many employees to produce the same amount of the same goods as in a comparable American factory. The reason is Japan's traditional system of 'lifetime employment' with lay-offs or dismissals only for very serious misconduct. As a result most of Japanese industry is grossly overstaffed, and thousands of people for whom there are no jobs are kept on doing almost nothing in the plant or office. Very few Japanese employers know (just as very few American employers know) that it costs three to five times a man's salary to have him on a job – in supervision, in space, in paper work and record keeping, in heat and light, in materials, and so on.

'Lifetime employment', in turn, means that a Japanese over 30 as a rule cannot change jobs. He is paid by his age rather than by the demands of the job he performs. He is assigned, however, to a job on the basis of length of service. A new employee over 30, therefore, could be given only beginner's work – and would get twice the starting wage. It is small wonder that no one will hire him. But then no one fires a man over 30; the firm just keeps him on the payroll and invents work for him.

As a result, older industries and businesses bear the heaviest burden of overstaffing; and the coal mines and railroads, as they are everywhere else, are in the worst shape of all. New industries and new businesses also have high costs because an artificially created 'labour shortage' steadily pushes up the wages that beginners can, and do, demand. Starting wages for school graduates have doubled in the last three years.*

* (Footnote 1971) And more than doubled again in the eight years since this essay was written.

The younger managerial and professional people in Japan are beginning to move from job to job in increasing numbers, though still only if their original employers permit them to do so. And many different ways to make the manual worker mobile are now being explored.

Some companies are introducing the Western system of paying for the job itself rather than for age and seniority. Others are toying with the idea of splitting between the old and the new employer the wage cost of any worker who changes jobs. The new employer would pay the base wage for the transferring employee; the old employer would pay the difference between that and the wage appropriate to the man's age. The Japanese are beginning to understand that industry has to separate the guarantee of a worker's income – which ought to be maintained – from the stranglehold the job has on him. The worker ought to be freed from the restrictions that penalize him and make it impossible for him to move into a better-paying job in an expanding industry.

But lifetime employment is much more than a matter of money. Until World War II it was almost entirely restricted to white-collar workers. Manual workers didn't achieve it until after the war and then only through bitter labour struggles. To them it represents, therefore, status and acceptance by society. An emotional issue anywhere (as witness our steel strike of 1959 over 'featherbedding' or the long and bitter fight of the Flight Engineers), employment security is pure dynamite in Japan. The longest and most violent strike in Japanese labour history was settled only two years ago, after virtually a whole county had stayed out for eighteen bitter months in protest against a management decision to retire with a generous severance allowance 2,000 coal miners in an exhausted pit. Yet, according to a recent government study, there are another 60,000 coal miners – one-third of the total – for whom there is no real work, though they all have 'full-time jobs'.

The problem of distribution costs is just as serious, and it too is as much a social as an economic problem. The distributive system of Japan is essentially what it was a hundred years ago – it is still a multitude of small middlemen who live on a pittance but who when laid end to end represent a staggering waste.

What adds difficulty to problems of employment security and distribution is the position of these issues on the Japanese political map. On the one hand, employment security is a sure-fire issue for the Left – indeed almost its only domestic issue with mass appeal. On the other hand, the millions of small wholesalers and retailers, who constitute the distribution system, are the solid voting core of the conservative government in power.

Yet these concrete social issues, as full of explosives as they are, frighten the Japanese less than the impact of foreign competition at home on their traditional mercantilism – which has all the force of an unwritten constitution. Opening the home market would surely upset the subtle three-way partnership among government, large business, and small business on which Japan's entire economic development has been based. It would force Japan to abandon the policy under which government prods industries to be productive and competitive for export, while it protects inefficiency on the home market. It would break up the peculiarly Japanese arrangement under which the large producers are hot and hard-hitting rivals yet maintain a price-umbrella for the small fellow. Above all it would force Japan to let the market decide what should be produced and how it should be priced – questions traditionally decided by political and national considerations.

OLD SLOGANS AND A NEW GENERATION

Many Japanese leaders believe that their economy must become an integrated part of the world economy anyhow, and fast. They maintain that Japanese industry badly needs the challenge of competition. The costs of automobile production – and with it car prices – would drop a full third, for instance, if Japan's 'Toyo-pet' had to compete with the English Ford, the French Renault, the German Volkswagen, and the American compact car. (Japanese heavy trucks and motorcycles – both export products – are already competitive.) These Japanese believe that their mercantilist economic policy, their employment practices, and their distributive system not only have been made completely obsolete by Japan's economic growth but are fast becoming serious obstacles to further growth. They are convinced that Japan would immediately benefit from economic integration with the West as much as Europe has already benefited from the Common Market. And in all probability they are right. Unless Japan wants to choke off her economic growth and prosperity she will have to become an open competitive economy. But if she does, tremendous political pressures will build up that will challenge political courage, vision, and leadership.

There are predecents for political leadership of rare ability in Japan's modern history. One occurred in the late nineteenth century when, in one generation, a ruling class of warrior-noblemen voluntarily abdicated, abolished a tribal feudalism a thousand years old, and turned the country into a modern state. No such leadership emerged between 1890 and 1940. But after World War II Shigeru Yoshida, Japan's prime minister from 1947 to 1957, again provided leadership of high courage and vision.

But whether similar leadership emerges now or not, the shape of Japanese politics will inevitably change. The defeat of World War II created new institutions and new slogans, but few new values. Even those values of the past that were neither nationalist nor militarist were discredited. The great majority of Japanese found comfort instead in work and its discipline. As in Germany, the job of rebuilding the country became for the time being an end in itself. A much smaller minority, needing absolute beliefs and commitments, took refuge in the only available orthodoxy, which was Marxism. It is no accident that the very same groups that had been the most fanatical nationalists under the old régime – especially students and professors – became the most dedicated Marxists under the new.

Today, the Liberal-Democrats (as the conservative party is called) win every election with monotonous regularity. But the static positions bequeathed by the Defeat and the Occupation show every sign of breaking up. Japan today gropes for new political values and new political directions. This is true on the Right as well as on the Left.

Now the job of rebuilding the country has been done. While the great majority wants more worldly goods (and especially wants to be able to buy and drive an automobile) economic recovery is no longer the great national task. And the Marxists in Japan may be where our own American Marxists were in the late 1940s, after the Henry Wallace campaign for President. Their god has been shown to have clay feet.

The president of the Zengakuren – Japan's Left-wing and fellow-travelling student federation, which staged the riots against President Eisenhower's visit in 1960 – returned last August from a 'Peace Rally' in Moscow with an amazing tale. The Moscow police, he said, took him and a number of his colleagues behind the Tomb of Lenin on Red Square, gave them a severe beating, and then hung them upside down for half-an-hour or so. All this for daring to stage a 'ban-the-bomb' rally. It is hard to believe that even Communist police could be quite so stupid. But it is even harder to believe that Japanese students could be so naïve as to think that Russia would encourage a demonstration against nuclear testing which condemned indiscriminately US and Soviet tests. Yet this is what Japan's Marxists (except for their very small core of hardened professionals) really did believe. And this belief is crumbling rapidly under the impact of the ideological conflict between Moscow and Peking, which, seen from Tokyo, is hot, bitter, and irreconcilable.

This does not mean that the Japanese Left will cease to be anti-American. Indeed the less dependent on Moscow (or Peking) it is, the more dangerous it may become. It is its subservience to the Communists – and especially to the Russians – which, more than anything else, has kept the Left from gaining a majority of the national vote. Should the Left ever become genuinely 'neutral' it may well get into power and the consequences for US strategy and foreign policy in the Far East may be serious.

But if a split opened in the ranks of the governing conservative party – caused, for instance, by a fight over the future of the small retailer – it could be equally serious for us.

IN SEARCH OF CERTAINTY

Right and Left may, however, look quite different in tomorrow's Japan. The most remarkable political phenomena in Japan today are not political parties or politicians but two religious sects, both of a strong fundamentalist cast: Ten Rikyo, a kind of Japanese Seventh-day Adventists, and Soka Gakkai, a schismatic Buddhist sect, somehow reminiscent of both the Mormons and Father Divine.

When the American Occupation took a religious inventory in the late forties, neither sect was even an independent, let alone a major group. Today each has millions of fanatical members. Ten Rikyo is not directly active in politics, though its members are expected to 'vote for what is right'. But Soka Gakkai polled four million votes in the Senate elections last July.*

Both sects fully accept modern industrial civilization and

* (Footnote 1971) And got up to seven millions in the 1969 elections.

are, in general, 'for progress'; both are strongly anti-Communist and professedly anti-nationalist. But they are concerned less with issues than with the ethical, moral, spiritual
values of politics, and attack all existing parties as unprincipled. Indeed, 'Soka Gakkai' means 'creation of
values'. All experience with such movements in other countries would indicate that these two will come to grief as soon
as they get into the practical and grubby business of politics
– which is probably why Ten Rikyo carefully sidesteps any
political responsibility. But such movements are a warning.
Their rapid growth and their ability to attract members
from all classes – students, for instance, and unskilled recent
immigrants from the countryside into the big cities, the
maids, chauffeurs, and laundresses – attest both to the
yearning for values, for commitments, and to disenchantment with today's politics and parties.

To meet this real need and opportunity for responsible
political leadership in Japan, there is an entirely new generation grown to manhood since the war. But there is also real
danger. If Japan fails to integrate herself into the Free
World economy – no matter whether it is the West or her
own social problems that keep her out – she will be pushed
towards close economic ties with Soviet Russia. Especially
in Siberia, the Soviet Union has an insatiable appetite for the
'advanced' products Japan has to sell, from chemicals and
turbines to railway rolling stock, trucks, and transistors. The
only trouble from Japan's point of view is that Russia does
not have anything to sell back to Japan but wants long-term
credits which Japan simply cannot give. Yet, if driven to the
wall, the Japanese might begin to buy raw material from
Russia even though the prices would be high and the supply
quite unreliable. Or Russia might use her gold stock to pay
Japan.

Trading with Russia would not require that the Japanese
sacrifice any of their traditional politico-economic practices;
they would not have to admit manufactured foreign goods to

the home market, or change their methods of employment or reform their distribution system. It would actually strengthen Japan's mercantilist policy. For these reasons conservative groups, determined anti-Communists at home, send trade mission after trade mission to Moscow, in the hope of finding an 'Eastern alternative' to economic integration with the West, which they fear as a threat to their traditional practices and institutions. They are willing to admit that trade with Russia would stop Japan's further economic growth, but they may regard this as a lesser evil.

Such a shift in Japan's economic alignment, even if totally without effect on her foreign and military policies (which, of course, would be quite unlikely) would be a major catastrophe for Japan but an even greater one for the Free World. The balance of economic power – now heavily with the West – would shift sharply towards the Soviet bloc. Worse still would be the psychological impact of such a shift. Japan, as the only non-Western country that has actually accomplished economic development, is the test case for others. If even Japan cannot achieve membership as an equal in the Free World economy, what chance is there for the poorer and far less developed countries ranging from Yugoslavia and Peru to Nigeria and Malaya?

DO WE REALLY MEAN IT?
There is much the West – and specially the United States – can do to help Japan make the decisions that are right both for her and for the Free World. We can prevent stupidity and racial prejudice (especially of the unconscious and therefore doubly dangerous kind that is so common in Europe) from pushing Japan against her own economic self-interest away from the Free World. If we do not, there is real danger that the Europeans, if only out of widespread ignorance of Japan and of her economic strength, will exclude her.

Even more important is that we recognize Japan's

importance to the West. Perhaps because post-war Japan has not been a 'problem' our policy-makers have not paid much attention to her – less for instance than to India or to the New African nations. We have seen Japan primarily in the light of our own strategy – as a permanent American military base and as a potential military ally. We tend to forget that Japan is also a great power, an ancient culture, and a prime symbol of 'economic development' to hundreds of millions of non-Europeans.

'The individual American who shows an interest in Japan – her history, her economy, her arts, her universities, her religion – may do more to tie us to the Free World than all the politics of your government', remarked a prominent Japanese banker, inclined, as a rule, to shrug off such 'intangibles'.

Finally we need to realize that Japan is not a 'European' country and neither can nor should try to become one. Every responsible Japanese gets the shivers when someone in Bonn, London, or Washington talks of the 'Atlantic Community'; he knows that no semantic sleight of hand can make Japan border on the Atlantic or trace her culture back to the 'Judeo-Christian heritage' of our college catalogues. No matter how Westernized her economy, how technically educated her people, how advanced her physicians and scientists – her roots of culture and history, art and religion, script, literature, and language are not European but Asian. A viable modern society in Japan must embrace both her Western civilization and her Asian culture.

There are signs that the Japanese begin to understand this – the appeal of the two religious sects discussed earlier lies largely in the stress they place on both ancient religion and ethics and modern economics, industry, technology, and science. There are signs that Japan can synthesize East and West. At least in painting – Japan's most representative and most truly national art – a whole generation of good young artists are now 'abstractionists' in the Western sense and yet unmistakably 'Japanese': 'calligraphers' in the best Japanese tradition and yet, unmistakably, schooled in Braque, Matisse, or Jackson Pollock. There are other signs of this breakthrough – in the movies, in ceramics, in architecture. The West has never before had to accept a non-European culture and country as an equal, let alone as a leader. We do, of course, pay lip service to such equality – but Japan waits to find out whether we really mean it.

The big job from now on, however, will have to be done by the Japanese themselves. Of course, their success will depend on an expanding world economy which tends towards being more rather than less liberal. But more important will be Japan's courage and vision in the management of its own domestic affairs – in government, in politics, and in business. Most important: Japan must solve her problems in a manner both 'modern' and 'Japanese'.

Tough as it undoubtedly is, the job is probably neither as big nor as difficult as what Japan has already accomplished since 1952. But it will not only be Japan that will be put to the test in the next ten years. Above all, it will be the West and its values that will be on trial in this new 'post-Western' world of ours. Modern Japan is both leader and criterion.

10. What We Can Learn from Japanese Management

[From *Harvard Business Review*, March–April 1971]

- Making effective decisions;

- Harmonizing employment security with labour-cost flexibility, productivity, and acceptance of change;

- Managing and developing the young managerial and professional employee.

These three areas surely rank high on any list of management concerns.

In each, Japanese management, and especially Japanese business management, behave in a strikingly different fashion from Western management, American or European. The Japanese apply different principles and have developed different approaches and policies to tackle each of these problems. These policies, while not *the* key to the Japanese 'economic miracle', are certainly major factors in the astonishing rise of Japan in the last hundred years, and especially in Japan's economic growth and performance in the last twenty years.

It would be folly for the West to imitate these policies. In fact, it would be impossible. Each is deeply rooted in Japanese traditions and culture. Each indeed applies to the problems of an industrial society and economy values and habits developed far earlier, by and for the retainers of the Japanese clan and their relationship with their lord; by the Zen priests in their monastery; or by the calligraphers and painters of the great 'schools' of Japanese art. Yet the principles underlying these Japanese practices deserve, I believe, close attention and study by managers in the West. They may point the way to a solution to some of our most pressing problems.

WHAT 'CONSENSUS' MEANS

If there is one point on which all authorities on Japan, Western or Japanese, are in agreement, it is that Japanese institutions, whether businesses or government agencies, make decisions by 'consensus'. The Japanese, we are told, debate a decision throughout the organization until there is agreement on it. And only then do they make the decision.

This, every experienced manager will say, with a shudder, is not for us, however well it might work for the Japanese. This can only lead to indecision, or politicking, or at best to an innocuous compromise which offends no one but also solves nothing. And if there were proof needed for this, the history of President Johnson's attempt to obtain a 'consensus' would supply it.

But even the most cursory reading of Japanese history, or the most superficial acquaintance with Japanese businesses or government agencies today, shows the opposite to be true in Japan. What stands out in Japanese history, as well as in today's Japanese management behaviour, is the capacity for making 180-degree turns, that is, for reaching radical and obviously highly controversial decisions.

No country, for instance, was more receptive to Christianity than sixteenth-century Japan. Indeed, the hope of the Portuguese missionaries that Japan would become the first Christian country outside of Europe was by no means just wishful thinking. Yet the same Japan, in the early seventeenth century made a 180-degree turn, within a few years completely suppressed Christianity and shut itself off from all foreign influences, indeed from all contact with the outside world, for 250 years. Then, another 250 years later, in the Meji Restoration of 1867, Japan executed another such 180-degree turn when it opened itself to the West – again something no other non-European country managed to do.

Or, take some present examples from business and economics. Toyo Rayon, the largest Japanese manufacturer of man-made fibres, made nothing but rayon as late as the mid-fifties. Then when it decided to switch to synthetic fibres, it did not 'phase out' rayon-making as every Western company in a similar situation has done. It closed its rayon mills overnight, even though, under the Japanese system of employment, it could not lay off a single man. The Ministry of International Trade and Industry (MITI), as late as 1966 when I discussed this matter with its officials, was adamantly opposed to any Japanese companies going 'multinational', and making investments in manufacturing affiliates abroad. Three years later, by 1969, the same officials in MITI working for the same conservative government, had turned around completely and were pushing Japanese manufacturing investments abroad.

The key to this apparent contradiction is that the Westerner and the Japanese mean something different when they talk of 'making a decision'. With us in the West all the emphasis is on the answer to the question. Indeed our books on 'decision-making' all try to develop systematic approaches to giving an answer. To the Japanese, however, the important element in decision-making is defining the question. The important and crucial steps are to decide whether there is need for a decision and what the decision is about. And it is in this step that the Japanese aim at attaining 'consensus'. It is indeed this step that, to the Japanese, is the essence of the decision. The answer to the question, that is, what the West considers the 'decision', follows.

In this process that precedes the 'decision', no mention is being made of what the answer might be. This is strenuously kept out for an elementary reason. It would force people to take sides; and once they have taken sides, a decision would be a victory for one side or a defeat for the other. Thus the whole process is focused on finding out what the decision is really about, not what it should be. Its result is a meeting of the minds that there is indeed need for a change in behaviour.*

This takes a long time, admittedly. Indeed the Westerner dealing with the Japanese is thoroughly frustrated during this period. He does not understand what goes on. He has the feeling that he is being given the run-around.

It is very hard, for instance, for an American executive to understand why the Japanese with whom he is negotiating, say about a licence agreement, keep on sending a new group of people every three months who start what the Westerner thinks are 'negotiations' as if they had never heard of the subject, take copious notes and then go back home, only to be succeeded six weeks later by another team of new people from different areas of the company who again act as if they had never heard of the matter under discussion, take copious notes, and go home in turn. Actually – though few of my Western friends believe it – this is a sign that the Japanese take the matter most seriously. They are trying to involve the people who will have to carry out an eventual agreement into the

* We actually have a complete account of this process at work – though it is not about a business decision. It is about the decision to go to war against America in 1941. (*Japan's Decision for War*, Records of the 1941 Policy Conferences. Translated and edited by Nobutaka Ike, Stanford University Press, 1967.)

process of obtaining consensus that a licence is indeed needed. Only when all the people who will have to carry out the agreement have come together on the need to make a decision, is the decision made to go ahead. Only then do 'negotiations' really start – and then they usually move with the speed of lightning.

It is only when the whole group has thoroughly understood what the decision is all about and when everybody knows that a decision is really appropriate, that the Japanese reach the point we mean when we talk of a 'decision'.

Only they no longer call it a 'decision'; they call it – and they are right – the action stage. At this point top management then refers the 'decision' to what the Japanese experts call 'the appropriate people'. Who the 'appropriate people' are is a top management decision. And it determines, in effect, what specific answer to the problem will be worked out. For, of course, in the course of the discussions leading up to 'consensus', it has become very clear what basic approaches certain people or certain groups are taking to the problem. Top management, by referring the matter to one or the other, in effect, picks the answer – but an answer which by now will not surprise anybody any more. This 'referral' to the 'appropriate people' is as crucial as the parallel decision in the American political process which so totally baffles any foreign observer of American government – the decision to which committee or sub-committee of the Congress a certain bill is to be assigned. Again, this 'decision' is not to be found in any of the books on American government and politics – yet, as every American politician knows, it is the crucial step which decides whether the bill is to become law and what form it will take. Similarly in Japan this top management decision – not mentioned in any Japanese books on government or business to my knowledge – decides what the actual answer to the question will be.

What are the advantages of this process? And what can we learn from it?

In the first place, it actually makes for speedy decisions, and, above all, for effective decisions. It might seem like a most time-consuming process. And indeed it takes much longer in Japan to reach a 'decision' than it takes in the West. But we in the West then spend years on 'selling' a decision. We make the decision first and then begin to work on getting people to act on it. And, only too often, as all of us in the West know, the decision is either sabotaged by the organization or, which may be worse, it takes so long to make it truly effective that it has become obsolete, if not indeed wrong, by the time the people in the organization actually make it their own behaviour, actually make it operational. The Japanese, by contrast, spend absolutely no time on 'selling' a decision. Everybody has been pre-sold. Also, of course, in their process it has become clear where in the organization a certain answer to a question will be welcomed and where it will be resisted. Therefore, there is plenty of time to work on persuading the dissenters, or on making small concessions to them which will win them over without destroying the integrity of the decision.

Every Westerner who has done business with Japan has learned that the apparent inertia of the 'negotiating stage' with its endless delays and endless chewing over of the same cud, is followed by a speed of action that leaves him hanging by the ropes. It may take three years to work out that licensing agreement during which there is no discussion of terms, no discussion of what products the Japanese plan to make, no discussion of what knowledge and help they might need. And then, within four weeks, the Japanese are ready to go into production and make demands on their Western partner for data, information, and people which he is totally unprepared to meet. Then it is the Japanese, by the way, who complain, and bitterly, about the 'endless delay and procrastination' of the Westerner. For they understand our

way of making a decision, that is, our way of making the
decision first and implementing it later, just as little as we
understand the Japanese way. which puts making the decision effective *before* making the decision itself.

In fact, the Japanese approach goes to the heart of
making effective decisions. This is not what the right answer
is, but what right behaviour follows from it. It is not derived,
as our approach to decision-making is, from mathematics
where the right answer is an end in itself and where *quod
erat demonstrandum* ends the decision-making process. It is
derived from seeing the decision as a process in which the
desired end-result is action and behaviour on the part of
people.

The Japanese process is focused on understanding the
problem. It almost guarantees that all the alternatives are
being considered. It rivets attention to essentials. It does not
permit commitment until we truly have decided 'what is the
decision all about'. As a result, it may come up with the
wrong answer to the problem – as was the decision to go to
war against the United States in 1941. But it rarely comes up
with the right answer to the wrong problem. And that, as all
decision-makers have learned, is the really dangerous course,
the really irretrievably wrong decision.

Above all, however, the system forces the Japanese to
make big decisions. It forces them to make fundamental
decisions, not to say radical ones. The system is much too
cumbersome to be put to work on minor matters. It takes far
too many people far too long to be frittered away on anything but truly important matters leading to true changes in
the policies and behaviour. Small decisions, even if obviously needed, are very often not being made at all in Japan
for that reason.

With us it is the small decisions which our process finds
easy to make, decisions about matters that do not greatly
matter. Anyone who knows Western business or Western
government agencies, knows that they make far too many

small decisions as a rule. And nothing, I have learned, causes as much trouble in an organization as a lot of small decisions. Whether the decision is to move the water cooler from one end of the hall to the other, or whether it is to go out of one's oldest business makes little emotional difference. One decision takes as much time and generates as much heat as the other. One might as well get something for that agony of change in institutional and managerial behaviour. This, however, means that one doesn't make small and frequent decisions. One makes the big ones. And this is what the Japanese process achieves.

I once watched a Japanese company working through a proposal for a joint-venture received from a well-known American firm, a firm by the way, with whom the Japanese had done business for many years. They did not even start out by discussing the joint-venture. They started out with the question: 'Do we have to change the basic directions of our business?' As a result, the 'consensus' emerged into a decision to go out of a number of old businesses and start in a number of new technologies and markets, with the joint-venture – which was established and has been doing very well – then as one element of a major new strategy. But until the Japanese understood that the decision was really about the direction of the business, and that there was need for decision, they did not once, among themselves, discuss the desirability of the joint-venture, or the terms on which it might be set up.

In the West we are moving in the Japanese direction. At least this is what all the 'task forces', 'long-range plans', or 'strategies' are trying to accomplish. But in the first place, we do not build into the work of these 'task forces' the 'selling' which the Japanese process builds in before the decision. This explains in large measure why so many of the brilliant reports of these 'task forces' or 'long-range planners' never degenerate into action but remain plans. At the same time, we expect these 'task forces' or 'long-range planners' to come up with 'recommendations', that is, to commit themselves to one alternative. To the Japanese, however – and they are right in that – the most important step is the understanding of the alternatives available. With us, as every observer of the process knows, the 'task forces', or the 'long-range planners' tend to start out with an answer, that is, with a 'recommendation' and then try to find documentation for it. The Japanese are as opinionated as we are. But because they discipline themselves not to commit themselves to a recommendation until they have fully defined the question, and because they use the process of obtaining 'consensus' to bring out the full range of alternatives, they are far less likely to become prisoners of their preconceived answers than we, in our decision-making process, are likely to be.

MYTHS AND REALITIES OF 'LIFETIME EMPLOYMENT'
Just as everyone has heard about 'consensus' as the basis for Japanese decisions, everyone, in Japan as well as in the West, knows about Japanese 'lifetime employment'. And again, what most people think 'lifetime employment' is, is as much a misunderstanding as the common reading of 'consensus'.

To be sure, most employees in 'modern' Japanese business and industry have a guaranteed job once they have come on the payroll.* While they are on the job, they not

---

* This, however, requires considerable qualification. Women are always considered 'temporary' rather than 'permanent' employees. Most of the employees of Japan's 'traditional businesses', especially the pre-industrial workshop industries such as lacquer-making, pottery, or silk weaving, are hired and paid by the hour. And even in 'modern' industry, there is a substantial, though slowly shrinking, body of employees – 20 per cent or so – who by unilateral management decision are considered 'temporary' and remain in this category even though they may have been on the job for many years.

only have practically complete job security endangered only in the event of a severe economic crisis or of bankruptcy of the employer. They also as a rule are being paid by seniority with pay doubling about every fifteen years regardless of job.

But instead of a rigid labour cost structure, Japan actually has remarkable flexibility in her labour costs and labour force. What no one ever mentions – and what, I am convinced, most Japanese do not even see themselves – is that the Japanese retirement system (or perhaps it should be called the Japanese non-retirement system) not only makes labour costs more flexible than they are in most countries and most industries of the West, it also harmonizes in a highly ingenious fashion the workers' need for a guarantee of job and income, and the economy's need for flexible labour costs. Actually most Japanese companies, especially the large ones, can and do lay-off a larger proportion of their work force if business falls off than most Western companies are likely or able to do. Yet they can do so in a fashion in which the employees who need an income the most are fully protected. The burden of adjustment is taken by those who can afford it and who have alternate incomes to fall back on.

Official retirement age in Japan is 55 – for everyone except a few who, at age 45, become members of top management and who are not expected to retire at any fixed age. At age 55, so you are being told, the employee, from floor sweeper to department head, 'retires'. Traditionally he then gets a severance bonus equal to about two years of full pay.*

Considering that life expectancy in Japan is now fully up to Western standards so that most employees can expect to live to age 70 or so, this seems wholly inadequate. Yet no

* Many companies, strongly backed by the government, are now installing supplementary pension payments which, however, by Western standards are still exceedingly low.

one complains about the dire fate of the pensioners. More amazing still, one encounters in every Japanese factory, office, or bank, people who cheerfully admit to being quite a bit older than 55 and who quite obviously are still working.

The rank-and-file employee – blue collar or white collar – ceases to be a permanent employee at age 55 and becomes a 'temporary' employee. This means, in the first place, that he can be laid-off if there is not enough work. But if there is enough work – and of course Japan, these last twenty years, has had an acute labour shortage – he stays on, very often doing the same work as before and working side by side with the 'permanent' employee with whom he has been working for many years. But for this work he now gets at least one-third less than he got when he was a 'permanent' employee.

The rationale of this is fairly simple. The man, the Japanese argue, has something to fall back on – the two-year pension. This, they freely admit, is not enough to keep a man alive for fifteen years or so. But it is usually enough to tide him over a bad spell. And since he no longer has, as a rule, dependent children or parents whom he has to support, his needs should be considerably lower than they were when he was, say, 40 and had, as a rule, both children and parents to look after.

If my intent were to describe the Japanese employment system, I would now have to go into a great many rather complicated details, such as the role of the semi-annual bonus.* But I am concerned only with what we in the West might learn from the Japanese. The main interest of the Japanese system to us, I submit, is the way in which it satisfies two apparently mutually contradictory needs: the need to provide job and income security, and the need for flexible and adaptable labour force and labour costs.

In the West, during the last twenty-five years, more and

* I give some notes at the end of Chapter 8, above.

more employees have achieved income maintenance that may, in many cases, exceed what the Japanese worker gets under 'life-time employment'. There is, for instance, the Supplementary Employment Compensation of the American mass-production industries which, in effect, guarantees the unionized worker most of his income even in fairly lengthy lay-offs. Indeed it may well be argued that labour costs in American mass-production industries are more rigid than they are in Japan, even though our managements can rapidly adjust the number of men at work to the order flow, in contrast to the Japanese practice of maintaining employment for 'permanent' employees almost independent of business conditions. Increasingly, also, we find in the heavily unionized mass-production industries, provision for early retirement such as was written in the autumn of 1970 into the contract of the American automobile industry. Still, unionized employees are being laid-off according to seniority, with the ones with the least seniority going first. As a result, we still offer the least security of a job and income to the men who need a predictable income the most, the fathers of young families who, of course, are also the ones who still might have older parents to support. And where we have 'early retirement', it means, as a rule, that the worker has to make a decision to retire permanently. Once he has opted for early retirement he is out and unlikely to be hired back, let alone at his age, to be hired by another employer. As a result, our labour force – and this is just as true in Great Britain or on the European Continent – lacks the feeling of economic and job security which is so pronounced a feature of Japanese society.

We pay, in other words, for a high degree of 'income maintenance' and have imposed on ourselves a very high degree of rigidity in respect to labour costs. But we get very few of the benefits. Above all, we do not get the psychological security which is so pronounced in Japanese society, the deep conviction of a man of working age that he need not worry about his job and his income. Instead we have fear – fear of the younger men that they will be laid-off first, just when the economic needs of their families are at their peak; fear of the older men that they will lose their jobs in their 50s and then be too old to be hired. In the Japanese system there is confidence instead, in both age groups, confidence of the younger men that they can look forward to a secure job and steadily rising income while the children are growing up; confidence on the part of the older men that they are still wanted, still useful, but also not a 'burden'.

In practice, of course, the Japanese system is no more perfect than any other system. There are plenty of inequities in it; and the treatment of the older people in particular leaves a great deal to be desired – especially in the small workshop industries of 'pre-industrial' Japan and in the multitude of small service businesses. But the basic principle which the Japanese have evolved – not by planning rationally, but by applying traditional Japanese concepts of mutual obligation to employment and to labour economics – seems to make more sense and works better than the expensive patchwork we have applied to symptoms of the problem without, however, coming to grips with the problem itself. Economically, it might be said, we have greater 'security' in our system – we certainly pay more for it. Yet we have not obtained what the Japanese system produces, the psychological conviction of 'lifetime employment', that is, of job and income security.

There is today talk – and even a little action – in American industry of 'reverse seniority' to protect newly hired blacks with little or no seniority in the event of a lay-off. But we might altogether consider applying 'reverse seniority' to older men past the age of greatest family obligation now that so many labour contracts provide for 'early retirement' after age 55. And the pressure for such 'early-retirement' provisions will predictably rise as the number of young men entering the labour force for the first time goes up sharply the next few years. Men who have the right to an 'early-retirement' pension may be expected to be laid-off first – today their seniority gives them all but absolute job security. By the same token, however, these men might have the right – today normally denied them completely – to come back out of 'early retirement' and be re-hired first when employment expands again. Indeed some such move that strengthens the job security of the younger, married employee with his heavy family-burdens, might well be the only defence against pressures for absolute job guarantees that could otherwise impose on America the rigid labour costs with which folklore endows the Japanese economy.

But even more important as a lesson to be learned from the Japanese is the need to shape benefits to the needs and wants of specific major employee groups. Otherwise they will be only 'costs' rather than 'benefits'. In the West – and especially in the United States – we have, in the last thirty years heaped 'benefit' upon 'benefit' to the point where the 'fringes' run up to a third of total labour cost in some industries. Yet practically all these 'benefits' have been slapped on across the board whether needed by a particular group or not. The one exception I can think of are maternity leaves. But teenage girls who only want to stay till they find a husband are made to pay into the pension plans. Private health insurance does not, as a rule, provide any protection against the costs of illness to an employee out of work, when, however, he needs such coverage the most. But most of the plans provide full benefits to the non-working dependents of an employed worker even though, with today's wages, most employees, when fully employed themselves, could well pay for routine illness in their families despite soaring health-care costs. In fact, underlying our entire approach to benefits – with management and union in complete agreement, for once – is the asinine notion that the work force is homogeneous in its needs and its wants. As a result we spend fabulous amounts of money on 'benefits' which have little meaning for large groups, sometimes even the majority, of employees, and leave unsatisfied genuine needs of other, equally substantial groups. This is in itself a major reason why our benefit plans have produced so little employee satisfaction and psychological security, and why an increase in one kind of benefit leads immediately to demands for new and different benefits to 'equalize' the benefit-position of some other group, the old or the young, the skilled or the unskilled, and so on.

What management and union alike might learn from the Japanese experience is to mould benefit plans so that the same amount of money can, flexibly, provide the maximum in true 'benefit' for different employee groups with different needs and wants according to their stages in life and family cycle.

It is the psychological conviction of lifetime employment that underlies what might be the most important 'secret' of the Japanese economy: cheerful willingness of the employee to accept continuing change in technology and process, and the acceptance of increasing productivity as good for everybody.

There is a great deal written today about the 'spirit' of the Japanese factory. But far more important than the company songs workers in big factories sing at the beginning of the working day is the fact that Japanese workers show little of the famous 'resistance to change' which is so widespread in the West.

The usual explanation is 'national character' – always a suspect explanation. That it may be the wrong one is indicated by the fact that acceptance of change is by no means general throughout Japan. The Japanese National Railways, for example, suffer from resistance to change fully as much as any other railway system, the American railroads, for instance. But the numerous private railways which criss-cross the densely populated areas of Japan seem to be relatively free from it. That the Japanese National Railways are as grossly overstaffed as any nationalized industry in the world may be part of the explanation; the workers know that any change is likely to create redundancy. More important is the fact that the industries in Japan which, like the Japanese National Railways, suffer from resistance to change, are also the ones that are organized according to Western concepts of craft and skill. The industries which apply Japanese concepts, as do the private railways as a rule, do not suffer from resistance to change, even though their employees also know that the company is overstaffed rather than understaffed.

The secret may lie in what the Japanese call 'continuous training'. This means, first, that every employee, very often up to and including top managers, keeps on training as a regular part of his job until he retires. This is in sharp contrast to our Western practice where we usually train a man only when he has to acquire a new skill or move to a new position. Our training is 'promotion-focused'; the Japanese training is 'performance-focused'. But also the Japanese employee, on all levels is, as a rule, being trained not only in his job but in all the jobs on his job level. The man working as an electrician will automatically attend training sessions in every single skill area in the plant. But so will the man who pushes a broom. Both of them may stay in their respective jobs until they die or retire. In fact, their pay is independent, in large measure, of the job they are doing, and is geared primarily to the length of service, so that the highly skilled electrician may well get less money than the floor sweeper. But both are expected to be reasonably proficient in every job in the plant which is, generally speaking, on the same level as their job (which in a plant means all rank and file, blue collar, jobs, for instance). The accountant in the office is similarly expected to be trained – or to train himself through a multitude of correspondence courses, seminars or continuation schools available in every big city – in every single one of the professional jobs needed within his company: personnel, for instance, training, or purchasing. And so it goes all the way to top management.

The president of a fairly large company who once told me casually that he could not see me on a certain afternoon because he attended his company's training session in welding – and as a student rather than as an observer or teacher – is of course the exception. But the company president who takes a correspondence course in computer programming is fairly common. And the young personnel man does so as a matter of course.

It would need a fat book on Japanese economic and industrial history to explain the origins of this system – though in its present stage it is just about fifty years old and dates back to the labour shortages during and right after the First World War. It would take an even fatter book to discuss the advantages, disadvantages, and limitations of the Japanese system – and the limitations are very great indeed. The young technically trained people, the young scientists and engineers, for example, resent it bitterly and resist it rather successfully. They want to work as scientists and engineers and are by no means delighted when being asked to learn accounting or when being shifted from an engineering job into the personnel department. Similarly, such highly skilled and highly specialized men as papermakers, running a big paper machine, or department-store buyers are not, as a rule, expected to know other jobs or to be willing to fit into them. But even these specialists continue, as a matter of routine, to perfect themselves in their own speciality, long after any 'training' in the West would have ended, indeed, normally, for the rest of their working lives.

One result of this practice is that improvement of work and process is built into the system. In a typical Japanese training session, there is a 'trainer'. But the real burden of training is on the participants themselves. And the question is always: 'What have we learned so we can do the job better?' Most of the participants, in other words, know the job – have indeed been doing it for many years. As a result, the new, whether a new tool, a new process, or a new organization of the work, comes out as 'self-improvement' week after week, month after month. A Japanese employer who wants to change the process to introduce a new product or a new machine does so in and through the training session. As a result, there is usually no resistance at all, but acceptance. Indeed, Americans in the management of joint-ventures in Japan always report that the 'bugs' in the new process are usually worked out, or at least identified, before it goes into operation on the plant floor.

A second benefit from this is a built-in increase in productivity. In the West we train until a 'learner' reaches standard performance. Then we conclude that he has mastered the job and needs new training only when he moves on or when the job itself is being changed. Our 'learning curve' reaches the 'standard' after which it stays on a plateau. Not so in Japan – and the Japanese understanding is more realistic, more in tune with all we know about 'learning'. The Japanese of course also have a standard and a 'learning curve' leading up to it. Their 'standard' as a rule is a good deal lower than the corresponding standards in the West; the productivity norms which have been satisfying most Japanese industries in the past are, by and large, quite low by Western measurements. But the Japanese keep on 'training'. And sooner or later, their 'learning curve' starts breaking out of the plateau which we in the West consider permanent. It starts to climb again, not because a man works harder, but because he starts to 'work smarter'. In the West we are satisfied if the older worker does not slacken in his productivity. This is a problem, too, in some Japanese industries; young women assembling precision electronics, for instance, reach the peak of their finger dexterity and their visual acuity around age 20 and, after 23 or 25, rapidly slow down. (One reason why the Japanese electronics industry works hard to find husbands for the girls and to get them out of the factory by the time they are 21 or 22). But by and large the Japanese would say that the older employee is more productive; and their figures would bear this out. With pay based on seniority, the output per yen may be much higher in a plant in which the work force is largely new and young. But output per man-hour is almost invariably a good deal higher in the plant that has the older work population – almost the exact opposite of what we in the West take for granted.

In effect, the Japanese apply to work in business and industry their own traditions. The two great skills of the *Samurai*, the member of the warrior caste which ruled Japan for 300 years until 1867, were swordsmanship and calligraphy. Both demand 'lifetime training'. In both one keeps on 'training' after one has achieved mastery. And if one does not keep in training, one rapidly loses one's skill. Similarly the Japanese schools of painting, the Kano school, for instance, which dominated Japanese official art for 300 years until 1867, taught that even the greatest master spends several hours a day copying, that is, keeps in 'continuous training'. Otherwise, his skill, and above all his creativity would soon start to go down. And the greatest Judo master still goes through the elementary exercises every day – just as, of course, the greatest pianist in the West does his scales every day.

'One difference I find hard to explain to my Western colleagues,' said one of the leading work study engineers of Japan to me one day, 'is that we do exactly the same things that the work study engineer does in Detroit or

Pittsburg; but it means something different. The American work study engineer lays out the work and the worker. We must lay out the work. In respect to the worker, we are teachers rather than masters. We try to teach how one improves one's own productivity and the process. What we set up is the foundation; the edifice the worker builds. Scientific management, time and motion studies, materials flow – we do them all and no different from the way you do them in the States. But you in the States think that this is the end of the job; we here in Japan believe it is the beginning. The worker's job begins when we have finished engineering the job itself.'

'Continuous training' in Japan goes a long way towards preventing the extreme specialization and departmentalization which plague us. There are no craft unions or craft skills in Japanese industry (the most significant exception are the Japanese National Railways which imported craft specialization from Great Britain and Germany, together with their steel rails and locomotives, and which are perhaps even more fragmented by craft and jurisdictional lines than American or British railroads are). Craftsmen, in the early days of Japanese industrialization, flatly refused to work in the new factories which, therefore, had to be staffed by youngsters, fresh from the farm, who had no skills and who had to be taught whatever they needed to know to do the job. Still, it is not really true, as Japanese official doctrine asserts, that 'men are freely moved from job to job within a plant'. A man in a welding shop is likely to stay in a welding shop and so is the fellow in the next aisle who runs the paint sprays. There is much more individual mobility in office work, and especially for managerial and professional people. A Japanese company will not hesitate to move a young manager from production control into market research, or into the accounting department. Yet the individual departments in the office tend to be rigidly specialized and highly parochial in the defence of their 'prerogatives'. The tunnel vision that afflicts so many people in Western business is, however, conspicuously absent in Japan. The work study engineer I quoted earlier insisted meticulously on the boundaries between work study and other engineering personnel. He himself never worked in any other function, from the day he graduated from engineering school to the day when, at age 55, he was made president of an affiliate company within his group. Yet he knew the work of every other function. He understood their problems. He knew what they could do for his work study department and what, in turn, the work study engineer had to do for them. He is the purest of specialists in his own work, and yet he is a true 'generalist' in his knowledge, in his vision and in the way in which he holds himself responsible for the performance and results of the entire organization.

This he himself attributes to the fact that – as he laughingly admits, very much against his will in the earlier years – he was subjected all along the way to 'continuous training' in all the work going on at his job level. When he was a junior work study engineer, he took part in the training sessions of all juniors, whether engineers, accountants, and salesmen, and so on, all the way through until he became a member of top management. And then he joined, voluntarily, a top management group which meets two evenings a week, usually with a discussion leader from the outside, to train itself in the work of top management.

We in the West emphasize today 'continuing education'. This is a concept that is still alien to Japan. As a rule, the man or woman who graduates from the University never sets foot on campus again, never attends a class, never goes back for 're-treading'. Normal education in Japan is still seen as 'preparation' for life rather than as 'life' itself. Indeed Japanese employers, even the large ones including government, do not really want young people who have gone to graduate school. They are 'too old' to start at the bottom. And there is no other place to start in Japan. They expect to work as 'specialists' and to be 'experts' rather than submit to training by their employer. Indeed the resistance to the highly trained specialist is considered by many thoughtful management people in Japan to be a major weakness of Japanese business, and even more of Japanese government. There is little doubt that, in the years to come, 'continuing education' will become far more important in Japan than it now is, and that, at the same time, the specialist will have to become far more important as well. But at the same time, Japan's 'continuous training' has something to teach us. We in the West react to 'resistance to change' and 'productivity' largely along the lines of Mark Twain's old dictum about the weather. We all complain but no one does anything. The Japanese at least do something – and with conspicuous success.

'Continuous training' is not completely unknown in the West. A century ago it was developed by the fledgeling Zeiss Works in Germany and applied there to *all* employees in the plant even though most of them were, of course, highly skilled glass-blowers and opticians with many years of craft training behind them. The world leadership of the German optical industry until World War I – if not until World War II – rested in large measure on this policy which saw in high craft skill a foundation for, rather than the end of, learning. With craft jurisdictions in the US (and even more in Britain) frozen in the most rigid and restrictive union contracts, this probably could be done today, however, only in mass-production industries with plant-wide or, at least, department-wide seniority.

But it could be done – and should be done – with the non-unionized, the clerical, supervisory, professional, and managerial employees. But here, where union restrictions cannot be blamed, managements are today busily working at creating departmentalization, specialization, and tunnel vision.

Sure, there is a good deal of 'continuous training'; companies not only have massive training programmes themselves but many encourage, through tuition refund, for instance, their younger technical, professional, and managerial people to keep on going to school and to continue their education.

But in all too many cases, the emphasis in these programmes is on a man's becoming more specialized and on *not* learning the other knowledges, skills, and functions. In most of the training programmes I know – and I know quite a few – the emphasis is entirely on the one function in which a young man already works; at most he is being told that 'other areas are, of course, important'. But then he is enjoined to learn more market research or more tax accounting or more work study engineering. As a result he soon comes to consider the other areas as so much excess baggage. And when we have to introduce something truly new – the computer is the horrible example – we bring in a whole raft of new specialists, with the predictable result that the newcomers are both ineffectual, since no one knows what they are trying to do, and resented, because they present a threat to everybody. Surely this management-imposed departmentalization and narrowness has been one of the major reasons for the difficulties we are having with the computer, let alone with the computer specialists.

And when it comes to education outside, in evening courses at the local university, for instance, a young man's supervisor will (practically all my students tell me that) push his subordinate into taking more work in his speciality and away from anything else. To be sure, company policies invariably make no such distinction in offering tuition refund – but the supervisor, as a rule, has to approve the young man's programme before the company will pay for it.

The rule should be the opposite: once a young man has acquired the foundations of a speciality, he should be systematically exposed to all the other major areas within the business – whether in his company's training courses or in 'continuing education' outside. Only this way can we hope to prevent tomorrow's professional and managerial people from being as departmentalized, as riven by 'jurisdictional demarcations', as confined in their vision to yesterday, as we have encouraged the skilled worker to become.

THE CARE AND FEEDING OF THE YOUNG

The House of Mitsui is not only the oldest among the world's big businesses; it dates back to 1637, half a century before the Bank of England was founded. It also was the largest of the world's big businesses until the American occupation split it into individual companies (and today, when these companies have come back together into a fairly close confederation, it may well be again the world's biggest business). In all its 300 years of business life, Mitsui never had a single chief executive (the Japanese term is 'chief *banto*', literally 'chief clerk') who was not an outstanding man and a powerful leader. This accomplishment no other institution can match, to my knowledge; neither the Catholic Church, nor any government, army, navy, business or university.

If anyone asks how to explain such an amazing success in executive development and selection, one always gets the same answer: 'Since earliest days the chief *banto* – himself never a member of the Mitsui family but a "hired hand" – had only one job: manager development, manager selection, and manager placement. He spent most of his time with the young people who came in as junior managers or professionals. He knew them. He listened to them. And as a result, he knew, by the time the men reached 30 or so, which were likely to reach top management, what experience and development they needed, and in what job they should be tried and tested.'

At first sight, nothing would seem less likely to develop strong executives than the Japanese system. It would rather seem to be the ideal prescription for developing timid men selected for proven mediocrity and trained 'not to rock the boat'. The young men who enter a company's employ directly from the university – and by and large, this is the only way to get into a company's management since hiring from the outside and into upper-level positions is practically unknown – know that they will have a job till they retire, no matter how poorly they perform. Till they are 45, that is, for the first quarter-century of their working life, they will be promoted and paid by seniority and by seniority alone. There seems to be no performance appraisal, nor would there be much point to it when a man can neither be rewarded for performance nor penalized for non-performance. Superiors do not choose their subordinates; the personnel people make personnel decisions as a rule, often without consulting the manager to whom a subordinate is being assigned. And it is, or so it seems, unthinkable for a young manager or professional to ask for a transfer, and equally unthinkable for him to quit and go elsewhere.* Indeed, every young managerial and professional employee in Japanese organizations, whether business or government, knows that he is expected to help his colleagues look good rather than stand out himself by brilliance or aggressiveness.

This goes on for twenty to twenty-five years, during which all the emphasis seems to be on conforming, on doing what one is being asked to do, and on showing proper respect and deference.

Suddenly when a man reaches 45, the Day of Reckoning arrives when the goats are divided from the sheep. A small, a

---

* This is changing, especially for highly trained technical people – but very slowly. It would still be almost unheard of for a young man to take a job in another company except with the express permission of his previous employer.

very small, group is picked to become 'Company Directors', that is, top management; they can then stay on well past any retirement age known in the West, with active top management people in their 80s by no means a rarity. The rest, that is, from 'Department Director' on down, stay till they are 55, usually with at best one more promotion. Then they are being retired – and unlike rank-and-file employees, their retirement is compulsory.*

To an outsider who believes what the Japanese tell him, namely that this is really the way the system works, it is inconceivable on what basis this crucial decision at age 45 is being made, yet it results in the emergence of the independent and aggressive top managers of Japan's businesses who have pushed Japanese exports all over the world and who have, in the space of twenty years, made Japan the third ranking economic power in the world when, at the eve of World War II, Japan was not even among the first dozen or so in industrial production or national capital and product capital.

It is precisely because Japanese managers have 'lifetime employment' and can, as a rule, neither be fired nor moved, and because advancement for the first twenty-five years of a man's working life is through seniority alone, that the Japanese have made the care and feeding of their young people the first responsibility of top management. The practice goes back at least 400 years, to the time of Hideyoshi, the military dictator who organized the retainers of the military clan, the

* There is a third category which, while very small in numbers, is of great importance and highly visible. Some members of upper middle management, that is, 'Department Heads', when they reach 55, are being moved into the top management of a subsidiary or affiliate where they can stay on without age limit. This is reserved for senior men who, while outstanding in their own work, are too narrowly specialized to move into the top management of the parent company. It explains, by the way, though only in part, why Japanese large companies have so many ostensibly independent subsidiaries and affiliates.

Samurai, in tight hereditary castes with advancement from one to the other officially not permitted. At the same time, the government of the clan had to find able people who could run the clan's affairs and who had to get opportunities at a very early age without offending higher ranking but less gifted clan members.

Today, of course, it would not be possible any more for the chief *banto* of Mitsui to know personally the young managerial people as his predecessor did a few generations ago. Even much smaller companies are much too large and have far too many young managerial and professional employees in their ranks. Yet top management is still vitally concerned with them. But it discharges this concern through an 'informal network' of senior middle management people who act as 'Godfathers' to the young men during the first ten years of their career in the company.

The Japanese take this system for granted. Indeed, few of them are conscious of it. As far as I can figure out, it has no name – the term 'Godfather' is mine rather than theirs. But every young managerial employee knows who his 'Godfather' is, and so does his boss and the boss's boss. The 'Godfather' is never a young man's direct superior and, as a rule, not anyone in direct line of authority over the young man or the young man's department. He is rarely a member of top management and rarely a man who will get into top management. Rather is he picked from among those members of upper middle-management who will, when they reach 55, be transferred as 'top management' to a subsidiary or affiliate. In other words, these are people who know, having been passed over at age 45 for the top management spots in their own company, that they are not going to make it in their own organization. Therefore, they are not likely to build a faction of their own and to play internal politics. At the same time, these are the most highly respected members of the upper middle-management group, the people who are known, trusted, and looked up to by the entire organization.

How the individual 'Godfather' is actually chosen for a young man, whether by formal assignment or by informal understanding, no one seems to know. The one qualification that is usually mentioned is that he be a graduate of the same university from which the individual young man graduated himself – the 'old school tie' binds even more tightly in Japan than it ever did in England. ('The Harvard Business School Alumni Association is the only truly Japanese institution outside of Japan,' a Japanese friend of mine often says, only half in jest.) But everybody inside the company knows who the 'Godfather' of a given young man is and respects the relationship. During the first ten years or so of a young man's career, he is expected to be in close touch with his 'Godchild', even though he may have in a large company a hundred such 'Godchildren' at any one time. He is expected to know the young man, see him fairly regularly, be available to him for advice and counsel, and in general, look after him. He has some functions which outside of Japan 'Godfathers' don't normally have, such as to introduce the young men under his wing to the better bars on the Ginza and to the right bawdy houses. But then learning how to drink in public is one of the important accomplishments the young Japanese executive has to learn. If a young man gets stuck under an incompetent manager and wants to be transferred, the 'Godfather' knows where to go and how to do something which officially cannot be done and 'is never being done'. Yet nobody will ever know about it. And if the young man has been naughty and needs a good spanking, the 'Godfather' will give it to him in private. By the time a young man is 30, the 'Godfather' knows a great deal about him.

It is this 'Godfather' who sits down with top management and discusses the young people. Again this may be

completely 'informal'. Over the saké cup, the 'Godfather'
may say quietly, 'Nakamura is a good boy and is ready for a
challenging assignment', or 'Nakamura is a good chemist,
but I don't think he'll ever know how to manage people', or
'Nakamura means well and is reliable, but he is no genius
and better not be put on anything but routine work'. And
when the time comes to make a personnel decision, whom to
give what assignment and where to move a man, the personnel people will quietly consult 'Godfather' before they
make a move.

How the system works a personal experience of mine may
illustrate. A few years ago, I found myself, by sheer accident, a temporary 'Godfather'.

One of my ablest students in twenty years at New York
University's Graduate Business School was a young
Japanese, let me call him Okura. The son of a diplomat,
he went to Oxford for his undergraduate work and took
the Japanese Foreign Service examination which he
passed with honours. But then he decided to go into
business instead, came to our Graduate Business School
in New York, and went to work for one of Japan's big
international companies. A few years ago, while I was in
Japan, he came to see me. I said, 'Okura, how are things
going?' He said, 'Fine, but I think I may need some help;
this is why I have come to see you. Not having gone to
school in Japan, I do not really have anyone in my
company who feels responsible for me. All our management people have gone to school in Japan. As a result,
there is no one in upper management who can tell the
personnel people that I am ready for a managerial job in
one of our branches abroad. I know they considered me
when they filled the last two vacancies in South America,
but no one knew whether I wanted to go there, whether
I was ready, and altogether what my plans were. I know
that you are going to have lunch with our Executive Vice-

President in a day or two, and, having been my professor, you can speak for me.' I said, 'Okura, won't your Executive Vice-President be offended if an outsider interferes?' He said, 'Oh, no. On the contrary; he'll be grateful, I assure you.' And he was right. For when I mentioned Okura's name to the Executive Vice-President, his face lit up and he said, 'You know, I was going to ask you to do us a favour and talk to Okura-san about his plans. We think he is ready for a big management assignment abroad, but we have no way of talking to him; none of us went to the same university he went to.' Three months later Okura was posted to head the company's branch office in a fairly important country in Latin America, Peru or Chile, if I remember rightly.

In the West where relationships are far less formal, the 'Godfather' as a source of information on the young people may not be important. But we need, just as much as the Japanese – if not more so – the senior manager who serves as a human contact, a human listener, a guide for the young people during the first ten years or so in business. Perhaps the greatest single complaint of the young people in the large organization today is that there is nobody who listens to them, nobody who tries to find out who they are and what they are doing, nobody who is their 'Godfather'. The idea which one finds in all our management books that the first-line supervisor can actually fill this role is simply nonsense. The first-line supervisor has to get the work out. All the sermons that the 'supervisor's first job is human relations' won't make it so. Above all, a supervisor will, of necessity, hang on to a good man and will not let him go. He will not say: 'You have learned all there is to learn in this place.' He will not say: 'You are doing all right, but you really don't belong here.' He will not ask a young man: 'And where do you want to go, what kind of work do you want to do, and how can I help you to get there?' In fact, the supervisor is almost bound to consider any hint of a desire to change or to transfer on the part of a young and able managerial and professional subordinate a direct criticism and an attack on himself. As a result, the young managerial and professional people in American business and industry (but also in Europe) 'vote with their feet'. They quit and go elsewhere. The absence of the human contact, of the guide, the counsel, the listener, is a main reason for our heavy turnover among the young educated employee. Whenever one talks with them, one hears: 'The company is all right, but I have nobody to talk to.' Or, 'The company is all right, but I am in the wrong spot and can't get out of it.' 'I need someone to tell me what I am doing right and what I am doing wrong, and where I really belong, but there isn't anybody in my company to whom I can go.' They do not need a psychologist. They need a human relationship that is job-focused and work-focused but still available to the individual, accessible to the individual and concerned with the individual. And that the Japanese – precisely because of the impersonal formality of their rigid system – have had to supply a long time ago. Because they cannot admit officially that this system exists, they have set it up the right way. For it is clearly the strength of their system that this 'Godfather' function is not a separate job, is not a part of personnel work, and is not entrusted to 'specialists', but that, on the contrary, it is discharged by experienced, respected, and successful management people.

But it is not only the young people in the American – or European – company who need a point of human contact, a counsellor, a 'guide for the perplexed'. Today senior managers need even more to establish communications to them from the young. The influx of the young, educated people is only beginning – for it is only now that the combined effect of the post-war 'baby boom' and of the 'educational explosion' are beginning to hit the management ranks. From now on, for ten years or so, the number of young entrants into technical, professional, and managerial work (i.e. of young men and women with a higher degree) will be very much larger than it has been so far when the college-educated still, largely, came from relatively low birth years. The first really high birth-year, the babies of 1950 will only graduate from college this year and next. And however little we really know about the young, we do know that they are different – in their expectations, their experiences, their knowledge of the world, and their needs.

In a number of companies, especially a few large ones, with whom I have been working these last few years, the attempt has been made to have senior executives meet, fairly regularly, with younger men – outside of office hours and without respecting lines of function or authority. In these sessions the senior man does not make a speech, does not 'communicate'. Rather he asks: 'And what do you have to tell me – about your work, about your plans for yourselves and this company, about our opportunities and our problems?' These meetings have not always been easy going. But the young people, though at first highly suspicious of being patronized, after a while came to look forward to these meetings, indeed to clamour for them. The real beneficiaries, however, have been the senior executives. The 'Godfather' concept of the Japanese may be too paternalistic for us in the West; it may even be too paternalistic for the young Japanese. But that the young managerial and professional people should be the special concern of senior men is an idea which we might well use, especially in this age of the 'generation gap' and of the change from a manual work-force to a highly educated knowledge work-force.

Any Japanese executive who has read this piece will protest that I grossly over-simplify, let alone that I have omitted most of the salient features of Japanese management. Any Western student of Japan who has read so far will accuse me of being uncritical. But my purpose in this article was not to give a scholarly analysis of Japanese management or even to attempt an explanation of Japan's managerial performance. I am fully aware of the many frustrations of the young manager in Japan, and altogether of the tremendous tensions in Japanese economy and society created by the Japanese economic achievement – tensions which are so great as to make me highly sceptical about all those current predictions that the 'twenty-first century will be Japan's century'. (Indeed, if I were a Japanese, this prediction would scare me out of my wits.)

Whether anyone can learn from other people's mistakes is doubtful. But surely one can learn from other people's successes. The Japanese policies discussed here are certainly not 'the key' to Japan's achievement; but they are major factors in it. They are equally not 'the answer' to the problems of the West. But, I submit, they contain answers to some of our most pressing problems, help for some of our most urgent needs and point to directions we might well explore. It would indeed be folly to imitate the Japanese; but we might well try to emulate them.

11. Keynes: Economics as a Magical System

[From the *Virginia Quarterly Review*, Autumn 1946]

This is the earliest of all the essays in this book, having been written in 1946, shortly after Keynes's death. Now it is frequently referred to in the literature; but at the time it was first published it had no impact and received little attention. Keynes was highly controversial then with a large and vocal minority of economists still holding out against the 'Keynesian Revolution'. But it was not the proper, let alone the fashionable thing in the forties to criticize Keynes and his economics for not being 'radical' enough to see Keynes's essence in the attempt to maintain the classical, free economy and to preserve the principles of laissez faire. *Even less fashionable was it then to predict that Keynesian economics could not and would not control the economy and, above all, not control cyclical swings.*

The most discussed economic theory of today, that of Milton Friedman of Chicago, addresses itself, however, precisely to the points made in this essay. Friedman, for all that he is considered a 'non-Keynesian', shares the Master's aim: to keep a self-governing economy that does not require continuous government interference. However, he proposes to achieve this by direct mechanical determinism, that is, by the direct provision of money, rather than by the means I called 'magic' in this essay, that is by Keynes's manipulation of 'confidence'. Whether this will work better than Keynes is yet to be seen.

This essay could not be written today – the economy of the world and our view of it are so totally different from the situation of the immediate post-World War II years. Still, I believe the essay projects fairly the fundamental problems and attitudes of the years between the two world wars, the period for which Keynes was 'Merlin, the wizard'. This essay therefore enables us to see where the mass changes have occurred and where we today have to do new thinking. Today the main concern would no longer be the fear of depression and unemployment as it was in 1946. Uncontrolled and apparently uncontrollable inflation would take pride of place. No longer can we, as all of us did in 1946, assume that government spending on defence and armaments has the same economic impact as any other government expenditure and that it is the size and direction of the deficit that alone matter. The last ten or fifteen years have clearly validated the traditional wisdom which considers armaments 'unproductive', that is, as economically harmful and a depressant to the economy. Finally Keynes himself, were he still alive today, would probably be at work on productivity as the key element in economic theory and economic policy. Keynes himself would probably now switch from 'macro-economics' to 'micro-economics'.

The influence and reputation of John Maynard Keynes are not explained by his having been a great economist, nor did his importance lie primarily in his economic theories. He was indeed a very great economist, in all likelihood the last of the 'pure' economists of the classical school, at once the legitimate heir and the liquidator of Adam Smith. But he was above all the representative political thinker of the inter-war period; he expressed perfectly its attempt to master what it knew to be a new world by pretending that it was the old one. Keynes's work was built on the realization that the fundamental assumptions of nineteenth-century *laissez-faire* economics no longer hold true in an industrial society and a credit economy. But it aimed at the restoration and preservation of the basic beliefs, the basic institutions of nineteenth-century *laissez-faire* politics; above all, it aimed at the preservation of the autonomy and automatism of the market. The two could no longer be brought together in a rational system: Keynes's policies are magic – spells, formulae, and incantations, to make the admittedly irrational behave rationally.

Keynes's theoretical analysis of the new social and economic reality is a masterpiece that will endure. His conclusions from this analysis proved wrong, however; the economic policies which gave him his reputation and influence have failed. When he died in the spring of 1946 he was apparently at the peak of success and power: the chief financial adviser of his government, a peer of the realm, the almost undisputed master of the schools, especially in this country. But his very disciples, while using Keynesian terms, methods, and tools, were actually abandoning fast both his economic policies and his aim.

I

Keynes, who could write prose of a rare lucidity if he wanted to, chose to present his theories in the most technical and most jargon-ridden language, but his central ideas are quite simple.

Classical economics knew neither money nor time as factors in the economic process. Money was the 'universal commodity', the symbol of all other commodities but without any life or effect of its own. It was convenient and necessary but only an accounting unit to keep trace of what went on in the economy of 'real' goods and 'real' labour;

price was simply the rate at which one commodity could be exchanged against all others. The money of classical economics is very much like the ether of classical physics: it pervades all and carries all, but it has neither properties nor effects of its own. And the classical economist was also very much like the physicist of his age in his concept of time: while everything happens in time, time itself is not a factor in the events themselves. This is no accident; classical economics were patterned consciously on the model of Newtonian physics, in structure as well as in its basic assumption of a mechanical and static economic universe.

Keynesian theory is based on the assertion, axiomatic in an industrial age, that the economic process is not only in time but largely determined by time, and that the economic expression of the time factor is money. To the classical economist money was the shadow of existing goods. Actually money, especially the bank deposits which are the money of a credit economy, is created and comes into being in anticipation of goods to be produced, of work to be performed. This means that money is not determined mechanically and according to economic rationality, but psychologically and socially on the basis of confidence in the future. Time thus enters into every economic transaction in the form of fixed money obligations for the investments of the past on which the present is based. These money obligations for the past actually are the largest single factor in the economic transactions of every member of an industrial society, for the cost of everything we use, whether a house, a loaf of bread, or a hired man's labour, is made up very largely of the money obligations for the past. Money, instead of being an inert and propertyless expression of economic transactions, influences, moulds, and directs economic life; changes in the money sphere cause changes in the 'real' economy. We live at the same time in two closely interwoven but distinct economic systems: the 'real' economy of the classics – an economy of goods, services, and labour,

existing in the present and determined mechanically; and
the 'symbol' economy of money, heavy with the obligations
of the past and determined psychologically by our
confidence in the future.

It is no belittling of Keynes to say that these insights did
not originate with him but were the work of a whole generation of economic thinkers before him, especially of his two
countrymen Hawtrey and Withers, of the Swedes Cassel and
Wicksell, and of the German Knapp. But Keynes syn-
thesized their isolated observations and thoughts into one
system, and developed a theory of the dynamics of the economic process from them: and it is this theory we usually
mean when we talk of 'Keynesian economics'. The assumptions of the classics had made it virtually impossible for
them to understand how a depression could ever happen
except as a result of physical catastrophes such as an earthquake or the destruction of war. Also, they were entirely
unable to explain how a depression could last: if only left
alone it had to correct itself. With the new understanding of
the autonomy of the monetary sphere as his starting point,
Keynes could give the first adequate theoretical explanation
of the vital phenomena of depression and unemployment.

The first answer was Keynes's most famous theory, the
theory of over-saving. Any saving is by definition a surplus
of productive resources – goods, labour, equipment – over
current consumption. For the classics that meant that,
unless physically destroyed, any saving must automatically
be 'invested', that is, used for future production. This, however, ceases to be true as soon as we bring in money as
autonomous, as having an economic reality of its own. Then
it becomes possible for savings not to be invested but to
become mere money savings, with the productive resources
they represent left unused and unemployed. Keynes asserted that the modern economy had an inherent tendency
towards over-saving.

Of even greater importance was his explanation of the

unemployment of a chronic depression. In the universe of classical economics a long-term depression simply could not happen; before a maladjustment could reach depression proportions it would have been corrected by the infallible and automatic mechanism of falling prices and falling costs. Yet long before 1929 long-term depressions had become far too familiar for their existence to be denied except by the most bigoted academician. Hence, orthodox economics had to engage in a search for the criminal conspiracy that prevented 'natural' adjustment and correction. Price monopolies, unions, government intervention through relief payments, subsidies, and tariffs – these and all the other measures by which society seeks to protect itself against the social destruction of a depression, became diabolical forces; and the resulting persecution mania of the economists who saw the cloven hoof in the mildest attempt at controlling economic forces soon made it impossible to base economic policy on the classical theories, even though these theories themselves were still generally accepted. From 1870 to 1930 economic policy was without proper theoretical basis. The ruling theory could not justify any of the measures actually taken; and as any economic policy that was possible politically was open to condemnation on theoretical grounds, theory furnished no guidance to distinguish between beneficial and destructive policies. Out of social necessity every economist in office had to do things he opposed in his writings; the resulting blend of cynicism and bad conscience finally gave us that evil genius of old-school financial economists, Dr Schacht.

But with money a factor, the automatic and infallible adjustment becomes the exception rather than the rule. In a credit economy prices and wages cannot adjust themselves very readily; they must be comparatively inflexible. For a very large – the largest single – part of all costs is the money obligation for the past. This obligation is unaffected by changes in the present value of money as the goods and services it represents were produced in the past at past prices and wages. We may add – though this may be going beyond Keynes – that prices and wages are also hard to adjust downwards because money has a social meaning, independent largely of its purchasing power; it buys not only goods but prestige. This is especially true of the lower income levels where the weekly money wage represents a definite social position.

For these reasons, the adjustment in a depression will not, in the modern economy, take the form of lower prices and lower wages. Prices and wages will tend to stay up. Hence the adjustment will take the only form possible: lower employment both of men and of capital equipment. And, unlike the adjustment through lower prices and wages, unemployment not only does not tend to correct the depression, it tends to make the disequilibrium permanent.

Actually, under modern conditions prices will fall, though not as evenly as they should – and with significant exceptions in the capital goods fields. But wage rates will not go down. In the first place, the wage-earner has usually much less margin between his income and his fixed obligations than the industrialist; hence the economic factors militate against wage cuts. Secondly, the political pressure of organized labour is much more effective in modern society than the economic power even of the strongest monopolist. Hence the maladjustment will not only not be corrected in the 'normal course of events'; it will become worse. The point at which new investments again become profitable will recede into the distance. From this follows one of Keynes's most important and, at first sight, most paradoxical conclusions: that we have to raise prices in a depression in order to obtain the very effect orthodox economics expected to get from falling prices.

II

These general theories have been justly criticized for their narrow emphasis on the monetary phenomenon to the exclusion of everything else. The monetary factor is probably only one of the causes of a depression, though perhaps a central one, rather than, as Keynes asserts, always and everywhere the only cause. But aside from this not unimportant question of emphasis, the Keynesian theories have been almost universally accepted. And with these basic theories a great many economists also accepted at first his economic policies. But, as most of the disciples have begun to find out, Keynes's economic policies do not follow from his basic theories; indeed, they are hardly compatible with them. His policies were really dictated by his political aim, not by his economic observations. His attempt to bring the two together into one whole, to make the policies emerge as the inevitable conclusion from the theories, may very well explain the tortuous and tortured style of his later writing, his increasing reliance on purely formal arguments, and his excessive use of mathematical techniques.

According to Keynes, the economic theorist, the level of business activity is determined by the amount of investment in capital goods which in turn is determined by the confidence which leads businessmen to borrow for expansion. Business activity depends in the last analysis on psychological, that is on economically irrational, factors. According to Keynes, the economic politician, the very confidence which creates credit is itself strictly determined by credit. Keynes offers two answers to the question of what causes confidence. He asserts that confidence is a function of the interest rate: the lower the rate, the greater the confidence. He also asserts that confidence is a function of consumer spending: the higher consumer purchases, the higher the investment in capital goods. In his theories Keynes seems to have wavered between these two answers;

politically, it does not make too much difference, however, which explanation is preferred. Both lead to pretty much the same conclusion: the quantity of money or credit available determines the degree of confidence, with it the rate of investment, and thus the level of business activity and of employment. Hence Keynes's monetary panacea for booms and depressions: in a boom, prevent maladjustment through 'draining off' purchasing power into a budget surplus; in a depression, cure maladjustment by creating purchasing power through budget deficits. In either case the quantity of money automatically and infallibly regulates confidence.

Keynes starts out with the statement that human behaviour in economic life is not, as the classic economists assumed, determined by objective economic forces, but that, on the contrary, economic forces are directed, if not determined, by human behaviour. He ends by asserting as rigid an economic determinism of human behaviour and actions as any Ricardo or Malthus ever proclaimed. By this assertion Keynes's entire economic policy stands and falls. And it is this assertion that was conclusively refuted by the experience of the New Deal. The New Deal – at least from 1935 to 1939 – was based on deficit spending which created consumer purchasing power and forced down the level of interest rates. Neither brought about a resumption of investment or a significant cut in unemployment. With the credit pumped into the banks, business promptly repaid its old debts instead of borrowing for new investments; and the money paid out by the government to the consumers flowed back to the banks almost at once to become 'over-savings'.

The faithful Keynesians have been hard pressed to explain away what happened. Their favourite argument is that political opposition to the New Deal offset the economically created confidence. But this defence is not permissible, let alone convincing. Either confidence can be created by creating credit and purchasing power regardless of the way business or any other group feels about governmental policy, or Keynes's economic policies are wrong. And confidence has been conclusively proved not to be producible by a cheque-writing machine.

Most of the disciples of ten years ago have drawn the conclusions from this experience. They are still Keynesians in their theoretical analysis, but no longer so in their policies. They continue to express their thoughts in monetary terms but they no longer talk about the interest rate or even about budget deficits or surpluses. Consumer purchasing power and 'confidence' have all but disappeared from their vocabulary. The programme of the most influential group of Keynesian economists in this country – as written by Alvin Hansen of Harvard into the original draft of the Full Employment Bill – provided that, in times of depression and unemployment, the government shall *produce* capital goods through public works and government orders in a quantity sufficient to bring the total capital goods production to a level which gives full employment. Whether this is done with or without a deficit, at a high or a low interest rate, is of very minor importance; what matters to the neo-Keynesian of today is not monetary policy but capital goods production. This shift denies both Keynes's economic concepts and his over-all political goal.

In fact, this shift even caught up with Keynes himself. Ironically enough, the very event which brought him official recognition and honours showed up the shortcomings of his theories and policies. In the course of World War II, Keynes became the official financial adviser to his government, and director of the Bank of England, a member of the peerage. For the first time his native country officially adopted Keynesian ideas as the basis of its financial policy: the measures outlined in his little pamphlet, *How to Pay for the War*, were adopted almost unchanged by the British government. But the war also showed, especially in Britain, that monetary policy is quite subordinate and that, by itself, it achieves very little. England's war production was obtained not by directing the flow of money, credit, and purchasing power, but through physical controls of men, raw materials, plant equipment, and output which could have worked almost as well with a different monetary policy – in Nazi Germany they worked without any monetary policy at all. And now that the war is over, the watchword of English economic policy is not credit, interest rate, or purchasing power, but 'productive efficiency'.

III

In the popular mind Keynes stands for government intervention in business. This may well be a correct evaluation of the ultimate effect of Keynesian economics; but if so Keynes achieved precisely the opposite of what he intended to achieve. For the one passionate aim of his policies was to make possible an economic system free from government interference, a system determined exclusively by objective and impersonal economic forces. 'The free market is dead, long live the free market', would be a fitting motto for his entire work.

Keynes's basic insight was the realization that the free market of the classical economists fails to adjust itself automatically as predicted because the economic forces of demand and supply, cost and price, are over-ridden by the psychological forces of money and credit. From this basis several conclusions as to economic policy would have been logically possible.

Keynes could have argued that conscious political action had to achieve by braking through the money wall what the market forces should have achieved by themselves. That would have been an economic policy of direct government intervention into *production* through public works and public orders rather than a policy of credit creation; and it is precisely what most of the neo-Keynesians advocate today.

Such a policy would restore the supremacy of the 'real' system but at the price of its political independence.

Keynes might also have arrived in logical development from his premises at a policy in which governmental action is used only to induce private business to build up reservoirs of capital goods production for use in a depression, for instance, through a system of tax rewards for building up reserves in good years to be coupled with stiff tax penalties incurred if these reserves are not used for employment – creating new investments in a depression. He might even have come to the conclusion that the proper policy is psychological rather than economic, i.e. propaganda to create confidence; the German economist Knapp, whose ideas had great influence on Keynes, actually gave this answer.

The one conclusion which logically and theoretically it seems impossible to derive from Keynes's premise, is the one he actually did derive. But it was the one and only conclusion which gave Keynes the desired political result: the maintenance of a *laissez-faire* political system in which only objective economic factors determine the economy, and in which man's economic activities are entirely under the control of the individual, not under that of the government.

If the liberal state of nineteenth-century *laissez-faire* was a night-watchman protecting the peaceful and law-abiding burgher against thieves and disturbers of the peace, Keynes's state was a thermostat protecting the individual citizen against sharp changes in the temperature. And it was to be a fully automatic thermostat. A fall in economic activity would switch on credit, a rise would cut it off again; and in a boom the mechanism would work in reverse. In contrast to the nineteenth-century state, Keynes's state was indeed to act positively; but the actions as well as their timing were to be determined strictly by economic statistics, not subject to political manipulation. The only purpose of these actions was to restore the individual's freedom in the economic sphere, that is, the freedom from all but economic factors, from all but economic considerations – with 'economic' referring to the 'real' economy of the classics.

The economic system of orthodox economics had been a machine built by the 'divine watchmaker', hence without friction and in perpetual motion and perpetual equilibrium. Keynes's system was a clock, a very good and artful clock, but still one built by a human watchmaker, and thus subject to friction. But the only actions required of the watchmaker were to wind, to oil, and, where necessary, to regulate the clock. He was not to run it, he was only to make it fit to run itself; and it was to run according to mechanical laws, not according to political decisions.

Keynes's basic aim of restoring by unorthodox methods the orthodox automatic market system, his basic belief that his methods were objective, non-political, and capable of determination by the impersonal yardstick of statistics, show best in his last major work: the 'Keynes Plan' of an international currency and credit system proposed in 1943. This plan projected his policies from the national into the international sphere. It proposed to overcome international depressions and maladjustments by the adjustment of prices and purchasing power through international credit creation. The agency which was to be in control of this international currency and credit was not to be a world government, but an international body of economic statisticians governed by index numbers and almost entirely without discretionary power. The result of this international system and its main justification was to be the restoration of the full freedom and equilibrium in international trade and currency movements.

Critics have rightly pointed out that Keynes was naïve to a degree amazing in such an accomplished and experienced political practitioner, in believing that his system could really be immune to political manipulation. It may be possible to obtain objective statistics. But to be meaningful, statistics have to be interpreted by human beings; and interpretations will differ radically with the political beliefs and desires of the interpreter – as witness last year's forecast of ten million unemployed in the United States before the spring of 1946, made in good faith by government experts interested in setting up a planned economy.* Also, even impersonal and objective control is still control; and it is an old political axiom that a government that controls the national income, i.e. the livelihood of the people, inevitably controls the souls of the people. Keynes's political system in which the state has the power to interfere in the individual's economic activities but refrains from using it, is thus a very different thing from his ideal, the state of nineteenth-century liberalism which was without power of interference.

But the decisive criticism of Keynes's argument is not that there are flaws in it, but that it is an irrational argument. It says in brief: we have proved that the factors that control economic activity are economically irrational, i.e. psychological factors; *therefore* they themselves must be controllable by an economic mechanism. But this 'therefore' is not of the vocabulary of reason, not even of that of faith; it is the 'therefore' of magic. It is on this very belief that the admittedly irrational can be controlled and directed by mechanical means, that every system of magic is based. The Keynesian 'policies' in spite – or perhaps because – of their elaborate apparatus of mathematical formulae and statistical tables, are spells. Because of this the fact that they failed once, in the New Deal, means that they have failed forever. For it is of the nature of a spell that it ceases altogether to be effective as soon as it is broken once.

But it was precisely its irrationality that made Keynes's policy so convincing to the generation of the long armistice. After the first World War the Western world suddenly awakened to the realization that the basic nineteenth-cen-

* (Footnote 1971) Actually 1946 was a year of acute labour shortages.

ury assumptions no longer applied. But it refused to face
he necessity of new thought and decision. The timid pulled
he featherbed of normalcy over their eyes and ears to sleep
on a little longer. The courageous accepted the new situation
out attempted to avoid facing it by finding a formula, a
mechanical gadget, a spell in other words, which would
make the new behave as if it were the old. One example
would be the labour policy of the New Deal. It started with
the realization that social and political relationships, rather
than the purely economic nexus of the pay cheque, are the
essence of modern industry. But it concluded that the mechanical device of 'equal bargaining power' on economic
issues would do the trick. Another example is in the field of
international relations. Here the first World War had clearly
shown that peace cannot be based on the concept of equal
sovereign states whose internal and external policies are
nobody's business but their own. The answer was a strictly
mechanical formula, the League of Nations, which represented nothing but the equal sovereign states in their fullest
equality and sovereignty, which was neither a super-govern-
ment nor a super-court, not even an alliance of the Great
Powers, but which was expected, in some magical way, to
overcome sovereignty.

We can trace this desire for a mechanical formula to make
the new function like the old, to make what was irrational
on the old assumptions again behave rationally, into fields far
removed from politics. It explains, for instance, the tremendous appeal of Freudian psychoanalysis as a cure-all. Freud
had had the insight to see the fallacy of traditional, mechan-
ist psychology – the same psychology on which the classical
economists had based themselves, incidentally. He realized
that man is not a bundle of mechanical reflexes and reac-
tions but a personality. But he avoided facing the problem –
a philosophical or religious one – by asserting that this personality is determined biologically, that it operates through
the grossly mechanical forces of repression and sublimation,

and that it can be controlled by the mechanical technique of analysis.

But the area in which the desire for a magical system was greatest was that of politics. And in the political field Keynes's economic policy was the most accomplished, the most brilliant, the most elegant attempt to make the impossible again possible, the irrational again rational.

IV

In the field of economic thought, Keynes was both a beginning and an end. He showed that classic economics no longer apply and why. He showed that economic theory has to give an answer to a new problem: the impact of man, acting as a human being and not as an economic machine, upon the economy. But he contributed little or nothing to the solution of these new problems; he himself never went beyond the classic methods and the classic analysis. Indeed it may be said that he held back economic thought. Before he came to dominate the scene we had made promising beginnings towards an understanding of the human factor in economic life in such books as Knight's *Risk, Uncertainty and Profit*, and Schumpeter's *Theory of Economic Dynamics*, both written before the first World War; and at the Harvard Business School, Elton Mayo had begun his pioneering studies of the relationship between worker and production. Keynes's influence, his magnetic attraction on young men in the field, made theoretical economics again focus on the mechanical equilibrium and on a mechanical concept of economic man determined by impersonal and purely quantitative forces.

Keynes's main legacy is in the field of economic policy. He has formulated our tasks here – even the term 'full employment' is his. But his only contribution to a solution – by no means an unimportant one – was to show us which way we cannot go; we cannot, as he did, assert that economi policy is possible without a political decision. We may decide perhaps that the state has to assume direct economic control of production – the decision of most of the neo-Keynesians. This decision raises the question of how political freedom can be maintained in such a state. It also brings up the equally difficult question of what the state is to produce and who is to decide on it; so far no state, whether capitalist, fascist, or socialist, has been able to overcome unemployment by direct government intervention except through producing armaments and armament plants, that is, through a war economy.

Or we can decide that the state has to create by political means the conditions in which a free-enterprise economy will itself prevent and overcome depressions. Such a policy is not impossible to devise on paper. We would need a fiscal policy that recognizes that industrial production extends over the business cycle, rather than one based on the fiction of the annual profit. We would need a policy of definite encouragement of new ventures and of capital investment in bad years. And we would need a labour policy which, while restoring the flexibility of wages through tying them in with productive efficiency and with business profits, gives security through such employment guarantees as an annual wage. But all this raises the question of how such policies, which demand of all groups that they subordinate their short-term interests to the long-term good of the whole, can be realized in a popular government based on sectional groups and subject to their constant pressure.

But Keynes himself cannot help us to make these decisions, or to answer these questions.

12. The Myth of American Uniformity

[From *Harper's Magazine*, May 1952]

Myths are re-enactments of basic experience. The 'Myth of American Uniformity' is seen in this essay as a re-enactment of a basic European experience, what one might well call the experience of the nineteenth century. It is also seen, however, as a symbol of a basic American experience, again the experience of America's nineteenth century. Whether today, almost twenty years after this essay was written in 1952, these are still the formative experiences of the two continents, is not certain. Yet though Europe has supposedly 'Americanized', the European still tends to see uniformity where the American sees diversity, and diversity where the American tends to see uniformity. Europe knows a great deal more about America than it did twenty years ago – and America knows a good deal more about Europe than it did then. But do the two understand each other better than they did then?

I

'How can you Americans stand all this uniformity?' Every one of the dozens of visitors from all over Europe who, during these past few years, have discussed their American impressions with me, has asked this question in one form or another. Yet what makes every single one – businessman, clergyman, or scientist; teacher, lawyer, or journalist; labour leader or civil servant – come to me for information is bewilderment, if not shock, at the incomprehensible and boundless diversity of this country.

'But *somebody* must lay out the standard curriculum for the liberal arts college. If the federal or the state governments do not do it, who does?'

'In what grade does the American high school student start Latin? How many hours a week are given to it? And what works of Shakespeare are normally read in the American secondary schools?'

'It can't really be true that there is no one labour union policy on work study. I am told that some unions actually insist on a time and motion study of each job, some unions acquiesce in it, and others refuse to allow any work study engineers. But surely no union movement could possibly operate pulling in opposite directions on a matter as important as this?'

'Please explain to us what American managements mean when they talk of "decentralization". Wouldn't this mean that different units of a company would do things differently, adopt different policies, follow different ideas? And how could any management allow that and still keep its authority and control?'

The going gets really rough when the talk turns to political institutions or to the churches. That it makes all the difference in the world what congressional committee a pending bill is assigned to, will upset even the urbane visitor – if indeed he believes it. And among the most frustrating hours of my life was the evening I spent with a Belgian Jesuit who insisted that there must be one simple principle that decides when and where agencies of the Catholic Church in this country work together with other faiths, and when not. The only comfort was that he obviously had got no more satisfaction from his American brethren in the order than from me.

Yet it is quite clearly not in diversity that the visitors see the essence of America. They are baffled by it, shocked by it, sometimes frightened by it. But they don't really believe in it. Their real convictions about this country come out in the inevitable question: 'But don't you find it trying to live in so uniform a country?'

It is not only the casual visitor, spending a few weeks here, who believes in 'American uniformity' despite all he sees and hears. The belief survives extended exposure to the realities of American life.

A few months ago a well-known English anthropologist, reviewing an exhibition of American paintings for a most respectable London Sunday paper, explained the 'mediocrity of American painting' by a reference to 'the uniformity of the American landscape – all prairie and desert'. One might remind the reviewer that nothing is more startling to the immigrant who comes to America to live than the tremendous variety of the landscape and the violence of contrasts in the American climate, soils, geology, fauna, and flora. Or one might reduce the argument to its full absurdity by asking which of these sons of Kansas, for example, is the typically uniform prairie product – William Allen White,* Earl Browder,† or General Eisenhower. But the essential fact is not that the argument is nonsense. It is that Geoffrey Gorer, the anthropologist, knows this country well, and that the newspaper that printed his nonsense is unusually knowledgeable about things American on the whole. Yet though they know all about New England or Virginia or Minnesota or Oregon, though they probably also know about the artists who paint in the desert of Cape Cod – or is it a prairie? –

* A progressive Republican newspaperman and small-town publisher of great political influence in the first four decades of this century and comparable, perhaps, to a highly respectable 'dissenter' of the late Victorian days.
† For many years the Secretary-General of the American Communist Party and Stalin's most faithful American follower.

they immediately think of 'uniformity' when something American needs explanation.

Or take the case of the young Danish lawyer who came to see me just before sailing back home. He was going to stay just a few minutes as he had only one question to ask. In the end he stayed almost the whole day – yet left with it still unanswered. His question? In one plant of the American company where he worked for seven months as a trainee, he found that output standards for the workers were set by a joint management–union committee. In another plant of the same company, located just a few miles away and organized by the same branch of the same union, output standards, he found, were considered strictly a 'management prerogative', with union action confined to formal protests against management decisions. He was sure he must have been mistaken in his observation; at the least, management and union must both be eager to have a uniform policy, whereas both seemed perfectly happy with the existing 'disorder'. I could not convince him that this was a fairly common situation all over the country. He left, certain that our labour relations must be uniform, at least within an industry, let alone within one company or one union.

And the 'productivity teams' that have come over from Europe to study American methods these past few years insist in their reports that one of the basic reasons for the greater productivity of American industry is the 'standardization' of the individual manufacturer on a very small number of models or lines. Yet most of the productivity reports themselves contain figures which show the exact opposite to be true: the typical American automobile manufacturer (even the smaller one), the typical shoe manufacturer, or the typical foundry turns out more models than its European counterpart. The people who write these reports seem quite unconscious of the contradiction.

Clearly, 'American uniformity' is an axiom for the

European, before and beyond any experience. It is indeed the one thing the European *knows* he knows about this country. There are today plenty of people in Europe who know that not all Americans are millionaires – though there are still far too few who know from first-hand experience how high the standard of living of the American worker really is. There are even some Europeans who have come to suspect that race relations in this country are quite a bit more complex than in the books of Richard Wright or James Baldwin. But it is a very rare European indeed – if he exists at all – who does not *know* that America is 'uniform'.

II

How is this dogma to be explained? The standard answer is that there is an outward sameness, a uniformity to all things material in this country. I have been sceptical of this answer ever since, a few years back, a magnificently accoutred cowboy, complete from white ten-gallon hat to woolly chaps and silver spurs, complained to me bitterly about the 'uniformity' of the American costume, and contrasted it with the picturesque leather pants, white knee stockings, and green braces of the Austrian students among whom he had spent a few months before World War II. The 'cowboy' was an earnest young social worker riding the range in the great cow centre of Chicago. And he delivered himself of his plaint on the way from a lecture on psychology to one on urban community problems during a YMCA conference. His excuse for his dress – had he felt the need for any – would have been that he went folk- and square-dancing both in the morning, before the day's lectures, and in the evening. But the Austrian students – I did not have the heart to tell him – wore their leather pants because they possessed at best one good suit and had to go easy on it.

Altogether there is as little diversity in Europe's outward

material appearance as there is in this country. People all through Europe, right through the Iron Curtain, dress pretty much alike. And when they don't – surely even the quaintest Sunday costume of a Slovak maiden can hardly rival the colours of a Californian going out on the golf course, or the ties a Mid-western salesman wears on his rounds.

Our towns and cities, ugly indeed, are not as much uniform as they are nineteenth- and twentieth-century towns and cities. Even in Europe it is primarily the old cities which look different. At least I know nothing in this country to rival the bleak monotony of sooty brick and broken chimney pots of the railroad ride into London, or the pea-in-the-pod uniformity of the famous Dutch housing developments with their endless rows of identically neat bungalows. And even the sun-drenched limbo – frowzy palms and peeling stucco – of the middle-class sections of Los Angeles offers occasional variety and architectural surprise compared to the numbing greyness through which one drives from the airport into the city that to most Americans stands as the symbol of European diversity: Paris.

When it comes to manufactured goods there is actually more diversity in this country than Europe has ever known. The variety of goods carried by our stores is the first thing that impresses any visitor from abroad. Nor is this a post-war phenomenon. As far back as 1938 one of the leading department store chains in England studied the Sears Roebuck catalogue and concluded that in every single category of goods the American mail-order business, for all its 'standardization', offered a wider range of goods in far more models than any European retailer could obtain from European manufacturers, let alone afford to carry.

But, you may say, when the European talks about 'American uniformity' he is not thinking of the material and outward aspects of American life, but of American culture and society. And here the dogma of American uniformity becomes totally incomprehensible. For it is in the non-material realms – in religion, political institutions, education, business life, even in entertainment – that the diversity of this country most deeply confuses the visitor from the other side.

Well-informed Europeans have heard that this country's political life is founded on pluralism and that our religious organization knows no rules – though they seldom seem to realize that these facts alone deny the legend of American uniformity. Most of them, however, believe that this country has uniformity in education. A hand-picked team of British educators, scientists, and industrialists who recently studied the relationship between industry and the universities in this country, obviously took uniformity for granted – though every single fact in their own report contradicted the assumption. Actually the diversity in politics and religion here is as nothing compared to the riot that prevails in education – the matrix of society.

There are colleges which look with distrust upon any book written later than 1300, are pained if they have to teach anything that is at all tainted with 'usefulness', and occasionally even dream of going back to teaching in Latin. There are other colleges – giving the same BA and enjoying the same acceptance by the general public – in which a student can earn a degree through courses in night-club etiquette, horseback riding, and fashion drawing. And in at least one Southwestern university you can now get a PhD in square- and folk-dancing; last summer I was shown with great pride the first accepted doctor's thesis, a formidable tome of 652 pages, mostly footnotes, on 'the Left-Turn Hopsa Step in Lithuanian Polkas'. Greater still is the diversity among different kinds and types of colleges, and among private schools, church schools, and state schools, let alone such phenomena, totally incomprehensible to any visitor from abroad, as the half-private, half-state university, or the church-supported but non-sectarian college. Some of the larger 'liberal arts' colleges have flourishing engineering schools of their own, and one large engineering school, Carnegie Tech in Pittsburgh, also runs a first-rate art and music school. And how can one explain to a European, accustomed to a Ministry of Education, the role of the private foundations, such as Ford, Rockefeller or Carnegie, and their power?

It is scarcely possible to talk about trends in American higher education, so mixed are the currents. Many engineering schools for instance have lately broadened their curricula to include more and more of the arts and humanities; but Columbia University – itself preponderantly dedicated to the liberal arts – has just announced plans for the most highly specialized Engineering Center. The University of Chicago has for some years now been admitting freshmen after only two years of high school (i.e. at age 16), with the avowed aim of making the undergraduate college an intermediate rather than a 'higher' institution; whereas other well-known schools, in order to make 'higher education' really 'high', increasingly prefer men in their early twenties who have spent a few years at work after leaving high school.

Nor is the situation any more uniform in secondary schools (i.e. the local schools in the age group 15–18). Within thirty miles of New York City there are schools so progressive as to live up to the caricatures in the funny papers of the twenties, and others so conservative as to justify every word of the progressives' indictment of the traditional schools. I have taught college freshmen from public schools who had learned more mathematics than most college curricula offer, and others who had come from schools with an equal reputation where mathematics, beyond long division, was an 'elective' and was taken only by children planning a career in science or medicine. There was one proper Bostonian who could remember only one American President, Benjamin Franklin*; the main educational dish

* Who, needless to say, never was President.

served at his very proper-Bostonian school had been a rich
stew called 'civics' which contained odd pieces of almost
anything except the history of his own country. And I have
taught other freshmen whom school had given a sound
knowledge of historical facts and even the thrill of history.
Yet every one of these high schools is unmistakably and
characteristically 'American'.

Even less compatible with the myth of American uniformity
is the reality of American literature – and if education is the
matrix of society, literature is its truest reflection. How 'uniform' for instance are the American writers who emerged in
the literary explosion of the nineteen-twenties: Sinclair
Lewis, Hemingway, Willa Cather, John Dos Passos, Wolfe,
Faulkner, T. S. Eliot, Robert Frost, Carl Sandburg? A more
diverse lot, in style, mood, and subject matter, could hardly
be imagined; and the diversity becomes the greater the more
names are added: Sherwood Anderson, for instance, or
Ellen Glasgow, Dashiell Hammett or H. L. Mencken, Scott
Fitzgerald, Ezra Pound, Eugene O'Neill, or e.e. cummings.
And just how 'uniform' are the three magazine successes of
the same decade, the *Reader's Digest*, *Time*, and the *New
Yorker*? The educated European knows American literature and avidly reads our magazines; a good many American writers may indeed be better known in Europe than
here. Yet if there is one thing he is sure of it is the 'standardization' of the American mind.

   Writers and journalists, it may be said, are non-
conformists to begin with. Well, what about entertainment
in America? Our radio stands perhaps first among the targets of the European critics of 'American uniformity'. If
everything they are saying about it were true, it still would
not account for the twenty-five or thirty-five stations – one
in almost every major city – which offer 'serious' music
eight to twelve hours a day. None of the 'serious' or 'high-
brow' programmes of European radio systems draws

enough of an audience to exist without heavy subsidies. But a great many of the two or three dozen 'serious' radio stations in this country manage to operate at a profit, though they are supported only by advertisers who are unlikely to be interested in anything but a listening audience large enough to justify the investment.

One station, WABF in New York, is even running an entire Sunday of music without any advertising, financed solely by voluntary contributions from its listening audience.

And how is one to explain that young people weaned on 'Good Night, Irene', the 'Hit Parade', and the 'Lone Ranger' rush headlong into chamber music, as listeners and, increasingly as players, as soon as they reach college? Walking across the campus on a fine spring evening one hears classical music, from Buxtehude to Bartok, streaming out of every other open window. Symphony orchestras are appearing in small towns as well as in large cities. And instead of being subsidized, these American orchestras are supported as they are formed by voluntary community action; the *Wall Street Journal* reports that more money is spent on symphonies than on basketball.

But what should completely destroy the European's concept of American uniformity is the diversity existing in industry. The fact that in this country business and industry are part of the country's culture is to the European the most remarkable thing about the United States – to the point where he greatly overstates the extent to which America has become a 'business society'. The European business men and labour leaders who have been touring this country under the auspices of the Marshall Plan these last four years all report as their central finding the experiments in new techniques, new products or processes, in accounting or in labour relations, in organization structure or in foreman training, carried on in almost every company they visit. No two, they find, do the same things. In the words of one of these teams, 'Every

American company feels that it has to do something different to stay in the race'. Many teams feel that American competition is too 'extreme'; and when pressed to explain why they use this term, they talk about the demands on managerial imagination and worker adaptability made by the need always to do something different and something new. The same sort of variety is found in our labour relations. In Europe relations between management and union tend to be rigidly and uniformly moulded by a central association of industries negotiating with a central federation of trade unions: the individual employer or the individual union branch pays dues but is otherwise inert. Not so here.

Some of the members of these teams even feel that we carry diversity too far to be efficient. 'I have seen a dozen plans for management development in as many companies', one of the senior men in British industry told me. 'Every one – Standard Oil, Ford, Johnson & Johnson, DuPont, General Electric, the Telephone Company – has a plan of its own, a staff of its own, a philosophy of its own. That just makes no sense. Why don't you fellows get together, appoint a committee, and have them work out the *one best plan* which everybody could use and which could be run centrally by a few top-flight people?'

It is not even true that within the American plant there is more 'standardization' than elsewhere, as we have all come to believe. The figures tell a different story. In this country of mass-production a larger proportion of the workers in manufacturing industries are what the census calls 'skilled workers and foremen' than in any other country on which we have data. And we have an even greater number of men, proportionately, in executive, technical, and managerial positions. In other words American productive strength lies in higher capital investment per worker and better management; better planning, better layout, better scheduling, better personnel relations, better marketing – all of which mean more skilled and more trained people rather than more unskilled repetitive work.

III

I am not discussing here the *quality* of American culture, whether it be crude, shallow, vulgar, commercialized, materialist, or, as the Marxists maintain, full of 'bourgeois idealism'. My concern here is solely with the prevailing European conviction of American uniformity. And that conviction is an obvious absurdity. Nor could it be anything else considering the pragmatic bent of the American people and their deeply ingrained habit of voluntary and local community action and community organization.

Indeed any serious student of America has to raise the question whether there is not *too much* diversity in this country. There is the danger that diversity will degenerate into aimless multiplicity – difference for difference's sake. Jefferson, de Tocqueville, and Henry Adams, as well as recent critics of American education such as Robert Hutchins,* have seen in this the major danger facing American society and culture.

There is actually more uniformity in European countries, both materially and culturally, than in the United States. It may no longer be true that the French Minister of Education knows at every hour exactly what line of what page of what book is being read in every French school. But still, in education, in religious life, in political life, in business as well as in its cultural ideals, European countries tend to have at most a few 'types', a few moulds in which everything is formed. What then can the European possibly mean when he talks of the 'uniformity of America'?

He himself, as a visitor, unconsciously furnishes the answer in the way he sorts out his American experiences, in

* For many years President of the University of Chicago.

the questions he asks, in the answers he understands and those he doesn't. When he thinks of 'diversity' he tends to think of the contrast between the ways in which social and economic classes live. He is used to seeing a definite and clear-cut upper-class civilization and culture dominating. And that indeed he does not find in this country. Therefore the bewildering differences in American life appear to him meaningless – mere oddities.

I still remember how the sage of our neighbourhood in suburban Vienna, the wife of the market gardener across the street, explained the 'Great War', the war of 1914–18, when I was a small boy of ten or eleven: 'The war had to come because you couldn't tell maids from their ladies by their dress any more.' Frau Kiner's explanation of history differed from that offered during the nineteen-twenties by Europe's learned sociologists, whether of the Right or of the Marxist persuasion, mainly by being brief and simple. They all assumed that there must be a distinct upper-class way of life, an upper-class architecture, upper-class dress, upper-class goods in an upper-class market – and contrasted with it the 'folk culture' of the peasantry or the equally distinct ways of life of the middle-class and working class. Indeed that eminently sane (though notoriously Americophile) magazine, the London *Economist*, echoed Frau Kiner only a few months ago when it reported with apparent amazement that 'to the best of their ability – and their ability is great – the [American] manufacturers make clothes for the lower-income groups that look just as smart as those they make for the more fortunate' – and explained this perverse attempt to make maids look like their ladies as the result of the 'egalitarian obsession' of this country.

The class-given differentiation in Europe is even more pronounced in the non-material, the cultural spheres. One example is the tremendous importance of the 'right speech' in practically every European country; for the 'right speech' is upper-class speech. Another example is the extent to which European educational systems are based on the education of a ruling class. The Renaissance Courtier, the Educated Man of the Humanists, the Christian Gentleman of nineteenth-century England – the ideal types which embodied the three basic educational concepts of modern Europe – were all in origin and intent ruling-class types. The rising middle-class not only did not overthrow the class concept of education, it emphasized it as a symbol of its own emergence into the ruling group. Similarly, in Occupied Germany the working-class leaders – to the chagrin as well as the complete bewilderment of American educational advisers – showed no enthusiasm for the plan to convert the traditional *Gymnasium* into an American school. To deprive these schools of their ruling-class character would actually deprive them of social meaning for working-class children.

Europe has even succeeded in turning diversities and differences that were not social in their origin into class distinctions. One of the best examples of this is the way in which the 'gentry' and its retainers became identified with the Church of England while the 'tradesmen' went to 'Chapel' – a distinction that held till very recent times and is not quite gone yet.

Thus the European myth of American uniformity tells us less about America than about Europe. For it is based, in the last analysis, on Frau Kiner's belief that a class structure of society is the only genuine moral order.

That today the theme of 'American uniformity' is played on above all by Communist propaganda is thus no accident. For the 'proletariat' of Communist ideology is indeed a 'master class'. It is a reaffirmation of the European ruling-class concept and of its ruling-class way of life in an extreme form – only turned upside down. On this rests to a considerable extent the attraction of Communism for European intellectuals. There is an old Slav peasant proverb: 'There will always be barons for there must always be peasants.' All

Krushchev would have had to do to change it into an orthodox Soviet proverb would have been to change 'barons' to
'proletarian commissars'. And Frau Kiner's philosophy of
history he would not have had to change at all.

IV

But Frau Kiner's statement could never have been made in
this country, not even by a sociology professor in a three-
volume tome. Whether the United States really has no ruling
class – and therefore no classes at all – or whether, as the
Marxists assert, the classes are only camouflaged in this
country, one thing is certain: this country knows no distinct
upper-class or lower-class 'way of life'. It knows only
different ways of making a living.

Indeed there has been only one genuine ruling-class way
of life in this country since its beginning: that of the plantation aristocracy in the Old South between 1760 and
1860.* When the *nouveaux riches* in the period between the
Civil War and the first World War made the attempt to set
themselves up as 'Society' they failed miserably. They could
not even develop an upper-class American architecture –
and of all the arts architecture is the mirror of the way of
life. The tycoons had to be contented with imitation French
châteaux, Italian Renaissance palaces, and Tudor manors
– the white elephants which their servantless grandchildren
are now frantically turning over to monasteries, hospitals, or
schools. (It is not entirely an accident, perhaps, that the
people most eager to live today in the baronial halls of yesterday's capitalists seem to be Soviet delegates.) To find an
upper-class way of life the tycoons had to gate-crash the
Scottish grouse moors, the Cowes Regatta, or the Kaiser's
manoeuvres in Kiel. In this country it was difficult indeed to
lead a ruling-class life.

* And only one 'lower-class' way of life: that of their black slaves.

The closest we come today in this country to anything that might be called an 'upper-class way of life' is to be found in the top hierarchy of the big business corporations. The way people in some of these companies talk about the 'twelfth floor' or the 'front office' faintly echoes Frau Kiner's concept of the 'ladies'. At work the big business executive has indeed some of the trappings of a distinct style of living in the ceremonial of receptionist, secretary, and big office, in his expense account, in the autographed picture of the 'big boss' on the wall, the unlisted telephone, and so forth. But only at work. As soon as he leaves the office the 'big shot' becomes simply another business man, anonymous and indistinguishable from millions of others. And he is quite likely to live, like the president of our largest corporation, in an eight-room house in a pleasant and comfortable but not particularly swank suburb.

In fact, it does not even make too much sense to talk of this country as a 'middle-class' society. A middle-class has to have a class on either side to be in the middle. There is more than a grain of truth in the remark made jokingly by one of my European visitors, an Italian student of American literature: 'If there were such a thing as a working-class literature, *Babbitt* and *Arrowsmith* would be its model.'

V

Any European who has perchance read thus far, will growl that if Europe's mental picture of 'American uniformity' is absurd, America's mental picture of 'European class society' is absurder. And he is right. In fact, the one myth is the reverse of the other. To the American, for instance, 'class society' means a society without social mobility. But Frau Kiner was anything but respectable lower-middle class knowing its place. She was a successful social climber who had fought her way up from a sharecropper's shanty and a job as a scullery maid at 14 – and had pushed her man up with herself. And in those years after the first World War she was capping her social triumphs by marrying off her beautiful and well-dowered daughters to 'gentlemen' – elderly and moth-eaten, but undeniably 'gentlemen'.

Nor is a society in which an Eliza Doolittle can jump from slum waif to 'great lady' just by learning upper-class speech a society without social mobility. (Indeed there is no better sign of America's failure to understand Europe's 'class society' than our tendency to play *Pygmalion* as a farce and as a take-off on upper-class snobbery – whereas it is as much crusading pamphlet as comedy of manners, the only snobs in it being the class-conscious cockneys.) Altogether there has been tremendous social mobility in any Western or Central European country whenever there was great economic expansion: in Britain between the Napoleonic Wars and 1860, in Germany a generation later, in Bohemia – perhaps the most startling example – between 1870 and 1900. The central difference between America and Europe may well be in the *meaning* rather than in the *extent* of social mobility. When the boss's son is made a vice-president in this country the publicity release is likely to stress that his first job was pushing a broom. But when a former broom-pusher, born in the Glasgow slums, gets to be managing director in a British company the official announcement is likely to hint gently at descent from Robert Bruce.

I must break off here. Another European visitor has just come in for a chat, a young French philosopher, fresh from a six-month tour of American universities. I anticipate a pleasant and informative afternoon; the letter with which he introduced himself was interesting and intelligent. 'The thing that impressed me most,' he wrote, 'is that no university I visited tries to develop a "school of philosophy". On the contrary each tries to stress different views and different schools in its faculty – the exact opposite from what we would normally do.' Yet I know that sooner or later in the course of the afternoon he will ask me, 'Mr Drucker, don't you find it very trying to live in so mechanically uniform a country?'

Index

If you have enjoyed this PAN Book, you may like to choose your next book from the titles listed on the following pages.

Peter F. Drucker

THE PRACTICE OF
   MANAGEMENT   60p

'Peter Drucker has three outstanding gifts as a
writer on business – acute perception, brilliant
skill as a reporter and unlimited self-confidence
... His penetrating accounts of the Ford
Company, the retail enterprise of Sears
Roebuck, and most interesting of all, the
International Business Machines concern, are
worth a library of formal business histories' –
NEW STATESMAN

THE EFFECTIVE EXECUTIVE   40p

The author identifies five talents as essential to
business effectiveness: the management of
time; choosing what to contribute to the
particular organization; knowing where and
how to apply your strength to the best effort;
setting up the right priorities; and, collectively,
effective decision-making.

How these talents can be developed forms
the main body of this book and the author
ranges widely through the annals of business
and government to demonstrate the distinctive
skill of the executive.

Graham Turner

'The most dramatic industrial story that can possible have been written' – LORD ROBENS

THE LEYLAND PAPERS   60p

'It is the story of thwarted ambitions and industrial savagery ... the story of a human catalyst of all that is good and bad in the tough jungle of the business world, of political intervention, of secret meetings and corridor discussions that finally gave birth to the second largest motor manufacturer outside the States' – THE SPECTATOR

'Graham Turner pulls no punches ... eminently readable, a vital contribution to British Industrial history' – BOOKS AND BOOKMEN

Alvin Toffler

FUTURE SHOCK   50p

Future Shock looks at the human side of to-morrow from a present where concepts of knowledge, careers, friendship, even love and marriage are changing daily.

Future Shock is the disease of change. Its symptoms are already here.

'A book to change the future' – THE GUARDIAN
'The best study of our times that I know . . .'
                              LE FIGARO